A Dance Towards

A Dance Towards Forever

Alyson Root

ISBN-13: 9798359425964
Imprint: Independently published

Cover design by: Cath Grace @cathgracedesigns

Dedication

For my wife, without whom the book would never have happened.

Table of Contents

Prologue

12 years earlier

"Samantha!" Charlie shouted. "Please tell me you're doing what I think you're doing!"

Sam couldn't stop the wide smile forming on her face, even if she tried. "I am indeed my friend," she winked, turning her face back to the bare torso laid on the table in front of her.

With one big gulp, Sam swallowed the strawberry-flavoured shot which had been balancing on the young woman's body. The room erupted with shouts and screams of encouragement.

"Well, that was delicious," Sam whispered in the girl's ear, still laying in front of her. The young woman looked back hungrily at her. Sam gave her a quick peck on the cheek before turning back to Charlie with a shit-eating grin, oh, and an undeniable buzz from the half dozen strawberry shots coursing through her body. God, life was good at nineteen. With her body moving to the music, Sam danced her way over to her best friend.

Sam and Charlie had met on the first day of Freshers Week. They'd got on so well that by the end of the week, Charlie had offered Sam the spare room in her flat.

For Sam, it was a no-brainer. She could move out of her mum's house, for one. Secondly, Charlie's parents — who were ultrarich — were paying for everything. No rent, no bills, and one hell of a new friend. Sam was living the dream.

"You are like my gay hero," Charlie gushed at Sam as they settled against the kitchen worktop, pouring copious amounts of an unknown brown liquid into two plastic cups.

"Oh, I want a superhero name."

"Lady Leztacular!" Charlie cried as she jumped into the air, thrusting her fist skywards like a toddler on a sugar rush. Charlie was clearly starting to feel the effects of the alcohol she'd consumed.

"Keep that one on the back burner," Sam laughed, watching her friend attempt to do a superhero pose but failing. Charlie was about to respond, but was cut off by a very attractive young woman who stepped into the space between her and Sam.

"Hi," the woman purred, speaking only to Sam.

"Hi," Sam replied with a brief grin.

"Want to have a drink with me?" She was looking straight into Sam's eyes with a stare that conveyed pure lust.

"That sounds great, but I can't right now. I'm here with my friend, but thanks for asking." Sam reached around the woman to grab Charlie, hugging her tightly to her side.

"Well, that's a shame," the woman said, pouting her lips. Sam had never found pouting attractive.

"Maybe another time?" Sam winked and shot her a killer grin. Charlie could practically see the woman swoon on the spot.

Grabbing Charlie tighter, Sam moved them into the garden through the kitchen door. "You are going to have a string of broken-hearted girls pining after you when you leave uni," Charlie chuckled.

The air was crisp and cold as they stepped outside, a welcome break from the heat of the house. Sam enjoyed the party

2

atmosphere immensely, but there was only so much she could endure, given the number of bodies that were crammed into such a small space.

Sam took in a big lungful of air before slowly letting it back out. A sense of calm washed over her. Charlie had found a garden chair and had slung herself into it so her legs were dangling over one arm and her back rested against the other. "Nice garden," Charlie continued.

"Yeah, not bad." Sam followed Charlie's gaze. Her ears were ringing from the blaring music. They sat in silence for a few minutes, taking in their surroundings.

"Did I upset you?" Charlie whispered. More than a little tipsy now.

"What? No, of course not... It's just I don't want people to think I'm stringing women along. I certainly don't want any broken hearts when I graduate," Sam mumbled.

Sam was a confident woman. She never worried about putting herself out there. She loved talking and flirting with women, but she never led them on. She was always up front and honest about her intentions. The very last thing she wanted was for anyone to get hurt.

As well as her outgoing personality, Sam also had the looks. Standing just over 5'6", she had shoulder-length sandy-coloured hair which contrasted wonderfully with her bright blue eyes. Her toned athletic body was a real selling point, too. Oh, and don't forget the dimples.

"S, I was only kidding. You're the most respectful person in the world. I know you wouldn't hurt anyone. Sorry, I love winding you up a bit, that's all." Charlie spun herself off the chair with as much dignity as she could muster. Which wasn't very much by the look of her scrambling off the floor, trying to kneel next to Sam.

"Ten points for the landing on that one, mate," Sam laughed loudly. "You tit! Get up here." She scooped Charlie up from her knees — which wasn't particularly easy — Sam wasn't exactly sober herself.

3

"Listen S," Charlie slurred. "You got the gift with the girls. It's just how it is. You clearly can't help the fact that they become a puddle of goo when you flash your big blues."

Sam chuckled; the sight of drunk Charlie was becoming the highlight of her evening.

Sam knew only too well how this night would end and it would *not* be with a woman in her bed.

Nope, it would be with her slinging Charlie over a shoulder and carrying her back to their flat, probably holding her hair back as she upchucked.

However, the great thing about Charlie, no matter how drunk, she never quit. There was still plenty of dancing and drinking ahead of them.

"C'mon, lightweight," Sam grinned, propping Charlie up. "Time to get your groove on." They headed back inside, Charlie swaying against Sam's side.

The party was in full swing, and each room of the house was completely packed. They shuffled through the masses into the makeshift dance room that pulsed with bright lights courtesy of a disco ball and several strobe machines.

The floor was vibrating with the bass of the music. Sam watched Charlie perk up instantly. Her bestie was about to let loose. Sam laughed loudly as Charlie threw herself into the fold, hopping and thrashing her hands about having the time of her life.

Every person in that room was dancing as if it would be the last thing they ever did. It was intoxicating, and Sam loved every second. Song after song after song, they danced. It was fantastic.

What seemed like hours passed and Sam's feet were on fire. She'd be lucky if she could walk in the morning. She grabbed Charlie, who was trying to perform some sort of robot dance — unsuccessfully — and headed for one of the dingy sofas in the living room.

The crowd had thinned considerably. Around thirty people remained in the dance room; someone had lowered the music enough so that people could hear each other talk.

4

After roughly twenty minutes, a friendly face appeared in front of them. Sam and Charlie were still camped out on the beat-up sofa.

"Sammy and Char, where the fuck have you been hiding?" It was Danny, one of their classmates, that they'd befriended early on. He was as tall as a lamppost and built like a house. Most people who met him presumed he was on some sort of sports course, but in fact, he was a talented video and photo editor.

"We needed to take ten," Sam replied loudly, the music suddenly becoming louder.

"Right well, your ten is up. We're starting a new game and you have to play."

Sam enjoyed drinking games, but she wasn't sure Charlie was in the best shape to take part in the night's activities.

"Can we give it a miss?" She pleaded.

"Not a chance. Charlie can coz, well, she's hammered," Danny chuckled. They both turned in Charlie's direction, who, true to form, was passed out dribbling down herself.

Awesome, Sam thought to herself before shifting Charlie into a more comfortable position. Charlie was going to have the mother of all hangovers, and Sam didn't think adding a crick in the neck would help the situation much.

Seconds after tending to her best friend, Danny hauled her ass up from the low-set couch. "Put this on," he shouted, thrusting a blindfold over her head, covering her eyes. She could only see a small sliver of light below the fabric.

"What kind of game are we playing?" Sam laughed. Stumbling as someone guided her clumsily to the group on the dance floor.

Danny cleared his throat and commanded the room with his booming voice. "Okay, everyone; thanks to sexy Sammy here, we have the right numbers. There are twelve people, so we will have six people with blindfolds on and six without. The people without blindfolds must pick one person to be on their team. Remember, this is a drinking slash dancing game, so make sure whoever you pick has got the stomach and the moves."

5

After some shuffling movements, Sam was shoved forward, bumping into someone, only recognising them by their voice as they loudly declared, "I'm having sexy Sam."

Patrick, the man who had entirely deafened her by shouting right next to her ear, was one of Danny's best mates and a nice guy, quiet usually, but not the case after a few shots. "Listen here, sexy Sam."

"Can you just call me Sam?" she laughed.

"No, I cannot. It's your new title. You are now and shall forever be 'Sexy Sam', who will win this game and therefore the bottle of Jack that is up for grabs," he said drunkenly. "You are going to slam those three shots like a boss and, after, dance as if your life depended on it and you're going to look hot doing it."

"Why am I blindfolded for that?" Sam immediately questioned. It seemed highly unnecessary.

"It makes it more fun for the people watching," he cackled.

"Sweet Jesus," she moaned. "Should I dance alone or with someone?"

"I can't tell you that."

"Why not?" she questioned again, louder this time.

"I don't know. It isn't my game. I have no fucking clue what the rules are, so just shut up and win."

"This is the stupidest game I have ever played," she shouted.

"Are you shitting on my awesome dance slash drinking game?" Danny shouted back, laughing, "It took me two whole minutes to come up with it and I think it's brilliant!" he yelled proudly. The others in the room seemed to agree and started chanting, "dance and drink," over and over.

"Okay, get your blindfolded dance monkeys in front of their shots. After the countdown, you must down three shots as fast as you can, no spilling, and then head towards the music," Danny screamed in pure excitement. "One… Two… Three… GO!" The game was on.

Sam had no time to think; she shoved her hands out and grabbed whatever was in front of her. She found the shot glasses easily and sank them quickly. Twisting her body round, she followed the cheers and calls toward the music.

All evening, the music had been an eclectic mix and now was no different. They danced to pop, rock, reggae, and trance. Sam had zero idea who was dancing around her. Bodies collided as blindfolded drunkards navigated the tiny dance floor. Sam couldn't help but laugh along with everyone because the small group of dancers must have looked ridiculous to anyone that was watching.

Danny shouted to the crowd as the last beats of Oasis' "Wonderwall" finished. "Ok party people, last dance to prove yourselves, and to prove that the Jack belongs to you! Make it a good one."

"Nail it Sammy," she heard from somewhere behind her. Sam geared herself for the last song, which she was convinced would be an energetic one for the grand finale. The song started, but it was far from energetic. It was a slow number. She listened to the first few bars before she recognised it. "I will always love you" blared out from the speakers.

A warm rush of joy pounded through Sam's body because the version playing was not Whitney Houston. No, it was the queen of country music herself, Dolly Parton.

Yes! Now, this was Sam's kind of song, but she wouldn't win that bottle of Jack by swaying softly by herself. Oh no, she needed a partner. Reaching out, she grabbed the closest person to her and pulled them in, ready to make a show of it for the crowd.

As they came into each other, Sam's senses were overloaded. The scent of almonds and cherries with a hint of vanilla infiltrated her nose; it was delicious, unlike anything she had smelled before. The body she was holding was soft, a woman for sure.

Without realising it, Sam had shifted herself even closer. Her body's instincts were taking over. She wanted, no, *needed*, to be as close to this woman as possible. She could feel soft hair against her cheek.

7

Trying her best, Sam looked through the small crack at the bottom of her blindfold. She could see the curves of a long, soft neck and just the strap of a top. The woman who she held didn't back out of the embrace but gripped her hands to Sam's lower back. The move rendered Sam breathless.

The surrounding room fell quiet as they danced. The music played on, but Sam had shut it out as she felt the warm breath of her partner gently caress her ear. Energy simmered between them. Sam felt it in her very cells; this was the most sensual thing she had ever experienced.

Sam became conscious that her hands were gently rubbing up and down the woman's back. Her body felt so good. She was soft and slender. Her curves were a treat to the touch.

The woman must have been experiencing similar feelings because she explored Sam in the same manner, her hands gripping gently on Sam's hips and then sliding up towards her ribs. They were in a world of their own.

Their breaths became shallow; their hips pressed firmly together, ebbing and flowing in unison. The woman leant her head into Sam, gently brushing her nose just below Sam's ear. Sam was on fire.

Sam turned her head, wanting nothing more than to capture the mystery woman's lips, but before she could register another thought, music flooded her senses, and she was bombarded with shouts and wolf whistles.

The music had changed to a completely different song. Sam felt the woman back away, whilst softly whispering, "Mon Dieu," and then she was gone. Sam felt the loss immediately.

It took Sam a beat to get her bearings. She felt her arm being pulled, and she followed Danny's voice. "Ladies and Gentlemen, we have a winner!" He catapulted her arm into the air and whipped off the blindfold. The lights momentarily blinded her, but she quickly focused on the room. Her view was obscured though by the crown of partygoers who had surrounded her.

"Who was that?" She spluttered to Danny.

8

"Sorry, kid, no idea. She just ran off, but you two nearly set the fucking house on fire with that dance."

He had the biggest smile on his face that Sam had ever seen. "I thought you were going to drop down and get freaky in the middle of the dance floor," he laughed.

Sam smiled weakly as she continued to search the room for her dance partner. That had been one hell of a dance.

With no clue of the mystery woman's whereabouts, Sam made a beeline for Charlie. She needed to get her friend home, and then she needed to process that experience.

Chapter One

Present Day

The sound of rain beating down on Sam's loft window tore her from another restless night's sleep. Lying there with her eyes still closed, she listened to the rhythm of the droplets hitting the windowpane. It didn't take long before her head filled with thoughts, none of which gave her any inkling to leave her warm and comfortable bed.

As she continued to listen, she desperately tried to empty her mind of any negative emotions and land in a place of calm and tranquillity, her efforts were rudely interrupted by the bane of her life, that goddamn alarm on her phone, a shitty reminder of the day that lay ahead.

Reaching over to the empty side of her double bed, she fumbled for her phone that lay on the pillow. Still refusing to open her eyes, she jabbed at the area until the noise stopped.

After a few more minutes of stubbornness, Sam gave into the irritatingly responsible voice that told her she had to get up.

Sam stretched and rubbed her eyes. The room that she now called home slowly came into view. It was a small, yet spacious, area. The walls were off white with no pictures. The floor was covered with cheap carpet, but it was sufficient for Sam's needs.

The furniture that inhabited the room was a mismatch of vintage and modern. Her grandmother had passed the dressers down to her before she died.

There was a small chest of drawers that had seen better days. Two of the drawer fronts were loose and wouldn't shut properly. This was the only item in the room that Sam had picked out herself. The only thing in her room that made her *slightly* happy was the bed she was currently refusing to leave.

Sam had moved back into her mother's house twelve months ago after a brutal breakup with Jo, the woman with whom she thought she would spend the rest of her life.

January 15th would forever be known as one of the worst nights of her life so far. After finishing an extensive project that had meant long hours at work and no sleep, she and her small team had finally completed it, with a couple of days to spare, no less. She remembered feeling the relief that she wouldn't have to look at that damn project ever again.

Sam had joined her colleagues at the pub for a well-deserved drink. It was a ritual; nobody drank until the project was finished and then all hell would break loose.

Sam knew it would be an enormous blow-out, so she'd called Jo to let her know she would be home late and to expect her to be a mess.

After an hour, Sam had felt the lack of sleep catching up with her. She'd apologised to her colleagues — who gave her as much stick as possible — before heading home. Thankfully, her apartment was a five-minute walk from the pub.

A sharp pain stabbed Sam in the chest as she forced herself to think of anything else but the next part of that memory.

Dragging her body into a sitting position, she leaned against the headboard and picked up her phone to perform her usual morning routine of checking her Facebook account.

Sam scrolled through the posts, skimming stories from her friends of their wild nights out, or their child's first gurgling noise, which they swore were actual words because their six-month-old was a genius. It was a routine that only made her miserable.

Sam had no social life to speak of, and this was a great way for her to be reminded of that every morning. She threw her phone down again, slowly sliding out of bed, scouring the floor for clothes that would be acceptable to wear in public.

The clock read 7:30 a.m., which meant that her mum would have already been awake for a couple of hours and would be in her studio painting.

Taking her crumpled pile of clothes, she headed for the bathroom. The hot water from the shower soothed her, relaxing her tired body, giving her a few minutes of pleasure before the day began. Her few moments didn't last long; there came a loud thudding on the bathroom door.

"Sam, are you in there?" came a gruff voice that Sam recognised as Andrew, a recent graduate who was renting her mother's loft room.

Sam rolled her eyes before answering, "Andy, sod off. I will be ten minutes max!"

"C'mon, Sam, I need to take a piss."

Sam reached through the shower curtain and unlocked the door; Andrew barged in with such force Sam thought the door would come off its hinges. "Jesus, Andy, be careful, *I'm* not forking out any money to repair shit *you* break."

"Sorry, mate," Andrew replied as he stood at the toilet, letting out a sigh of relief.

Sam remembered their first meeting; she had turned up at her mum's front door in tears. Mascara running down her face as she ugly-cried in front of a tall, slim, and untidy looking man instead of her mother.

12

Sam recalled Andy's reaction to her and the state she was in; he looked alarmed at first but then simply called to the other occupant of the house, "Sandy, are you expecting a crying woman at the door today?"

Sam was still looking bewildered when her mum finally came to the door, and the unknown hipster slid away into the living room. Her mum explained she had met Andrew at a still life class — he was the model. Sam had instantly berated her mother for shacking up with someone younger than her own daughter, to which her mum had burst out laughing, explaining that he was the new lodger.

That was the day after the worst night of her life, and she always recalled with great affection how gentle Andrew had been with her; he'd sat talking to her as if he'd known her for years. They became good friends quickly, and she liked the fact that her mum had someone else around the house apart from her.

With a quick goodbye, Andrew left just as fast as he had barged in. Sam stood under the burning water for a few more seconds before concluding that she would have to get a move on herself.

With the coffee pot heating, Sam slumped at the breakfast bar, checking through her bag to make sure she had everything she needed for the day.

Pouring the black liquid into her Wonder Woman mug, she inhaled the steam, the smell instantly making her feel more alert. As she sipped, she felt the caffeine run through her body, jolting her to life.

The soft morning sun was pouring through the window; the rain that had woken her so abruptly had cleared, leaving a bright and clear morning in its wake.

Sam spent a few minutes looking into the back garden through the double French doors, watching the trees sway gently in the early morning breeze, her mum's wind chimes playing their sweet tunes. She hadn't noticed her mum emerging from her studio.

13

"Samantha, my little ray of sunshine," she gushed, squeezing Sam's face like a child, "your aura is looking lighter today."

Sam loved her mum more than anyone else in the world; she had raised Sam alone after her dad had passed away when she was still a toddler. Sandra was the most laid-back person Sam had ever met. She insisted everyone call her Sandy, even Sam, to which Sam, pointblank, refused.

Sandy Chambers was a small woman, only 5'2" in height. She barely reached Sam's shoulders. Her hair was always tied up in a twist, with either a pencil or an old paintbrush sticking out the side.

"Morning, Mum, how's the painting going?"

"It is going somewhere, my dear. I'm letting the paintbrush decide every stroke, so I'm not sure what I will have in the end," she said with a wistful smile.

Sandy was approaching sixty but had the mental age of a twenty-year-old. Sam had never seen her mum in any type of formal dress. She had wardrobes full of "Floaty Dresses" as Sam liked to call them. Most of her mother's clothes were decades old, bought in some small backstreet market in Budapest or Thaïland when she'd travelled as a young artist.

She watched her mother float around the kitchen, watering the plants that littered every surface, and putting down cat food for the strays. Nothing calmed Sam like her mum. She loved just watching her, always happy and relaxed. She enjoyed life. It was that simple.

"Do you want a chai tea, button?" Sandy chirped. It wasn't a nickname that Sam relished, especially at thirty-two years of age, but her mum loved the pet name and refused to stop using it no matter how many times Sam begged her.

"No thanks, Mum, I have my coffee," Sam smiled.

"Coffee isn't good for you; it won't help detox your body and mind, honey." Sam rolled her eyes. They had the same conversation every morning. Sam had never seen her mum drink anything but weird herbal teas, with things floating in them that looked like twigs.

"Okay, we know this conversation isn't going anywhere and you know I'm never going to drink that stuff," she said, pointing at her mum's mug. "Anyway, I'm going to be late. I'll call you later from work. Have a creative day." She walked over and kissed her mum, grabbed her keys and coat, and set out to face the day.

As she walked her daily route to work, her mind wandered back to the days that had offered her the promise of a beautiful future. There was a time when it felt like she had everything going for her. She had done well at school and then at the university where she'd studied art, earning a BA (Honors) in photography. She'd met Jo in her third year, and they were inseparable. They were in love, or so Sam thought.

After over a decade together, Sam was certain that they would stay together forever. She'd truly believed they were a perfect match. Until that dreaded evening when she'd returned to their beautiful two-bedroom flat to find clothes scattered about on the floor. Items that she recognised but were not hers and noises coming from their bedroom. She couldn't bear to relive those feelings again, yet every time her mind wandered back to that day, she felt the pain all over again.

Her memories were so vivid. She could still hear her footsteps echoing down the hall as she approached the room. Her heart raced as she opened the door to their bedroom. Standing there looking at Jo between her boss' legs, in their bed. Every detail, every moment of those few seconds, was ingrained in her mind.

As Sam gasped for breath, trying desperately to rid herself of that terrible memory, she realised she'd stopped walking and was standing in the middle of the street. A sudden pressure on her shoulder made her turn. It was Charlie, her best friend, looking at her with an odd expression on her face.

Charlie stood an inch smaller than Sam. Her hip length hair sat haphazardly on her head in a messy bun. Sam had always been a little jealous of Charlie's hair. It was jet black and perfectly straight, unlike her wavy mop.

As usual, Charlie was dressed in her cherry red Doc Martens, skintight black jeans and a slim-fit band T-shirt. Sam loved her dress sense. Charlie had found her style as a teenager and stuck with it. Sam could see Charlie in her seventies still rocking that look.

"What have I told you about standing in the middle of the street staring into space? You're scaring people! C'mon, I need coffee before we start."

She scooped Sam by the arm into the nearest coffee shop. "So, tell me what the hell that was all about," Charlie barked, hooking her thumb over her shoulder in the direction of the street they had just left.

"I was daydreaming," Sam quickly replied, knowing full well she wasn't going to get away with such a lame excuse. Charlie gave her a look that made Sam want to crawl up into a ball and disappear.

"Don't pull that bullshit with me! You were all dark and miserable about that waste of space again, weren't you? How many times, Sam, do we have to have this conversation? How many more minutes of your life will you spend thinking about that useless, cheating piece of —?"

"Leave it, Char, not now." Sam wasn't in the mood for this conversation. Her sharp tone made Charlie hesitate and finally give up on the conversation. Sam sighed, feeling desperately guilty for snapping at her best friend, who had been the one person other than her mother and Andrew that had supported her through the awful times following her breakup with Jo.

After a few minutes of awkward silence, Charlie spoke. "So, we meet the new boss today. I bet he's a moron."

Sam was thankful that they could move on to a subject that wasn't about her. "I don't know. His credentials are beyond impressive, and he is bringing some major clients with him," Sam responded with a smile.

Charlie didn't look convinced. "Hmmm, well, as long as he doesn't mess with my flow," Charlie muttered into her coffee.

Twenty minutes had passed since they sat down in the coffee shop and began talking about the new boss. Sam was feeling lighter, her brain no longer consumed with Jo. Instead, she was feeling a rush of excitement for the upcoming meeting with John, their new boss and the new owner of Bright Lights Photography.

"Right then, time to get going, woman," Charlie barked. If anyone else had addressed her as "woman," Sam would have been offended, but she was so used to Charlie it didn't phase her at all.

The walk from the coffee shop to work was short. Bright Lights Photography resided in a beautifully remodelled Victorian house. Well, the term house undersold it. The space was immense. The previous owner — and founder — had refitted the space to house editing suites and offices. They had also purchased the building next door. The rooms in that building were converted into photography studios.

As they rounded the corner into the office carpark, they both noticed the large and expensive-looking car parked across the two bays. "Shit, he's already here!" Charlie barked.

They both picked up the pace, which was difficult so early in the morning. The three flights of steep stairs — which on an average day they would have taken at a snail's pace — tested their fitness as they took them two at a time.

Sam reached the office before Charlie. She was in reasonably good shape, whereas her best friend arrived a minute later breathing heavily. "You need to stop smoking, woman."

"Oh, shut up and get inside," Charlie spluttered, barging past Sam through the tall oak door that led to their office.

The small space was packed with people. Sam and Charlie tried in vain to sneak in without being noticed.

"Ah, ladies, I'm so pleased you could join us."

They both froze in place and looked over to the tall, good-looking man who was in the centre of the office. He had to be John Spencer, the new boss and owner.

Sam quickly fumbled for some words. "Sorry, Mr Spencer, we–"

"First thing you ladies missed, I do not want to be addressed as Mr Spencer! John will do just fine, and who might you be?" he interrupted.

"Sam Chambers, and this is Charlie Baxter." Sam hoped that she sounded more confident than she felt.

"Ah, Sam and Charlie, I've heard good things about you two." Sam felt heat crawling up her neck; she knew her cheeks would turn a delightful shade of red now that all eyes were on her.

John surged forward with his speech, which Sam was eternally grateful for, as now every head had snapped back in his direction. She let her shoulders slump and tried to calm her nerves.

"I know it surprised many of you to hear that I would take over Bright Lights. Even though it is a smaller company than I am used to running, I truly believe that it is well worth my time and money. I have been tracking work coming out of Bright Lights for the past eighteen months, and I see nothing but potential.

"Now all I ask of you is to continue showing the world how talented you all are. I will try to speak to you all individually, but as you know, I have many other companies to oversee, so all I can say is that I will do my best." With that, John smiled and exited the room.

"You had to go for sodding coffee!" Sam jabbed at Charlie.

"Keep your knickers on. He was okay about it," Charlie quickly replied. She was right, but Sam hated being late and especially hated being the centre of attention, which unfortunately had just happened. She could still feel her face burning.

"Sam, for god's sake, relax. We need to get the *Bella Magazine* project started today, so can you stop worrying about people noticing you and crack on with organising the shoot?" Charlie huffed.

The next hour went by like any other. The office was buzzing with people discussing projects, going in and out presumably to and from the studios next door. This was something Sam enjoyed, watching people getting excited about photography; it gave Sam a sense of belonging.

"Sam, Charlie, can I grab you both for a second?" Neither of them knew the woman who had spoken. She must be part of John's team.

They shot a quick glance at each other before dropping everything and following the young woman who had spoken to them. They trailed behind her, almost colliding with each other, when she abruptly stopped outside the executive suite, which was on the top floor.

"John would like a word. Go straight in."

They hesitated, but with a brief nod from Cory — Sam spotted her name on her desk plate — they opened the door to John's office and stepped inside.

The room was light and modern; the new owner was putting his own touches to it, as there were dozens of framed photographs strewn across the floor and on the desk.

"Thank you for coming to talk to me. I apologise for the mess, but I like my offices to inspire me, so I need to choose just the right photographs."

Both women were silent. It was an odd feeling to be in the presence of one of the world's greatest entrepreneurs. Oh, and not forgetting richest people on the planet.

John Spencer was a self-made man. He became successful by turning small businesses — media based mainly — into empires. He was named as the youngest and wealthiest entrepreneur twice in three years, and he was only in his early twenties at the time.

John Spencer was the man that every business owner wanted to know and often wanted to be. He was known for his ruthless honesty and radical reconstructions. Sam could see why he had become so successful so quickly. He had an air of dominance, power, and confidence.

19

Sam had done her research. She knew that John had been married to his college girlfriend, and she knew he was now a widower. The papers reported on his wife's illness for months before her passing almost two years ago.

John was smartly dressed in a suit that probably cost more than Sam's annual salary. His hair was well groomed, and he looked just as fresh as he did all those years ago when he had first made a name for himself.

"Okay, let's get down to business. I'm going to be travelling for most of the year, which isn't ideal when you have just bought a company. So, therefore, I need to make some changes in staff positions quickly." John could tell he had made both women very nervous.

"Now don't panic, the changes are for the best I assure you!" John pressed on, "Charlie, you have done some fantastic work. I have been watching you closely for a while now. Your reputation precedes you, and I think your achievements should be recognised and rewarded." Charlie looked utterly stunned. "I'm making you the new lead photographer," he finished.

Charlie stood there for what seemed an eternity, staring at her new boss until she finally snapped out of it and gave a smile of disbelief.

"Excellent, I'll take that as an acceptance smile," John laughed. He turned his attention to Sam, looking a little less jovial. "Now, Sam, I have studied your work closely. You are *very* talented. However, over the past twelve months, your work has taken a turn, and not for the better."

Sam should have put money on being the one to get shafted. It seemed to be the theme of her life recently. Before she could comment, John continued, "I think it's important for you to tell me what you need to get you back to where you were a year ago." He looked directly into Sam's eyes, which made her feel uneasy, but she held his gaze.

"Uh, right," she muttered, not sure what she was supposed to say.

"So?" John questioned.

20

How the hell was she supposed to give him an answer? Could he turn back the last twelve months and stop her from getting her heart ripped out? Because that was the only thing that she could think of.

He was right. She knew her work had suffered because how could it not have? Sam was a passionate person—well, she had been until her passion had been brutally stripped from her. She had no idea how to get it back. She was barely existing as a semi-functioning person, nowhere near the level she needed to produce art as she'd done before Jo had destroyed everything.

She was taking too long to answer. She looked at Charlie for help, but it was too late. John had lost his patience. "I'm flying you out to Paris. Your flight leaves at five. Hélène will meet you at the airport and fill you in on the job."

Sam looked frantically at Charlie. Her brain couldn't process what he had just said. "Paris!? How long will I be going for?" she shrieked.

John could see the panic on Sam's face. "Sam," he barked, pulling her out of her downward spiral. "I'm sending you because I think you are right for this project. Helene has all the details. I know you are just the person for the job. Grab your gear and get ready."

"Sorry John, of course, I'll happily go. I'll begin prepping now." She turned and left the office with Charlie close behind.

Charlie and Sam sat at their desks, trying to take in the news. Charlie finally broke the silence. "Holy shit, this is huge!"

"Yes, it is," Sam replied, still shocked.

"Well, damn, I mean lead photographer." Charlie had delight etched across her face. "And you, flying out to Paris."

"I know. I mean, shit like this doesn't happen to me," Sam muttered.

"Oh, for Christ's sake, Sam, stop being so down on yourself. It's grating on me. Get your shit together, and do it with a smile," Charlie barked.

Charlie was right to call her out. She *was* feeling sorry for herself. She was thankful that her best friend was blunt enough to pull her out of her own self-pity.

After two short hours, Sam had her gear ready to go. She'd checked her bag a dozen times and was sure that she had packed far too much, although she didn't know what the project was or what equipment would be available to her, so it was better to be safe than sorry. She waited for Cory to bring her the details of her flight and then she would head off to the airport.

Just as she glanced at the clock, she saw Cory coming over to her desk. "Change of plan, Sam. You will take the Eurostar. Here is your ticket and itinerary. Your train leaves at six-fifteen. A car will pick you up at five." Cory dropped the paperwork on her desk and bustled off.

Sam packed her documents along with her equipment, shooting Charlie a look that conveyed her panic. Charlie, in return, gave her a warm and reassuring smile back.

The rest of the day went by quickly. Sam had taken most of the afternoon to go over her open projects with Charlie, who would most likely complete them. She handed over a few of her smaller jobs to a couple of other photographers that she trusted to do a good job.

With a few minutes to spare before the car arrived, Sam grabbed her things and headed over to Charlie. "Okay, I'm going. Wish me luck."

Charlie set down her pen, stood up, and pulled Sam into a hug that made her feel instantly better. "You got this," she whispered into Sam's ear.

Sam headed for the door with renewed confidence. Maybe, just maybe, her life was going to turn around for the better.

Chapter Two

It was unusually warm for the time of year in Paris. Anna rolled over again, trying to get comfortable, hoping that she would slip into a deep sleep soon. The day ahead would be so busy, she needed to be rested.

Listening to the noise coming from the street and the fan that was humming in the corner of her room, she finally felt herself drifting into darkness.

Anna recognised the room she was in. It was her childhood room at her parents' house, although it looked different. The walls were a different colour, and her single bed was now a double. She could hear music playing. It wasn't a song that she instantly recognised, but it was familiar.

There was a bright light shining through the shutters. She moved closer to the window to open them. The handle on the door turned. Anna swung around to see who it was, but she didn't recognise the woman standing in front of her. She was a little shorter than Anna, with sandy hair brushing her shoulders; she was dressed in formal attire, navy blue trousers and a jacket with a white shirt underneath. Anna noticed the shirt was unbuttoned just enough that she could see the curved shape of her breasts.

Without words, the woman took off her jacket and threw it onto a chair that Anna knew didn't belong in her room. The woman walked slowly toward her. As Anna looked into her eyes, she felt her own hands begin to unbutton her own shirt. Anna couldn't take her eyes off this woman. She had a rush of exhilaration surge through her body. She wanted nothing more than to have the stranger touch her.

The scene changed. Anna was no longer in her familiar bedroom but outside in the seering heat. Clear blue sky stretched above her, yet the woman Anna had seen in her room was there again, still walking toward her.

However, she no longer looked like she worked in an office. She was clad in a forest green bikini. Her skin shone in the light, her half-naked body glimmering under the sun. The stranger stood in front of Anna, looking into her eyes as if searching her very soul.

The stranger was stunning. Anna had never seen a woman who exemplified beauty like this. She felt a warm hand reach under her shirt, feeling every inch of her torso. She felt the hand move up, and she gave a long and sensual moan, her body longing to be devoured by this woman.

Anna took off her shirt, and the woman smiled, then leaned in and kissed her neck. Anna's bra fell to the ground, the same warm hand caressed her breasts.

Anna felt an unfamiliar sensation between her legs. She was excited, more excited than she had ever been before.

The stranger had worked her way down her torso, kissing her skin until she reached Anna's trousers. Anna looked down. The stranger continued to look into her eyes as her hands unfastened her trouser clasp.

Anna looked into the ocean blue sky, knowing any moment her wait would be over, she would feel unforgiving pleasure, a sensation so intense she wouldn't be able to stay silent any longer.

The stranger's warm, moist tongue intensified the wetness between her thighs as she explored Anna's folds. Inhaling deeply and with every nerve in her body singing, she let herself scream in sheer delight.

She jolted as she heard a voice talking to her. "Anna, wake up! Jesus Christ."

Anna lay there, her head spinning, panting as if she'd just run a marathon. "Sorry, go back to sleep," she whispered.

"We've a long day tomorrow. Keep it down."

The man lying next to her rolled over, muttering, but she didn't care. Anna stared at the ceiling, trying to catch her breath and trying to remember the face of the woman that had explored her in a way that no other person ever had. A few minutes passed. She was still panting, and in fear of waking him up again, she slid out of bed and went to the kitchen.

Standing in the darkness, she tried to clear her head. She opened the fridge to get some water. The light illuminated her naked body, beads of sweat glistened on her chest. The cold air escaping the open fridge felt heavenly on her burning skin. "Jesus Christ," she muttered to herself. Her body felt different, as if it was not her own. She could still feel a tightening between her legs. "Shake it off, it was a dream," she tried to tell herself in the small hope she could brush it off, but there was no denying the power of what she had just experienced.

She placed her cup quietly in the sink and walked back to her room. She lay down with her back to the man in the bed and closed her eyes, hoping that she would find herself under that blue sky again with her perfect stranger.

* * *

Anna sat in her favourite café, watching the crowds of people pass by. Lighting her fifth cigarette of the morning, she watched a homeless man searching the bins across the street. It was hard to see such poverty in such a wealthy city.

A few minutes passed as she continued to observe the world around her. A glance at her watch confirmed that her coffee companion was late. She knew Frédéric wouldn't be on time, he never was.

Looking in the direction she knew he would come from, she rolled her eyes when she saw Frédéric running across the busy street waving, his scarf half around his neck, half of it dragging behind him, his coat buttoned up incorrectly and his shoelaces catching under his feet.

"Bonjour Anna."

"You should say Bonsoir Frédéric! Why is it so difficult for you to arrive on time?"

Anna and Frédéric were both born in Paris to English parents that had moved over to France a few years before Anna was born. Although she and her brother were fluent in French, they spent most of their time conversing in English, as neither of their parents had done well at picking up the language.

It irritated Anna. Her parents had been living in the country for over thirty years and had made little effort to learn. It was normal now for Anna and Frédéric to talk in English whenever they spoke. However, they enjoyed breaking out into French when they were growing up, especially when it was to curse their parents.

Every Wednesday, Anna and Frédéric would meet at the same café to catch up. Once they had both finished university, their lives had started to grow apart. Frédéric began his job as a junior architect and Anna worked tirelessly for a small publishing company.

With only fourteen months between them, they were close throughout their childhood, and when it became apparent their lives were heading in separate directions, they made a point of meeting every week without fail.

"So," chirped Frédéric, "I have some news."

"Go on then. What's the big news this week?" Anna replied sarcastically. Anna's idea of big news and Frédéric's were vastly different. Anna lost count on the amount of times Frédéric had a "big announcement" only to find out it was something as ridiculous as him finding a new fabric softener.

"Don't say it like that," Frédéric replied, a little hurt. "Anyway, it's not what you think!" he added, going red in the face. He had Anna's full attention now. Frédéric rarely blushed.

"I've met someone, and I want you to meet her." This was the first time Frédéric had asked Anna to meet a woman he was dating. She knew it must be serious. Growing up so tightly together, they had promised each other that they would only meet partners if it were love, which as adults seemed a tad childish but nevertheless they'd kept their word, sort of.

Frédéric had met James—a handful of times—but Anna couldn't say it was because she was *in* love with him. It had just been the natural progression of their relationship. That was not in accordance with Anna's and Frédéric's agreement and it made her feel bad.

"Wow, this is huge Freddy."

"Please don't call me that."

"Sorry, I'm just a little shocked."

"She's great. I know you will adore her."

"Do you love her?"

"I do. She's the best thing that's ever happened to me," he smiled.

"Well then, I can't wait to meet her." She was so happy to see her little brother light up the way he did. "So, tell me all about her," Anna whispered with excitement.

Just as Frédéric was about to answer, his phone rang. Anna cringed. For some unknown reason Frédéric insisted on having the loudest ringtone possible, which meant everybody in a five-kilometre radius stopped to stare as it bellowed.

"Sorry, I need to get this," Frédéric apologised. He stood up and took the call a few feet away from the table. Anna took another sip of her coffee and began putting her belongings that lay on the small table into her bag. Frédéric wouldn't be staying for coffee. A few minutes passed before Frédéric returned to the table with an apologetic smile.

"It's okay, I know you have to go."

"I'm so sorry, there has been a major mistake on a set of blueprints, and if it's not sorted out this morning, I won't have a job this afternoon," Frédéric ranted. Anna kissed her brother and watched him leave. The alarm on her phone chimed. It was Anna's signal to begin her journey to work.

Lighting another cigarette, she walked down the street to the metro station. Anna enjoyed the routine. She had always liked to plan and keep to schedules. It was comforting knowing where she would be, and at what time she would do things. It helped her to stay calm.

For nine years, Anna had worked at Tower Publishing. First as a junior editor and now as the editor-in-chief. Most of the day was spent organising and liaising with the other editors. It was a tiring job, but the money was good and she got to spend her time surrounded by books which she adored.

Her apartment was crammed with books, most of which she had read several times. Her partner, James, did not enjoy reading. In fact, she wondered if they had any similar interests at all.

After a quick ride on the metro, she exited the platform and began the climb up to the street. The sun was shining as she exited the station. Unlike others, Anna enjoyed the walk from the station to work. She would sometimes get off the metro a couple of stops before hers just to enjoy the fresh air.

Today, however, she was keen to get to work. She had a long list of jobs to get done by the end of the day, which would mean another late night.

As she walked along the cobbled streets, she noticed the people rushing by, most of whom had headphones in, listening to music and avoiding eye contact with anyone else. Anna was no different. As part of her daily commute routine, she would also have music playing, often something soft to ease her into the day.

Her office was set in a beautiful part of the city, with every building showing off its glorious architecture. Frédéric loved to visit Anna at work just to look at the surrounding offices.

9:15 a.m., she had made it in good time. Stepping through the door, she was greeted by Kim, her personal assistant, who had been working for her for the past two years.

Kim had moved from England three years ago after finishing university. She was a short girl with long platinum-blonde hair. She was gifted with a body that would rival any 1950s pin-up model.

Anna had hired her on the spot after an hour-long interview, which was surprising because Kim's major at university was science — biology to be precise — and she had no experience as a PA, but something about Kim had made Anna feel good.

Maybe it was her sense of humour, or it could've been her unrelenting positive attitude and bubbly energy. Either way, Anna had made the right call hiring her. They were a perfect team.

"Here is your coffee. You have three meetings scheduled for this afternoon, but don't worry, I've kept them short! You have a reservation at two with Daniel and James has called three times already, but he thinks you are out of the office until midday, so won't call until then."

"Why does he think I'm out of the office until noon? He knows I plan to be here this morning?"

"That would be because I *told* him you were, so you could get some work done."

"Ah, I knew I hired you for a reason," Anna chuckled.

Anna sipped at her coffee and took in her surroundings. It was a morning ritual. She started it because of Kim.

Every morning Anna would come to work, throw her things down and start working immediately until one day she saw Kim standing by her own desk, looking around serenely. Anna had noticed her do it every morning for a week before she'd asked what she was doing.

"Why are you standing there like that?"

"I'm looking at everything," Kim replied with a smile.

"Well, yes, I can see that, but why are you doing that?"

29

"Because I work in a stunning city, in a beautiful office with a great boss! I take five minutes every morning to remember how lucky I am! Oh, and how grateful I am that everyone speaks English," she giggled.

Kim reminded Anna of her parents. She was useless at French, but she tried to learn, which was pleasing. From that day on, Anna would stand with Kim for five minutes, taking it all in.

"Right, work time," Kim interrupted.

"Yes, you're right." Anna let out a huff before settling down to work.

The morning progressed as planned, which Anna liked. She found it unnerving when her plans weren't followed. A couple of hours had passed, Anna had got through a large amount of coffee. Normally she restricted herself to three cups a day, but she had already consumed four.

Something was niggling at her. She couldn't help but feel she'd forgotten something important. It was unlike her to forget. She was far too organised for silly mistakes. Her head hurt. *Must be the caffeine.*

"Bonjour Anna." Marcus had walked in. He was the co-owner of the business. Up until two years ago, Marcus had shared ownership of the company with John Spencer and his wife, who was also Marcus' best friend Claire. Sadly, Claire had passed away after a brutal battle with cancer, leaving Marcus alone in the office. John still owned half the company, but was now a silent partner.

Marcus was in his late fifties, slim and balding. He was always dressed in the same brown cord trousers and jacket with a light blue shirt underneath, a multi-coloured scarf, and matching gloves. It didn't matter what time of year it was, he always wore the same outfit at the office.

Many of their clients thought he was a little strange, maybe eccentric, but it didn't matter. Anna admired him, and he had given her a chance to show him what she was made of.

"Bonjour Marcus, ça va?"

(Hello Marcus, how is it going?)

30

"Très bien, merci. Tu es prête pour ton voyage?

(It's going well. Are you ready for your trip?)

"Pardon?" Anna replied, looking very confused.

"Tu vas à Londres aujourd'hui, non? Pour un mariage il me semble? Tu as changé ton programme?

(You are travelling to London today, no? For a wedding, I thought? Have you changed your plans?)

Anna sat looking up at Marcus. She now understood the strange feeling she had and now knew the important thing she had forgotten.

"Oh, putain," she gasped. Within seconds, Kim was standing beside her.

"What's happened? Anna, are you okay?"

"Kim, my trip to London, it's today," Anna replied with panic in her eyes. This *never* happened to her. She was always so organised. "How did I forget?"

"Trip, what trip?" Kim flicked manically through her diary. Frantically searching for a note or scribble suggesting that Anna would travel that day. "I've got nothing down Anna, are you sure it's today? You would have told me."

Anna lowered her head into her hands. She remembered she was supposed to tell Kim three weeks ago about it, but something had distracted her before she had got round to it. Marcus looked at Kim and then back to Anna, shrugged, tilted his head, then continued on with his day as if nothing had happened.

"Jesus, okay, it's okay!" Anna was half talking to herself and half to Kim, trying to mentally check off everything she would need to do and everything she would need Kim to do before leaving.

"Kim, cancel my meetings, make something up and then call Daniel, send my deepest apologies, call James and ask him to throw some things into a bag for me. If he gives you any trouble, tell him I have been bogged down and need him to help me out with this *one* thing."

31

Anna's tone had become severe. Kim burst into action. Thankfully, she'd got a significant amount done on her list, which meant there was little for her to worry about and nothing that couldn't wait until next week.

"Oh, Christ," Anna blurted out.

"What, have you forgotten something else?" Kim was ready with her notepad and pen.

"I just remembered that the trip is a week long." Anna put her head back into her hands, letting out a groan of misery.

The thought of a full week with James' family made her stomach churn. She had only met them once, and that was by accident. Anna had just started dating James. They'd known each other for a little while, meeting through mutual friends. James had moved to Paris from New York. He was born in Cheshire, England, but studied in America, where he stayed until the pharmaceutical company he worked for offered him the opportunity to work in Paris.

Back then, Anna's mother had been grilling her every time she called about her love life — or, more like, lack of love life. Anna was all right on her own. She didn't have time for a relationship. She'd been that way since she could remember, having no desire to date.

After yet another interrogation from her mother, Anna had tried to appease the situation by telling her mum she was dating James, which wasn't entirely true, but he was the first guy she could think of. Knowing her mum would expect frequent updates on their budding relationship, Anna agreed to have a few drinks with him to keep up the charade.

After a couple of months and many drinks, they'd almost automatically become a couple. There was no awkward conversation about where their relationship was going or where they saw themselves in five years' time. They got on well. The sex wasn't great, but then again, Anna hadn't experienced the mind-blowing sex that all her friends had with anyone.

They'd moved in with each other after a year of dating, more for the financial benefits than any romantic notion. A week after

32

they'd started cohabiting—that's how James explained their situation—his parents took a trip to Paris for their wedding anniversary.

Anna had made it clear she didn't want to meet them. She was awkward with parents and didn't need the stress of it. James understood and didn't force the issue. He'd arranged to meet his parents for lunch, far away from their apartment. He'd explained Anna was very busy and wouldn't be able to make it.

Perfect plan, right? Wrong! His parents turned up at their apartment two hours earlier than the expected meeting time. Anna couldn't escape, she had no excuse. His parents stood at the door, looking at her dressed in pyjamas, ready to have a relaxing afternoon reading on the sofa with a bottle of red.

The meeting did *not* go well. Anna could feel the judgement oozing from every inch of his mother and nothing but chest stares from his father. Thankfully, that had only been a few hours of misery, but not this time! This time she had to endure a week because James' sister was getting married and he was the best man.

Kim stood looking at Anna with sincere sympathy. "Can I get you anything, maybe another coffee or a large whisky?" she grinned. There was nothing for it. Anna had no choice but to shut up and put up with the situation.

In what felt like a blink of an eye, the clock above her desk read one o'clock. Anna had to be at Gare du Nord at half past. Kim had done a fantastic job as per usual. She had arranged everything from getting Anna's bags packed to a car that would take her to the station.

Time for one last cigarette. There wouldn't be another chance for a few hours as James didn't like her smoking, so she avoided it when he was around.

Anna left the office and perched herself against a nearby lamppost. The sun shone brightly on her face. She lit the cigarette and took a deep breath. It felt good, relaxing. For a moment, the impending doom she felt was forgotten. She closed her eyes and listened to the city.

33

The warm breeze licked her skin, and in that instant, she remembered something, or should she say someone else, that had licked her skin with the same warm, delicious feeling.

With her eyes still closed, she could see a blurred vision of the stranger she had dreamt about. Her heart raced, and she could no longer hear the cars or people walking by, only the sound of her own breath.

"Anna?" Kim shouted from inside. Anna almost fell sideways from her perch. She gathered herself together and stubbed out her cigarette. "Sorry, didn't mean to make you jump. The car is ready for you," Kim chirped.

At one twenty-five, Anna arrived at the station. She saw James waiting for her, and he did *not* look happy. "Before you say anything," she began, "yes, I forgot, yes, I am sorry, and no, I do not want a conversation to take place." James huffed with aggravation, but didn't pursue it any further.

The check-in and security clearance was quick, and the train left on time. The journey was nothing to write home about. James sat on his phone scrolling and Anna looked out of the window for the better part of the train ride.

"At least something's going right today," James snapped as the train slowed in its approach to St Pancras. They were ahead of schedule. It was the first time he had spoken since entering the station in Paris, which was over three hours ago.

They gathered their things and shuffled along the aisle. It was the first time Anna had paid attention to James' luggage. He had his laptop case with him and his work phone.

"James, you told me not to bring work with me. Why the hell are they in your luggage?"

"I have no choice. We have a big meeting when I get back, and I have to be prepared," he said, blushing, knowing he'd been caught out. Just as they left the train and began walking towards the exit of the station, James's work phone rang. Anna shot him a look, which clearly communicated he was not to answer it. He rolled his eyes and answered, regardless.

As they rounded the corner, Anna almost tripped over her own feet. The woman she could see walking towards her with all sorts of paperwork and equipment looked *exactly* like the woman in her dream, the beautiful stranger.

Her breath caught, she was momentarily stunned. Anna diverted her gaze, not wanting to be caught staring. As she looked away, she could have sworn the woman stared back at her. James, however, hadn't seen her at all. He went barrelling into her, causing her to drop everything she was holding. Without bothering to check if she was okay, James continued on as if nothing had happened.

Anna couldn't quite believe what she was seeing. The woman who was now scrabbling around on the floor trying to pick up her belongings was stunning, just as Anna had remembered her. But how was that even possible?

Anna stopped, with the intention of going back to help, but she found herself staring at the goddess again, unable to move. James, however, wasn't messing around. He grabbed Anna by the arm and marched her out of the station. Her perfect stranger was now lost in the crowd.

Chapter Three

The journey to St Pancras was uneventful, which was pleasing because Sam couldn't deal with any more drama. When the car pulled up to the station, she took a deep, calming breath and got out. Excitement filled her up from head to toe.

Paying no attention to the people around her, Sam stared down at her tickets, all the time talking to herself in her head, checking off all the things she needed and reassuring herself that she had got it all with her. She turned the corner and in a split second noticed a woman looking at her, but before Sam could hold eye contact, she piled straight into a man talking on his very expensive-looking business phone. The collision sent Sam's gear and paperwork flying across the floor. The man in question continued to his destination without looking back.

Arsehole.

Sam scrambled to the ground, scooping everything up. Great, now she would have to go through everything again to make sure she hadn't lost anything important. Her irritation at the man was palpable. Why couldn't people be a little nicer? Would it have killed him to stop and help her?

As quick as her ire had risen, it faded as the face of the woman she had caught looking at her flashed across her mind. Phew, those were some gorgeous eyes. Damn it, now wasn't the time to be fantasising about sexy brunettes. She had a train to catch.

Once she'd collected herself together again, she proceeded to the security gate. Her ticket indicated she had priority boarding because she was travelling first class and therefore could skip the long lines. Oh, how the other half live.

Sam had never travelled first class, she'd never even travelled in business class before. Economy all the way. Not today, though. Today Sam was on her way to Paris in style, which made her overly excited, almost childlike.

She tried to hide her excitement—although she probably didn't do a good job of it—because, after all; she was an adult.

The security had still been a little unnerving. She always felt as if she was doing something wrong, especially when the security officer's eyed her up suspiciously. Her bags and equipment had gone through the x-ray with no issues, and the passport control had only taken a few minutes.

Sam had nearly half an hour before the train was due to depart, allowing her another opportunity to recheck all of her things, grumbling as she did. Although if she had forgotten or lost anything, it would be too late now.

When she was satisfied that everything was accounted for, she checked her watch. Her excitement was getting the better of her as the time ticked away.

Ten minutes passed before the announcer's voice crackled through the loudspeakers. The train was now boarding. Sam approached the train and began counting the carriages to see which one she would be in. As far as she could see, she would only have to walk a short distance, which was a relief. The heavy equipment was starting to hurt her shoulder.

First class was everything Sam hoped it would be. Large leather chairs lined the carriage. Businessmen and -women unloaded their laptops and organised their paperwork. It only took them a few minutes before they were busy working as if they'd never left the office. Sam found her seat and settled down. She also unloaded her laptop and plugged it in. *Might as well do something productive.*

Trying hard to concentrate, she looked through the latest images that had been shot a couple of days ago. Sam enjoyed having time to critique her own work. She wasn't the type of person to pick apart her work to be self-deprecating. She did it to improve her style and technique. It was imperative to continue learning. Each job she completed presented a learning opportunity in some way or another.

An hour passed, and the initial excitement still bubbled beneath the surface. She had to physically stop herself from grinning like an idiot when the steward approached her about the lunch menu.

After a very satisfying plate of gourmet cheese, red wine, and pudding, Sam surveyed her surroundings again. Everyone in her eyeline was still beavering away, some on their mobile phones, others operating tablets and laptops at the same time. Sam had done enough work for one day. She wanted to enjoy the experience of travelling.

Having not gone very far in a long time, she now welcomed the adventure with open arms. A split second later, her excitement was replaced with dread. She hadn't told her mother that she was leaving the country. "Shit, shit, shit," she muttered to herself as she began dialling the house number from her mobile.

Recapping the events of the day to her mum had helped rid Sam of her nerves that had been plaguing her since she'd accepted the assignment. Sandy had been over the moon that Sam was travelling. It didn't phase her in the least that Sam had forgotten to tell her before departing.

Hearing her mum's surprise and delight after being told about John and the changes he'd put into place left her feeling much better than when John had implemented the changes earlier in the day. That was Sandy Chambers for you, supportive, calm and full of positivity. By the end of the call, Sam felt giddy. She was going to Paris.

The light was fading as the train surged on. Sam had immersed herself once again into her work. She felt guilty watching everyone else working so hard. After a while, Sam checked her watch. "Surely we should be in France by now?" she muttered, craning her neck towards the window, trying to catch any sign that they had left England.

"The electricity pylons," she blurted out. A couple of people looked up from their machines inquisitively. Sam didn't care. Even though the landscape was very similar to England, the electricity pylons were very different. They looked like characters from the *Space Invaders* game. Sam had to stop herself from squealing.

As she watched the world rush by, she concentrated on the bright lights of the small villages that were rushing by. Her bum was getting numb, and all she wanted to do was find the nearest attendant and ask if they were nearly there yet. She chuckled at her own thoughts.

Fifteen minutes later, the announcer's voice crackled over the intercom. Sam had to strain her ears to understand what was being said. They would arrive in Paris Gare du Nord shortly, is what she could make out from the tinny voice.

Not knowing what to expect, Sam packed her things away, put on her coat and sat straining her eyes, trying to look for any signs that they were entering the city.

A few more minutes passed, and Sam felt the train slow. Within a couple of minutes, it was at crawling speed. All the other passengers started packing their belongings away. By that time, Sam had already left her seat and was waiting nervously by the door. She was one of the first passengers off the train, although it took her a little while to figure out which direction to go. She presumed that Hélène would have a sign or something to identify herself.

Following the other passengers along the platform, she turned into the main hall where a small crowd of people were standing waiting for their respective friends, family and clients. To the left of the group stood a very elegant woman holding a sign that read "Samantha Chambers" in big, bold letters. Instinctively and out of nerves, Sam waved frantically until she realised how absurd she looked.

"Helene, I presume?" Excitedly, she thrust her hand forward for a traditional handshake.

Helene looked amused. "Samantha, it's good to meet you," Helene replied smoothly with a gorgeous French accent. She clutched Sam's hand and then gently pulled her closer, giving Sam a kiss on each cheek. "That's how we say hello here." Helene's voice was all silky and French. Cue the swooning. Blimey, that accent did things to Sam.

Sam was happy and relieved that Helene seemed friendly. It made the whole situation a little less daunting knowing that she had someone she felt comfortable around to call on.

Sam followed Helene through the crowds of people and out of the station. Waiting for them was a private car, ready to take them to their destination, wherever that was.

Apart from the train times, Sam knew a grand total of zero about the project or client she was supposed to be working with. "So, er, what exactly will I be doing here?" She was trying not to sound how she felt, which was nervous and nauseous.

"Ah yes, I should probably brief you!" Helene chuckled, rooting through her very expensive-looking handbag. She pulled out a black folder and handed it to Sam. Her hand brushed against Sam's fingers and lingered for a few seconds.

The exchange sent a wave of electricity up Sam's arm. Sam looked from her hand to Helene, who was smiling sweetly at her. Shaking herself internally, Sam tried to focus as Helene explained her assignment.

"Rupert Downes, CEO of a leading pharmaceutical company in the US, is very rich, powerful and loves Paris. He's commissioned us, or I should say you, to be his personal photographer," she continued on as Sam flicked through the folder. "He wants you to capture the city, the good, the bad, everything!"

"That's a very vague and long list! How long has he commissioned me for?"

"As far as I am aware, there isn't a time limit. Oh, and the best part, there is no budget! You have free rein." Helene's smile grew exponentially when she saw Sam's eyes light up. It was every photographer's dream to have an unlimited budget.

"Wow, that's certainly exciting," Sam replied. "The only issue I can see is that I haven't packed to be here long term. To be honest, I grabbed my overnight bag I keep at the office. I have maybe three days' worth of clothes."

It had only just occurred to her that at no point had she asked how long she would be away. She hadn't planned for this. She'd been swept up in the moment and had forgotten to do anything practical.

"No need to worry, as I said, no expense spared!" Helene began rooting around in her handbag again, pulling out a set of keys and handing them to Sam, who looked thoroughly confused.

Helene explained the keys were for an apartment. "The apartment is yours for the duration of the job, along with a company credit card, so I suggest you do some shopping." This was too much to deal with. *Surely there must be a catch?* "I will show you the apartment, then I'll leave you to get settled in before we begin working tomorrow. I'll have you collected at 9 a.m. Henry, your driver, will take you to our version of Bright Lights."

Moments later, the car pulled up to a beautiful building that Sam thought looked typically French, although, in reality, she knew very little about French architecture.

A very polite young man who held the door for Sam and Helene manned the lobby. Henry followed close behind with all of Sam's luggage and equipment. Thank God, Sam couldn't imagine having to pick all that lot up again. Her back and shoulders were knackered.

At the end of the lobby, rows of gold plated letter boxes reflected on the polished marble floor. Everything about the place screamed money. There was a slight rumbling and a ping that made Sam turn to look. The doors to a small elevator slid open, a young couple stepped out casually talking to each other. As they approached, Sam and Helene were greeted with a polite "Bonsoir."

Sam smiled and went red. Another glaring issue that Sam hadn't thought through was the fact that she couldn't speak French, not in the slightest. She had always found languages hard.

During her French exam at school, she'd sat and stared at the teacher with a blank face, her mind devoid of anything remotely French. She recalled how the teacher had waited patiently for her to say something, anything, before realising that Sam would not be wowing her with any impressive language skills. She was therefore dismissed a mere five minutes into the exam. Needless to say that Sam got a big fat *U*.

"Helene, will I be working with many French-speaking subjects?" Sam enquired, hoping the panic she felt didn't resonate in her voice.

"That's entirely up to you. It depends on what you want to do, although I'm sure that Rupert will want models used in some shots," Helene replied as she headed for the little elevator.

"Right, yes, of course." Sam felt a knot in her stomach.

Helen turned to Sam just as the elevator door slid open. She could obviously see that Sam had clenched her eyebrows with stress. "Don't panic, we have many people that can help with any language difficulties. You are cute when you do the eyebrow thing."

Feeling reassured, and a little confused at Helene's behaviour, Sam followed her into the small elevator. There was not a lot of room and Sam felt Helene's front pressed against her back. *Jesus, are those her nipples?*

They reached the fourth floor, exited, and walked down a softly lit corridor. Only two apartment doors were visible. They reached the door furthest from the lift. Helene looked expectantly at Sam. It took her a few seconds to twig that she had the keys. With a grin and a little blush, Sam retrieved said keys and unlocked the door.

The apartment was breathtaking; no other word could describe it better. Each room was a well-planned mixture of modern and traditional design. The dark wooden floors shone under the expertly placed spotlights that were dotted all over the apartment. As they moved through the space, Sam's jaw dropped. Each room seemed more decadent than the last.

"La pièce de résistance" was her new bedroom. The room was enormous, a giant bed sat centre stage with two ornate bedside tables flanking either side. There were floor-to-ceiling windows that were sure to flood the room with tons of natural light in the daytime. A double set of doors led to a walk-in wardrobe that was almost the size of Sam's bedroom back in England.

For a split second, Sam caught herself thinking of Jo. It was instinctive to want to call her and tell her everything that was happening. It was like a hot knife stabbing her in the gut. The only thing that she could do was sit down.

"Are you okay?" Helene questioned; looking concerned.

"Yes, I'm fine, just a little overwhelmed," Sam lied. "It's a beautiful place," she added quietly, her eyes roaming, trying to take it all in. Her thoughts were racing through the events of that horrid night again. She had to get control of her mind.

Forcing herself, she stood up and went over to the window. The Eiffel tower stood in the distance, with its mesmerising light show in full swing. "Oh, wow," Sam gasped.

"Welcome to Paris," Helene whispered in her ear. Sam shivered, her body responding to Helene's closeness, which was closer than someone should be in a strictly professional situation. Sam turned her head slightly. She could smell Helene's perfume. Helene was looking straight into Sam's eyes. "Have you eaten?" The question took Sam by surprise.

43

"I had a quick bite on the train but nothing since," Sam replied, realising that she was starving.

"Dinner? I know a few decent places," Helene chimed as she moved away from Sam and towards the door.

"Yeah, sounds great." Did she say that with a bit too much enthusiasm? Truthfully, she was confused. Had she imagined that Helen had been flirting since the station? Was she that desperate for attention that she was inventing a beautiful woman coming on to her?

They walked for a few minutes, Sam following Helene, trying not to look like a complete tourist. Although it was unlikely that she'd succeeded, especially when she made little noises of surprise and excitement every ten feet.

They stopped at a small restaurant that doubled as a café in the daytime. Music played in the background. Each table was lit with small candles. Their table was tucked away in the back corner. It seemed intimate, and once again Sam puzzled over Helene's behaviour since they'd met. *She's definitely flirting.*

Sam picked up the menu and pretended to read it even though every word was in French and she had no clue what she was looking at. Helene smiled and giggled a little before reaching over and explaining each meal. As the evening progressed, Sam began to relax.

Everything had been delicious. The duck she'd picked was amazing and the wine that accompanied it had been divine. Sam couldn't remember the last time she'd eaten at a restaurant, let alone tasted such delicacies.

The conversation had been light and interesting. Helene was really fun to talk to. She put Sam at ease with her warmth and charm.

"I have seen some of your work. It's very good." Helene gave Sam a brief nod of praise.

"Thanks. I wasn't aware anyone had really seen it."

"Oh yes, John likes to get to know the people he will work with, and so do I."

"And how is it you came to work for John?" Sam enquired, fiddling unconsciously with the napkin on the table.

"John owns the company I work for, just like you." She said as she sipped her wine. Sam couldn't help but stare at Helene as she drank, the candlelight reflected in her eyes making them dance.

Helen was a little shorter than Sam; her hair was dirty blonde and fell down her back. Her eyes were a deep blue and a little mesmerising in the dim light.

She wore a form-fitting skirt that accentuated her legs and a matching blazer that tapered into her waist; she looked very smart and very sexy. The silk shirt underneath shimmered as she moved. Sam had to stop herself from looking at that shirt. It was *very* distracting.

"You're staring," Helene whispered.

"Shit, sorry. I didn't mean to." She could feel herself going red.

"It's okay, I don't mind," Helen whispered softly.

Sam wasn't sure if it was the wine that was giving her some courage and, frankly, she didn't care, because she knew she had to say something.

"Forgive me if I am completely wrong, but is it my imagination or are you flirting with me?" She sounded confident in her delivery. *Fake it 'till you make it, right?*

"Yes, I'm flirting," Helene replied with ease. "I have been flirting since the station. I wondered if you were picking up on it."

Sam sat there, looking stunned. "I thought I was imagining it."

"Are you okay with it?" Helene poured herself and Sam another glass of wine.

"Of course, I'm okay with it. Maybe a little surprised, but definitely okay with it." Sam smiled widely and then reached for her wine. However, before she could wrap her fingers around the stem, Helene had taken her hand. Sam looked at her, trying to read the situation. *Keep cool.*

45

"I don't want to seem too forward, well, no more than I already do." Helene grinned, "but how about I grab the check, and we go back to the apartment?" A jolt of excitement shot through Sam. She couldn't believe this was all happening.

"That sounds like a good idea." She was trying to sound seductive, although she wasn't certain she'd stuck the landing. Helene left the table to pay for their meal. Sam could feel her heart pounding. She hadn't had sex in a *very* long time, presuming that's where the night was heading.

Sam's mind raced. Her internal voice pointed out that she had *not* prepared her body for this. In other words, she was not properly groomed. She couldn't remember the last time she'd shaved her legs, let alone anywhere else. *This is going to be a disaster.*

Before she could have any more time to spiral, her phone rang. It was Charlie. Sam had forgotten to call her when she arrived.

Looking up to see if she could get Helene's attention, Sam began collecting her things. Helene looked over and saw Sam gesturing to her phone. Grabbing her coat, Sam headed outside.

"I am so sorry, Char."

"Oh no, don't worry, it's not as if I have been sitting wondering if you're alive or anything," Charlie tutted.

"I am here and safe. It's been crazy. I completely forgot to call you! Oh shit, I forgot to call mum as well."

"I've spoken to your mum, and she is far less worried than me. She told me you were 'on an adventure to soothe your soul'," Charlie chuckled.

Sam was relieved and amused. She could hear her mum saying those very words in her cheery and wistful voice.

"I really am sorry. Honestly, you won't believe what is happening."

"I'm listening." Charlie's interest was clearly piqued.

Sam recounted the entire day, starting from the train journey until the exact moment she picked up the phone. Charlie remained silent for a few seconds after Sam had finished telling her story. Suddenly, a burst of laughter rang out from the phone.

"What are you laughing at?" From where she was standing, there was nothing funny about the situation at all. Terrifying yes, funny no.

"This is exactly what you need!" Charlie exclaimed. "Someone to clear away the cobwebs," she continued to laugh.

"Char, that's disgusting."

"Oh, come off it, you sound a thousand times better just with a little flirting. Imagine what you will be like with a bit of the other." Charlie was so enthusiastic that Sam couldn't help but giggle.

Sam looked into the restaurant window. She could see Helene collecting her things and heading towards the door. "Shit, she's coming," Sam barked.

"Blimey, that was fast," Charlie howled.

"Be serious! What am I doing? This is insane. I've only known her for a few hours."

"Alright, calm down. You clearly want this, but it's new and you're scared. Don't spoil it for yourself. Take life by the ovaries and go for it," Charlie pleaded.

"I gotta go. I will call you tomorrow."

"Everything okay?" Helene stood close to Sam, her body heat was delicious.

"Completely fine, just my friend. Shall we go?"

"Absolutely," Helene smiled.

They walked in silence. Sam was too busy worrying to think of anything to say. They approached the apartment building, which made Sam panic more. Was she supposed to take the lead, considering it was her place they were going to?

Helene didn't hesitate for a second. Clearly, she wasn't feeling nervous. She walked straight in, greeted the doorman, and got into the elevator.

The apartment was warm and welcoming when they entered. Sam was feeling the effects of the wine. She steadied herself against the wall before dropping her coat onto the hook by the door. "Would you like a drink?" Sam called, noticing Helene had disappeared from view.

"No, thanks."

Sam hesitated for a minute. She wasn't sure what to do next. She followed Helene's voice into the living room, where she found her perched on the arm of the sofa waiting, with a look of concern or maybe worry in her eyes as she regarded Sam.

"Are you okay, you seem nervous?"

Sam cleared her throat. "I'm good. It's just that it has been some time since I–"

"We don't have to do anything, Sam," Helene interjected.

"I want to," Sam replied quickly. She needed to feel the warmth of another body touching hers.

Without another word, Helene walked over to Sam, took her by the hand, and led her to the bedroom. Helene dropped her hand when they stepped through the door. Walking a little further away, she turned around and began undressing. Never shifting her gaze from Sam.

Helene was graceful in her movements. Her long hair danced against her skin as she removed her shirt. Sam stood watching, taking her in. She was beautiful. She was also standing half-naked in a black lace bra. *Holy fucking shit.*

The time for watching was over. Sam needed to touch, be touched. She bridged the gap between them in two long strides. She reached out, allowing her fingers to glide over Helene's bare shoulders.

The subtle perfume that Sam had noticed earlier engulfed her now. It filled her with excitement. She could feel her body responding to the woman in front of her. Sam's fingers continued to caress.

Making her way around to Helene's back, she leaned in and brushed her lips against the side of her neck. Helene's reaction was instant. She turned and reached for Sam's shirt, ripping it open, causing several buttons to ping on to the floor. The delicacy Helene had shown a few seconds earlier had been replaced with an urgent hunger.

48

Following Helene's lead, Sam removed her own bra and threw it to the floor. Helene studied her body and then within seconds Sam felt lips wrap around her breast. Helene's tongue circled her nipple and an all too familiar but forgotten sensation travelled to her sex. The urge to be touched was overwhelming. A fire had been lit, and it was spreading rapidly.

"I want you inside me," Sam gasped. This was not a romantic act. It was primal. Sam didn't want to wait, she didn't want to be teased.

Helene continued to kiss Sam on her chest. Without halting her ministrations, she guided Sam's body to the bed, pushing her down, so she was lying on her back, her legs hanging off the end. They parted briefly only so Sam could remove her trousers and underwear.

Helene continued to explore with her mouth. It was pure ecstasy. Sam could feel her mind becoming clearer. No painful memories, no fear, just two bodies enjoying each other.

It was as if every one of Sam's nerves had electricity coursing through them. How could it possibly get any better than this? That question was answered when Sam felt Helen's fingers slide inside her. The sensation was overwhelming.

Helene pumped her fingers hard. Sam let out a loud moan. Her hips moved in time with Helen's hand. Sam knew she wouldn't be able to last very long. She could feel her body building up.

Gripping the bedcovers, Sam felt herself tighten. The orgasm took control of her entire body; she closed her eyes, letting it wash over every inch of her. At the precise moment that it was at its most intense, a face flashed across her mind. But it wasn't Helene or Jo. Who was the person invading this most intimate and vulnerable moment?

Who was the woman from the station?

Chapter Four

The drive from the station was longer than Anna thought it would be, and she was feeling irritated. James had been deep in thought for quite a while. He looked over at her with a reserved and worried expression etched across his face.

A second passed before he spoke. "What is the status of our relationship?" he shot at her. Anna blinked rapidly, not sure how to answer. "It's been a while now. Should we think about moving forward?" James remarked. "Anna, are you listening?" he barked.

"I don't understand why you want to talk about this now."

"Now is as good a time as any," he shot back.

"Things are fine how they are, aren't they?" she snapped.

James looked both angry and a little hurt. Anna felt guilty. He was a kind man and didn't deserve the way she spoke to him sometimes, but she wasn't ready for this conversation. In fact, she wasn't certain if she would ever be ready for it.

"Sorry, I'm not trying to be difficult." She just wanted to calm the situation and make James feel better. "I don't think this is the moment, that's all. I'm nervous about meeting your sister and let's be honest, I'm not the flavour of the month with your mum."

"It's not like I want to have specifics now. I just want to know that we can talk about our options."

"Options? James, we aren't organising a loan. We are talking about our future. I think we need to discuss it later when we can both give the subject our full attention."

"Fine," he shot back, his jaw muscles clenched tight.

They spent the rest of the journey in silence. Anna didn't enjoy arguing with him, but she preferred this to talking about their feelings. Life was simple with James. He wanted little from her and vice versa. Well, that was until he started asking about their "options."

A few miles later, James broke the silence again. "We've nearly arrived. I suggest the fact you forgot about the wedding should remain between us."

Anna said nothing but nodded her head in acknowledgement of his comment and continued to stare out of the window.

The countryside where James' parents lived was beautiful. Frost was visible on the trees; it had dropped to freezing now that the sun had set. If it hadn't been for the family visit, Anna thought she would enjoy visiting this part of England very much. "We're here," James mumbled.

As they approached the largest house that Anna had ever seen outside of a movie, she experienced crushing nerves. Anna's upbringing couldn't have been more different from this. Her parents owned a small little cottage in the middle of France. It barely fit all four of them when they were growing up.

James had seen her reaction and for the first time in a long time, smiled warmly at her. "Don't panic, you will be fine," he said calmly before exiting the car and heading to the boot. For a few seconds, Anna felt frozen in place. When James shut the back of the car, Anna was jolted into action.

51

Climbing out slowly, she reached for James' hand. She needed some reassurance. James seemed surprised but didn't pull back. They gripped each other's hands tightly as they headed for the front door. Ringing the doorbell, which produced an extremely obnoxious chime, they stood and waited.

Moments later, Anna saw a silhouette approach. Jillian. James' mum greeted them with a pursed mouth and the same judgemental look Anna had received the first time they'd met. *Great, let the fun times begin.*

Just as Anna remembered her, Jillian stood around 5'5" in an immaculately pressed skirt and blouse, her hair tied neatly into a bun on the back of her head. Anna wondered if she had a wardrobe full of identical outfits.

They greeted each other politely. However, that was the extent of the pleasantries. Anna knew Jillian didn't like her very much — that was no secret at all.

James was embraced warmly and quickly whisked away. Without hesitation, Anna followed. She was determined not to give Jillian any more excuses to dislike her.

Entering the living room, Derek greeted them — who, unlike his wife, looked quite different from the last time Anna had seen him. Standing at a good six feet, Derek now looked a lot more portly than before, his grey hair combed to the side, and his face had a permanent red glow.

Even though he was dressed in golf attire, Anna knew it was for show. James hadn't spoken a lot about his family, but he had mentioned his father's love of watching golf but his hatred of trying to play the game itself. Derek gave Anna an uncomfortably long hug before finally letting her go once his wife had glared at him.

The other person in there was a young-looking woman that Anna presumed was Jenny, the bride-to-be. Jenny was a petite girl with mousy brown hair shaved at the side, which was a surprise. The impression that she had about the Dunton family certainly didn't involve shaved heads.

James and Jenny were similar looking; however, Jenny shared her mother's thin frame and jawline. Wearing ripped jeans and a baggy T-shirt, Jenny looked out of place against her brother and parents.

"I'll introduce myself then, shall I?" she quipped at her brother. "Anna, it's a pleasure to meet you. I'm so happy that you could come with James."

"My pleasure," Anna lied with a smile that was a little too wide to be real.

"C'mon, I'll show you around the place," Jenny chirped, before she took Anna by the arm and led her out of the room. "Don't worry about mum; she is a snob, especially when it comes to the golden boy!" Jenny scoffed. "I heard about your meeting in Paris."

Anna gave a sheepish grin as Jenny laughed.

Sparing no detail, Jenny guided Anna around the house, explaining the history and sharing childhood stories. It was surprising just how different she was from James.

They entered the living room where the rest of the Duntons were sitting. "So, what do you think?" Jenny asked.

"It's a beautiful building," Anna replied. "My brother would love it here. He is an architect in Paris," she added. James gave her a smile as she sat beside him. Jillian continued to talk as if she hadn't noticed Anna speaking.

"Anna was just telling me about her brother. He's an architect," Jenny interrupted, her intention to force her mother to be polite and acknowledge Anna.

"That's a fine career," Derek replied.

"He is a brilliant young man."

"Yes, sounds like a respectable job," Jillian said stiffly. "We were very proud of James when he went into the pharmaceutical business. They highly respect him in the company," she added, looking at James with pride.

Anna couldn't help but discern that James really was the centre of his parents' attention. She felt bad for Jenny until she looked over at her and had to stifle a laugh. Jenny had seen the

53

adoring look her mother was giving James, but instead of looking hurt, she was making a gagging face, sticking her fingers into her mouth.

They spent the rest of the evening listening to James recall the past few months since he had seen his parents; meaning they had to listen to work-related stories, all of which Anna had heard several times before.

Anna learned about Jenny's fiancé Jack. He was the manager of the local animal shelter. That's where they had met. Jenny had worked in the shelter since she had left university where she had studied politics, something that she'd found she hated but finished to please her parents.

"So you understand why I'm not as celebrated as my dear brother," Jenny joked as they sipped on brandy in the parlour.

"I can't imagine your parents were too pleased," Anna remarked, making a point of whispering.

"Upset is an understatement. I thought mum was going to have a heart attack," Jenny giggled. "We exchanged a few choice words when I explained I would work with dogs and cats for minimum wage."

"What made you choose animals?"

"I love them more than people. It was always my dream job. In my final year of uni, I realised I couldn't choose a career based on my parent's approval," Jenny said a little louder than expected. Anna could see Jillian turn red, but continue to look as if she was in deep conversation with Derek and James.

"So why Jack?" Anna challenged playfully. She couldn't help but think back to the conversation in the car with James. She needed to understand how to know if the person could be "the one."

"There was never any question. We fit. He is my other half. You will meet him tomorrow before the rehearsal banquet."

"I very much look forward to it." If Jack was anything like Jenny, they'd get on wonderfully.

The evening drew to a close at 10 p.m. sharp. Jillian demanded that everyone retire to bed, as they had a busy day

54

ahead of them. No one argued, especially not Anna. She desperately needed to sleep.

James' room had been kept exactly the same as when he'd lived at home. Certificates and diplomas were displayed proudly on the walls, along with a vast amount of trophies and medals.

James threw their luggage on the floor and jumped onto the bed. It was clear to see that he was happy to be at home. Anna got the feeling it was more because of the unrelenting attention he received from his parents rather than because he missed being back in the UK.

"So, did you enjoy dinner?"

"It was delicious," Anna replied, sitting on the edge of the bed. She wished she could share a room with Jenny. She would have had more to say.

"Mum was telling me about the rehearsal banquet. You will sit at a different table to me, I'm afraid," he said as he undressed.

"Who will I be sitting with?" She wasn't in the least bit surprised she wouldn't be allowed near the family table.

"Not sure. The extended cousins, I think."

"Cousins, wow, I'm surprised. I would have thought your mother would have seated me at the 'friends of friends' table," Anna shot at him.

"Don't be like that!"

Anna couldn't bear to get into another fight, especially one that she knew she wouldn't win. She undressed and got into bed. A few minutes later, she felt James climb under the covers. They mumbled a halfhearted "Night" before rolling away from each other.

Anna woke early. She hadn't slept well. Although the bed was comfy, she'd struggled to settle down. With a heavy head, she sat up and switched on the lamp, waking James. "Shit, sorry." She quickly flipped the light off before James could moan at her.

The smell of coffee was extremely pleasurable as she made her way downstairs. Her body craved it, that and a cigarette. The last time she'd smoked was outside her office. When she entered the kitchen, she was relieved to see Jenny sitting at the table, reading a magazine. "You look rough," Jenny mocked.

"Bad night," Anna yawned. "Is there anywhere I can smoke?"

"Stand at the back door," Jenny said, without looking up from the magazine.

"Are you confident that's allowed?" Anna replied sarcastically. She felt as if she could be herself with Jenny, although she still scanned the area to make sure Jillian or Derek weren't in earshot.

"It's fine, that's where Jack stands," she smiled.

Anna headed for the door. The sun was still low. The light shone over the large grounds, highlighting all the little spiderwebs that were covered in morning dew and that hung from tree branches and bushes. Anna took a deep breath in. She welcomed the cold air.

Standing with her hot coffee in one hand, she lit her cigarette. The satisfaction was instantaneous. After she had inhaled for the third time in quick succession, she felt her head buzz. It didn't take her long to finish. She was sad that it had ended, but now her toes were becoming numb from the cold.

Anna sat at the table quietly, trying to wake herself up, knowing that she would need to be on top form to put up with another day of Jillian. James joined them in the kitchen, still wearing his pyjamas. He settled for a cup of tea and sat down next to Anna. "Where's mum and dad?"

"They went out. They shouldn't be too long," Jenny responded casually as she prepared breakfast for them all.

"When can we expect Jack?" he quizzed.

"Around half eleven, twelve. We're going to the shelter to check on Sid."

"I take it Sid is an animal and not an employee," James snorted. Jenny rolled her eyes at her brother.

"Yes, of course, he's an animal, you know, because I have told you about him, but I suppose unless the conversation is about you, you're not interested," she shot back without hesitation.

56

James looked wounded but kept his composure as he grabbed a newspaper that lay closed on the table. Jenny looked at Anna with a big smile and a wink. Anna returned the smile after making sure James wouldn't see.

Midday arrived at the sound of a car pulling into the driveway. Anna was having a pleasant morning with Jenny and James in the kitchen. It had been very relaxed. The breakfast that Jenny had made was delicious. Anna couldn't remember the last time she had eaten a full English.

Knowing that the day was about to go downhill rapidly, Anna steeled herself for the inevitable rudeness that Jillian was going to show her. She was pleasantly surprised, however, when a young man entered the kitchen instead. Jenny got to her feet and embraced him, kissing him repeatedly. Anna presumed he must be Jack.

Jack was only a little taller than Jenny. Similarly, he wore ripped jeans and a T-shirt like Jenny. His hair was longer than Jenny's. Tied into a scruffy bun on the top of his head, he looked as though he had just crawled out of bed. The image suited him; he looked stylish in his messiness. Jenny turned to Anna, glowing with adoration.

Witnessing Jenny's reaction to the man she loved gave Anna mixed feelings. She felt a sense of hope and sadness. Anna couldn't think of any time in her relationship with James that she'd ever looked at him the way Jenny was looking at Jack right then. She felt hopeful that one day she would have that look on her face, but would it be with James?

I doubt it!

"Jack, this is Anna, James' girlfriend and my new bestie."

Jack marched over and hugged Anna with so much enthusiasm it made Anna giggle. She laughed when he went straight over to James and did the same. "How ya doing, buddy?" He clapped James hard on the back, making him drop the newspaper.

James looked a little disgruntled. "Good, thanks. You?"

57

"Ah, all good! Marrying this one, so I'm on top of the world," he said, squeezing Jenny's bum and winking at her. Jenny returned to her seat as Jack made himself a drink. All ears turned to the kitchen door as they heard voices in the hallway. Jillian and Derek had returned.

Anna watched Jack put his cup down, look at Jenny and wink again. No sooner had Jillian stepped into the kitchen than Jack shouted excitedly, "Jillian," and with a huge smile and wide-open arms, he scooped her up into a behemoth hug. Jillian was taken completely by surprise. Her eyes went wide — almost comically — with shock. Jenny started laughing, with Anna and James following suit.

After a lengthy hug, Jack released Jillian and gave Derek a hearty handshake. He then returned to his drink as if nothing had happened. Jillian straightened her top, shot a glance at Derek, and then went into the pantry with the bags she was holding. Derek seemed less affronted than his wife. He settled down at the table, picking at the scraps from breakfast. "Are you ready for the rehearsal dinner, Jack?" Derek mumbled through a bit of toast.

"Banquet," Jillian corrected from inside the pantry. Jenny rolled her eyes.

"Of course, I have my bagpipes ready. I have been practising day and night," he said with a very serious look on his face. Jillian shot out of the pantry.

"I hope you're joking," she snapped.

"Yes, I am," Jack said bluntly. "It's actually a trumpet."

Jenny started laughing again. Anna was enjoying herself. After thinking that all of James' family would be like his mother, she was thrilled to know that they weren't all bad.

They spent most of the day talking about the rehearsal dinner, sorry "banquet". Anna couldn't see the point of it all. Why they needed to rehearse eating and drinking was beyond her. One thing that was for certain, if she ever got married, there would be none of this.

As the afternoon rolled into evening, the wedding conversations wore thin. Even Jenny was getting frustrated with her mum's constant pestering and questioning. Both women were relieved when Jillian insisted they leave to get ready for the evening's event.

Anna searched through her clothes, not knowing what had been packed for her. After a few minutes of rummaging through her suitcase, she was almost certain that James had left it to Kim to pack her belongings because she had some very well-thought-out outfits; she knew James hadn't got the fashion sense to have picked them out so carefully.

Eventually, after several minutes of going back-and-forth between two dresses, she picked her favourite black backless. The dress made her feel good. It hugged her in all the right places and accentuated her breasts. She always felt better about her body when wearing it.

Half an hour later, she was ready. Looking at herself in the mirror, she saw James enter the room. "Wow, you look great," he exclaimed.

"Don't seem so surprised," Anna replied, feeling a little embarrassed.

"I meant nothing by it. I just think you look good," James said, a little stung as he went to open his own luggage. Anna felt bad again. She wondered why she couldn't accept a compliment from him. The atmosphere had become tense. Not knowing how to make it better, Anna left James to get dressed alone.

Finally, everyone was ready to go. James, Derek, and Jack had enjoyed a small glass of whisky before Jillian practically threw them out of the house and into the waiting cars.

The country hall where the "banquet" was taking place was a short car journey away. They pulled into the large gravel car park. The valet service was under a large archway that was lit by grand ornate wall lamps. Small lanterns lit the pathways that led around the building and into the lush grounds. It was beautiful.

The inside was just as exquisite. A dozen tables were lined with white satin cloth, sparkling crystal glasses, and gold

59

cutlery. Candles positioned on each table gave the room a romantic glow. It didn't take long for Jillian to jump into action, ordering everyone to their seats as other guests began to arrive.

Anna was not in the least bit surprised to see that she was sitting far from the head table. She continued to look around the room, admiring the architecture and the decoration. The other members of her table seemed pleasant. They reintroduced themselves to each other with hearty handshakes and short stories of childhood mishaps they'd shared.

Anna sat quietly, waiting for her chance to introduce herself. A short, stout man was the first to talk to her. He introduced himself as Timothy Smith, a cousin from "up north." Anna spent a few minutes explaining her connection to the family.

"Blimey, I haven't seen little James for a long time," Timothy declared. "Paris, eh? He has done well for himself, and with you, too. Very good." Anna smiled politely. Timothy was a character, and another member of the family that seemed the opposite of James' parents.

With members of the table chatting away, Anna was quite content observing and listening as they made their way through the three course meal. The lamb was heavenly and even though it was hard to admit, Anna knew Jillian had good taste in food, because the menu she'd designed was sublime.

Anna was happy at her table of castaway family members. She had a very pleasant conversation with cousin Rebecca, who had spent some time travelling. Rebecca had visited Paris three times in two years. She seemed particularly taken with it. "It must be amazing to live there?" she gushed.

"I'm very fortunate," Anna replied. "When will you visit again?" She would happily meet up with Rebecca the next time she was in town.

"Maybe next year, I have my heart set on Indonesia next."

Before Anna could ask any more questions, Jillian stood up, tapping her glass, getting everyone's attention. The speeches were about to begin. Anna's mind wandered. She scouted the room and saw James deep in conversation with a very attractive blonde woman. They obviously knew each other well. James seemed very relaxed. Anna noticed they touched each other on the arm or the shoulder when they spoke.

"That's Amy," Rebecca whispered. "I think they dated at one point."

Anna didn't know how to respond. Should she feel jealous? She knew she didn't. She was happy to see James enjoying himself, even if it was with someone else.

Finally, after an achingly long time, the speeches ended, and after several minutes of applause, Jenny spoke. "Thank you all for coming. We can't wait to see you again for the actual event." Her happiness was paramount as smiled down at Jack. "Now that the formalities are over with, we would like to ask you to move to the next room for the disco." Jenny almost squealed in delight. Jillian didn't look half as impressed.

For a few minutes, there was an eruption of noise from chairs scraping along the floor as the guests made their way to the room located just behind Anna's table. Through the double doors, Anna could see lights shining as the music started up.

Everyone seemed in good spirits. Most of the guests headed for the bar first. Anna stayed in her seat, waiting for James. She looked around at the emptying room. He was nowhere to be seen.

Realising that he must have already gone through to the party, she promptly left her chair and headed for the disco. James was already at the bar, and he wasn't alone. Amy stood chatting away with him. Anna walked over and propped herself next to him. "There you are."

"Anna!" he replied, almost surprised to see her standing there. "I thought you had already come through," he lied.

Anna looked from James to Amy and back to James. James seemed to struggle with what to say, so she put out her hand and introduced herself. "Hi, I'm Anna."

"Right, yeah, sorry, this is Amy," James spluttered.

"It's a pleasure, Amy," Anna smiled.

61

"Nice to meet you too," Amy replied with a sweet smile. James stuttered his way through an explanation of how he knew Amy. Anna had the impression that he thought she would be angry with him, as if she had caught him doing something wrong.

"I hope James has bought you a drink?"

"Oh, yes, thanks, he just ordered."

"Did you want one?" It seemed he had forgotten to order one for his girlfriend.

"No, I had enough wine at dinner thank you. I'm going to look for Jenny to give my congratulations one more time." Anna replied, leaving James looking a little ashamed of himself.

For the rest of the evening, Anna wandered around, looking at everyone enjoying themselves. She especially enjoyed watching cousin Timothy demonstrate his dancing capabilities — or lack of.

Every so often Anna would glimpse James and Amy talking. She could see how happy he was with her. As far as Anna could recall, he had never mentioned Amy, but as she watched them, it was clear that they had history. They'd definitely dated, and Anna surmised it hadn't been casual either. That much was obvious as she watched them from afar.

When the last song ended, many of the guests had already left. Anna was bone tired. It had been an exhausting few days. James had joined her in the car park a few minutes later. Amy had left shortly before, and Anna noticed their hug had lasted a little longer than most friendly goodbyes.

The night had been a success. Even Jillian seemed a little more relaxed. The car journey back was quiet. Tiredness had taken hold of everyone. After a brief goodnight, everyone retired to their rooms. Anna threw her dress to the floor, pulled on her pyjamas and climbed into bed. It felt so good to be lying down.

James slipped under the duvet, but instead of turning in the opposite direction as usual, Anna felt him pull closer to her. Leaning in, he kissed her neck. His hand reached under her top and cupped her breast. He pressed himself against her. She could feel he was hard.

Taking his hand away from her breast, he pulled Anna's pyjama trousers down. Anna rolled over onto her back. James shifted slightly to position himself on top as he guided himself into her. He took his time building the rhythm.

James looked straight into Anna's eyes, but she felt as if he was looking straight through her. His eyes were vacant. He was disconnected. She could see that his mind was somewhere else. Anna could hear his breathing getting heavier, a slight moan in each breath. Screwing his eyes shut, he thrust harder.

Anna visualised her dream from two nights ago. She could see her stranger again. Closing her eyes, she focused on that face, looking at her so intensely. She felt a tightening. James felt it, too. He moaned harder, grabbing her backside as he thrust deeper inside. Anna was lost in her own head. It wasn't James fucking her; it was the woman from the train station.

James' body tensed. He was ready to come; Anna gripped the sheets as her own body prepared for the orgasm stirring low inside her body. In unison, they let out a final groan of pleasure. James waited a few seconds to catch his breath before he pulled himself away and rolled over onto his back.

Anna lay there breathing heavily, staring at the ceiling. James sat up and left the bed; he entered the Ensuite and shut the door. Hearing the shower turn on, Anna replaced her pyjama trousers, rolled over and turned out the light. Before she could stop herself, she sobbed, tears streaking down her face.

Chapter Five

The noise from the street woke Sam early. Her head felt fuzzy. She couldn't remember how much wine she had drunk in the restaurant, but she was sure it was too much.

It took her a few minutes to orientate herself to her new surroundings. Putting her feet on the warm floor, she yawned and stretched her body.

The floorboards gave a little creak as she tiptoed down the hallway to her enormous kitchen. After opening nearly every cupboard door, she finally found a glass. The only thing she could think of was how dry her throat had become. The water soothed her, but it hadn't quenched her thirst. Another glass did the trick.

When the memories from the night before came flooding back, she suddenly felt very awake. Sam crept back down the hall and poked her head around the door, looking at her new bed and the person occupying it.

Now that the alcohol had worn off, Sam was feeling less confident. Her brain went into overdrive trying to process what had happened. She didn't want to be caught staring so tiptoed back to the bed and slid under the duvet, feigning sleep, hoping that when Helene woke up she would take control of the situation and Sam could follow her lead.

Two hours passed as Sam lay there trying to think of every potential outcome she may face once Helene has risen from what seemed to be a deep slumber. As she checked the time on the clock above the bed, she felt Helene stir. Sam tried to stay as still as possible.

Helene sat upright, stretched, and rubbed her temples. After a minute Helene copied Sam's earlier movements, shuffling into the kitchen to pour herself a drink. Listening intently, Sam heard the tap shut off and the unmistakable creaking of the floorboard. "Morning," Helene yawned.

"Morning," Sam imitated, feeling her face redden.

"I think I'm a little hungover," Helene remarked as she lay back down, clutching her head.

"Me, too. My head is pounding a little." Sam tried to sound as normal as possible, even though her insides were squirming. They both lay silent for a few minutes before Helene rolled over and draped her arm around Sam.

A sudden loud ringing noise gave both of them a fright. *Who the hell is ringing the sodding bell?* Helene reached over to her purse and retrieved her phone. "That will be Henry, your driver. He will be here to take you to the office."

"Shit, what do we say?" Sam panicked.

"Why would we say anything?" Helene replied, looking a little confused.

"Of course, sorry, we need to keep it between us." They had just had a one-night stand, of course they wouldn't tell anyone. They had to work together.

"No, I didn't say that," Helene smiled. "I simply meant that we haven't got to explain ourselves to anyone. We are adults," she added before kissing Sam on the cheek.

65

"Oh, right, yeah," Sam blushed. She sat for a few minutes watching Helene gather herself before heading out of the bedroom towards the apartment door.

"Bonjour Henry."

"Bonjour Madame." A low voice replied.

Sam tuned out the conversation between Henry and Helene after the initial greeting. She moved over to the window and looked outside. Staring out at the city, Sam didn't notice when Helene returned. It was only when she felt lips on her neck that she pulled her gaze away from the wonders that lay beyond her window.

"I think you need to get ready," Helene whispered.

Sam's body ignited again as she felt Helene's breath in her ear. "Of course, time to work," Sam smiled, looking into Helene's eyes, still unable to fully grasp how she'd ended up in her current situation.

Thirty minutes later, they were both dressed and ready to go. Henry had waited patiently by the car. Sam could smell fresh cigarettes as he brushed past her to open the door.

Sam continued to act like a tourist, staring out of the tinted car window whilst Helene began working from her phone, answering emails, now and then cursing in French at something on her screen.

The car pulled onto a small cobbled road. The buildings on either side towered over them; each had a dozen arched windows and exquisitely sculptured facades. "Which one is the office?" Sam inquired.

"Both?"

"What, both buildings?"

"Yes, both buildings," Helen said with a smile, seeing Sam's reaction. "That one," pointing to the building on the right, "is where we have our studios and this one," diverting her gaze to the building to the left, "is for our office and editing suites" she finished.

"Impressive."

The inside was as spectacular as the exterior. The décor was similar to Sam's new apartment, classically elegant with a modern twist. Two receptionists busily answered the phones as they walked past. Helen gave a little wave, which was returned by both women simultaneously. "Clara and Bette," Helene remarked without looking back, Sam gave them a little smile.

Helene gave Sam a brief tour of their workplace before ushering her into a room that Sam surmised was Helene's office. "Sit down." Helene hung her coat on the back of her door before rounding her desk to take a seat. "So, how are you finding it so far?"

"So far, so good," Sam grinned. She was in her element.

"Sam, I think there is something I should tell you. I should have said it last night, before, well before we went to bed."

Sam's heart felt as if it were in her throat. She stared at Helene, hoping that she looked calm. "You're married."

"No, it's nothing like that," Helene laughed. "I'm technically your boss while you are working here."

"Oh!"

"It's not an issue for me. I just wanted to know how you feel about it?"

"I'm okay with it. We're professionals, and I don't think it would have changed anything if you had told me last night," Sam admitted truthfully.

"I'm happy to hear that," Helene smiled, and for the first time Sam saw vulnerability. "In the office, we are professionals. Work is work," she added.

"Not a problem." They looked at each other silently for a few seconds.

"Okay, let's get down to it then. You have the equipment. What else will you need?"

"A guide, I want to capture the entire city, not just the usual places that tourists see, so I need someone with intimate knowledge of Paris."

"You need Sébastien. He knows Paris like the back of his hand." Helene reached for her office phone that lay under a pile of paperwork. "Seb, can you spare a few minutes?" Moments later, the door opened. A tall, thin and kind-looking man stood in the doorway, his brown curly hair draped in front of his round glasses.

"Salut," he said happily, strolling over to Helene and kissing her on each cheek.

"Seb, this is Sam," Helen gestured.

"Very pleased to meet you," he said, holding Sam's hand to his lips.

"Pleased to meet you, too." She had never had someone kiss her hand before.

"Now, can you spare some time, Seb? Sam would like to begin her project by exploring the city. We both know that you are the man for the job."

"Of course. I cleared my calendar yesterday. I can read you like a book, Helene," he said, winking at Sam. "Everyone in the office is excited to meet you, Sam. We are all intrigued to meet the photographer that landed the Downes project."

"I didn't exactly land it. It came as a complete surprise, if I'm honest."

Sébastien smiled sweetly. "Of course you landed it. Nobody gets anything for free in this business, you know that," he exclaimed.

"Very true." Helene looked pointedly at Sam.

Usually—or more like "post Jo"—Sam would have felt uneasy, receiving a compliment. She found it difficult to believe what was said to be the truth, especially when it came to her work or her abilities as a photographer. But not today. Since arriving in Paris, she felt lighter, more positive. Bright Lights Photography seemed a lifetime away, and so did the memories.

Quickly putting any thought of the past to the back of her mind, Sam sat straighter and focused on the job at hand. "When can we get started, Sébastien?"

"Right now, let me grab my coat and we can get going. I saw Henry put your equipment next to your desk," Sébastien said, walking towards the door, looking expectantly at Sam to follow. Sam stood up, ready to leave.

"I just need Sam for a couple more minutes." Helene smiled at Sébastien as he left the room, nodding politely in acknowledgement of his dismissal.

"Here is your work phone. I have saved the essential numbers for you." She handed Sam the mobile in her hand. "Sébastien is great. He will look after you."

Getting up from behind the desk, she walked over to Sam. "If you need me, just call." She leaned a little closer. "Before you go, I realised I forgot to say… I really enjoyed last night. I hope it wasn't a one-off." She pressed her lips softly on Sam's.

Without hesitation, Sam rose to her feet. She pulled Helen close, holding her by the waist as she returned the kiss with force.

For a moment Sam had the urge to reach down and tug up Helene's skirt, which had been teasing her all morning. She wanted nothing more than to repeat last night's events, but a voice in her head reminded her she was at work, meaning she could not rip Helene's clothes off. Helene looked surprised when Sam stepped away. "What's wrong?" she gasped.

"We're at work," Sam replied, catching her breath.

"Right, of course." Helene cleared her throat and straightened her clothes.

"You know I want nothing more than to touch you." She didn't want Helene to feel rejected, but she knew she couldn't afford to mess this up by being unprofessional for her sake and Helene's.

"I know. You are right. We need to be sensible." She walked back to her seat, taking her place behind her desk.

"Can I see you later?"

"I think I can fit you in," Helen smiled before turning to the paperwork in front of her.

Smiling to herself, Sam left the office with a swagger in her step. She looked for Sébastien, who was waiting by the door, holding Sam's camera bag and tripod. "Ready to go?"

"Absolutely."

They left the office and walked along the cobbled street. There was no sign of Henry or the car. Clearly, they would see the sights by walking or public transport.

"If you want to feel Paris, no more cars!" Sébastien exclaimed, as if he had read Sam's thoughts. "If you must use a vehicle, it is the metro or the bus from now on," he added, crossing the street and turning the corner.

Sam was more than happy to stretch her legs. She remembered her first project for Bright Lights, which too had involved walking around a city, but the city she'd photographed then was nothing compared to Paris.

Restaurants and cafes lined each street, filled with people talking intensely with each other, sipping on coffee and smoking cigarettes. It was everything that Sam had hoped it would be.

They weren't heading in any specific direction; Sébastien was giving her the uncut tour, taking her to places that saw little tourists but held breathtaking sights.

It didn't take long for Sam to take numerous photographs. Buildings, streets, graffiti, the river — everything became her subject, and she revelled in it. No feeling on earth compared to this, the feeling of complete freedom, she thought as she focused on an old woman drinking an espresso with her dog sitting on the chair next to her basking in the sun.

Hours passed as they walked and travelled on the bus to different locations. Sam wasn't sure how many pictures she had taken, but she knew it was going to take her a long time to edit them all. As the sun set, they headed back to the office.

Sébastien was a great guy and a fantastic guide. Sam felt she had got to know him rather well over the course of the day. She'd listened to him talk about the city and stories of his time in Paris for hours. He was fascinating. They had spoken about her job at Bright Lights, his wife Charlie, and their unborn baby, who was only a few weeks away from making an appearance. It really had been the perfect first day.

"Helene is still here," Sébastien remarked as they dumped their gear on the closest desk. All the walking had taken its toll on them both. Sam looked toward Helen's office and saw a dim light shining through the partly open door.

"Thanks for today, Sébastien. I have had a great time, and I know I've got some great material to work with."

"My pleasure, and please call me Seb," he smiled, patting her on the shoulder. "I need to go. Anita will expect me home any second."

With a wave and a smile, Seb left, leaving Sam alone. The only thing on Sam's mind now was Helene and continuing where they'd left off earlier in the day.

As Sam approached the door, she realised Helen wasn't alone. Another voice, a familiar voice, came from the office. Sam knocked gently on the door. Helene opened it with a beaming smile. "Good, you're back." She reached for Sam's hand. "I have a surprise for you. There is someone you know who works here. I didn't tell you before because I didn't want to spoil it. She said that you worked together in the past," Helen finished, before pulling Sam into the room.

Confused, Sam looked towards the person sitting in the seat she had been sitting in a few hours earlier. The woman stood and turned to look at Sam. It was her; it was The Traitorous Bitch or Lauren, as everyone else that didn't despise her knew her as. Sam's world felt as if it was crashing down around her. She couldn't move. She could only look at the woman who had ripped her life apart.

Sam slowly turned to Helene, who had clearly seen Sam's face drain of colour. "This is cruel." Sam was desperately trying to stay in control of herself. She could feel tears welling up, but she was determined not to break down in front of them.

"What do you mean?" Helene replied, looking genuinely confused and concerned.

"Why on earth would I want to see her?" Sam spat at Helene, anger saturating every word.

71

"Sam, please," Lauren spoke, walking a little closer. Immediately reacting to Lauren's advance, Sam took a step back, her heart racing as she tore her hand from Helen's grasp.

"What is going on?" Helene barked at Lauren.

Before Lauren could answer, Sam ripped open the door and ran out. She couldn't hold the tears back any longer. She needed to be as far away from that room as possible.

The cold air hit her lungs as she crashed out of the main doors. She couldn't catch her breath. She felt hands grasp her arms gently. Pulling away, she fell to the floor. She was going to pass out.

"Madame Chambers," a familiar voice said. Sam looked up. Through tears, she could see Henry, her car driver, bent down beside her.

"I... need... to... go," Sam sobbed.

Without another word, Henry scooped Sam from the floor and gently helped her into the back of the car. Slowly, Sam calmed down. She took deep breaths, thinking of Charlie and what she would say to her if she were there.

By the time they had reached the apartment building, Sam was back in control. She wiped her tears and thanked Henry for his help. Sam could see that he wanted to enquire further, but he resisted and bid her a good night with concern stamped across his gentle face.

Sam headed for her apartment building. She had to use every ounce of strength she had to hold herself together and smile when she saw the doorman. Thankfully, there was no one else in the lobby or elevator. As the door to her apartment closed softly behind her, she clutched her stomach, trying with all her might not to vomit.

The phone that Helene had given her buzzed in her coat pocket. It stopped for a few seconds and began again. Throwing her coat to the floor, Sam entered the kitchen. She needed water. She could feel herself shaking. As she concentrated on drinking, her hand became steadier, her abdomen unclenched and she was able to stand a little straighter leaning against the kitchen counter.

The doorbell startled her. She closed her eyes, willing the person on the other side of the door to go away. Repeatedly it rang. "Sam, let me in," Helene shouted through the door. "Please, let me explain," she pleaded.

"Please leave," Sam called, her voice trembling.

"I'm not leaving until you listen to me," Helene replied forcefully.

"Please, Helene, not now," Sam replied weakly.

"I didn't want to do this, but clearly you leave me no choice," Helen shouted. The sound of the lock being opened made Sam move quickly to the hallway. Helene stood in the door, looking at Sam. A set of keys dangled from her finger. They stood for a few seconds looking at each other, this time though it was not with passion or lust but with panic, worry and pleading.

"What happened between you?" Helene was rooted to the spot. She could see that anguish on Sam's face.

"What, she didn't tell you?" Sam snapped.

"No, she didn't! She told me you worked together, that's it," Helene pressed. "I thought it would be a comfort to see someone you knew," she continued, wanting to get everything out before Sam barked at her again.

"Comfort," Sam screamed. "That woman ruined my life."

"Tell me," Helen said gently. "Please," she added as she walked over to Sam, pulling her into her arms.

"I'm not sure if I can," Sam cried, her body going limp against Helene's.

"Please," Helene repeated. Sam pulled herself away from Helene's embrace. She walked through to the lounge and sank into the sofa. Helene appeared a few minutes later, carrying an open bottle of wine and two glasses. "I think you need this."

Sam drained her glass and poured herself another. She could see Helen watching her patiently. "Did she ever mention someone named Jo?" Sam was unable to look Helen in the face.

"Yeah, Jo broke her heart."

Sam laughed. She couldn't stop herself. "Lauren had an affair with *my* girlfriend of ten years—Jo!" Sam choked, unable to believe what she had just heard.

"Oh," Helen replied quietly, "I had no idea." She placed her hand over Sam's.

"Lauren was my boss at Bright Lights. Jo was a freelance editor and would work for the company now and then."

"When did you find out about the affair?" Helen pressed lightly.

"My team had landed a big client. We had been working on the project for months. I came home early from celebrating its completion and I found them in our bed."

There was no use trying to hold back the memories anymore. They flooded into her mind, her body felt numb.

"They humiliated me. Everyone in the company knew. After I found out, they paraded themselves in front of me. They were so cruel."

"I'm so sorry." Helene held Sam close to her chest.

"How did you meet her?" A sinking feeling had replaced the hurt she had felt. She could sense something else was wrong.

"During a project in the south of France six years ago, before she secured a permanent position at Bright Lights," Helen replied vaguely.

"And she began working for you when?" Sam pressed, the bad feeling growing ever more intense as she looked at Helen, who had now turned pale and could no longer look Sam in the eyes.

"She doesn't work for me, Sam, she is my boss," Helen replied, her fingers fiddling with her top.

Sam felt her body slump, all her energy was gone, all her fight. "So that means she is my boss again?" Sam simply stated.

"There is more." Helene shifted uncomfortably in her seat.

"How could there possibly be more?"

"We had a relationship for six months."

Sam took a second to process what Helene had said. Suddenly, and without warning or understanding of her actions, she laughed uncontrollably. Of course, this was how it was going to go. Her life had been one shit show after the next for the past year. Why did she think travelling to Paris would change a damn thing?

After a few minutes, she was able to gain some control of herself. She took a few deep breaths before letting her head sag. "Well, it was good, while it lasted."

Chapter Six

The morning after the banquet was tense, Anna and James had exchanged only a handful of words. It was clear something had changed between them. Anna was thankful to Jenny for keeping her busy with wedding preparations. Every time Anna was alone, she thought of James, their relationship, and how lonely she felt.

"Is everything alright?" Jenny looked at Anna apprehensively.

"Oh, yes," Anna lied.

"You're a terrible liar, Anna," Jenny replied. "I don't know what's going on between you and James, but I think you should talk to someone. You look so sad," she added, gently pressing Anna on her shoulder.

Jenny was right. Anna felt as if she would explode if she had to keep these feelings inside any longer. Before she could stop herself, all the things she had been desperate to say for so long came spilling out. Jenny stood there looking a little shocked by the sudden outburst, but she remained her usual smiling self, taking in every word that poured out of Anna.

When all her thoughts and feelings had finished tumbling out, Anna deflated and became silent. She wasn't sure if she had made any sense. She'd spoken with such speed that Jenny might not have understood at all.

As soon as she'd gathered herself together, Anna looked at Jenny and let out a deep breath. She felt better, but that didn't stop her from worrying about Jenny's reaction. She had just told her boyfriend's sister that she didn't think they belonged together after all.

"How long have you felt this way?"

"I think we have both felt lost for some time. We have just existed together for so long that it has become normal. Something has changed between us since we have been here. I can't keep living like this," Anna sobbed.

Jenny embraced Anna, holding her tightly, gently stroking her hair. "Anna, speak to him now. Don't wait any longer," Jenny whispered as she comforted her.

"But the wedding is tomorrow. I don't want to ruin it for him or, more importantly, you," Anna replied weakly.

"Speak to him. Don't let this go on any longer. It isn't fair to either of you."

Giving her one last look and a kiss on the head, Jenny left Anna alone with her thoughts. She knew what she had to do, and she knew she had to do it immediately, before any courage she had mustered vanished.

James was sitting in the kitchen reading the morning paper. He peered over the top of the page as Anna entered the room. He continued to look at her as she sat in the chair closest to him. "We need to talk."

"Can it wait?" he replied coldly, his eyes returning to the sports section.

"No, it can't."

Sighing, he folded the paper and looked at Anna. "What do you want to talk about?"

"Us!" Her voice was steady, and she felt ready to say what needed to be said, what should have been said months ago. "Do you love me?"

James' face turned the same shade of red his mother did when she was uncomfortable. "What sort of question is that?" he snapped.

"It's one that you need to answer honestly, James," Anna replied calmly. "I'm not in love with you."

The conversation wasn't about hurting him, but she knew they had been lying to each other for so long that anything she said that resembled her true feelings would seem heartless. "I'm sorry if that is painful to hear," Anna pressed on. "I'm not trying to hurt you, but I need us to be honest with each other." She just needed him to understand. "It wasn't me you were fucking the last night. We both know it. I'm not mad, which is a problem, because if we *were* in love, James, that should have been a *big* problem."

James took a second to collect his thoughts, letting out another sigh. "No, I don't think we are in love, Anna." He thumbed the piece of bread that was left on his plate. "I'm sorry about last night."

"I am too. You are a good man James, you deserve more and so do I."

A few moments of silence passed. "What do we do now?" he looked up from the table to meet Anna's eyes.

"I think it would be best if I went home."

He blew out a breath. "Maybe that would be the best option. I'll handle mum."

Yeah, I'm positive she's going to be over the moon!

"Can you explain to Jenny as well? She has been so kind and I feel terrible about leaving a day before her wedding?"

"Of course, don't worry. We should talk again when I get back. Sort through everything." Anna nodded in agreement.

A few more moments passed as they looked at each other. Maybe they were actually seeing each other clearly for the first time. Anna stood and went over to James. She wrapped him in

78

a hug that she hoped conveyed her feelings for him. Even though they weren't in love, she appreciated him and the time they'd shared.

James held her tightly before letting go. He stood and left her at the table. Ann saw a tear fall down his cheek before he disappeared. She watched him leave, not sure if she should have stopped him, and tried to comfort him more. There was little point, though. They had said everything that needed to be said, for now.

Anna sat looking at the door for a few minutes. It finally dawned on her she had just changed the course of her life forever and without a single idea of what to do next. The banging of an upstairs door brought her back to reality. Even though she didn't have a plan, she knew she needed to get out of the house, away from James and his family, away from everybody for a while.

Less than an hour later, Anna had packed. She still felt awful for the timing of her personal breakdown, but Jenny was very kind and wished her well. The taxi pulled up twenty minutes later, which had felt like an eternity, as she stood outside the front door with her bags by her side. She felt eyes on her back from the top window. She was sure that James's mother was making sure that she *actually* left.

The taxi driver tried to strike up a conversation several times, but Anna's mind just couldn't focus. She was polite, but evidently not in the mood for chitchat. The driver turned up the radio and fell silent for the rest of the journey.

Anna let her mind drift, listening to the music as the world passed by. She hadn't noticed that the car had stopped until the driver cleared his throat. He helped her with her bags and then left her at the entrance to the train station.

Anna felt a sudden rush of relief. She wanted to hug the taxi driver, for no other reason than because he had *literally* taken her from a place of sadness and confusion to a place of possibility and adventure. At least that's how she saw it.

The next two trains were fully booked, leaving her no choice but to kill a few hours in the shops that were dotted around the station. Even though she had no life plan, she knew that going home was the first step. It was the only thing that made sense to her. If she was going to sort herself out, she needed to be in a place that comforted her. Paris was that place.

The time to get through security was short. Anna had hoped it would take a little longer. She wasn't sure she wanted to sit with her own thoughts for too long.

After collecting her belongings, she headed for the seating area. Mercifully, the Eurostar waiting area was quiet, allowing her to choose a seat furthest away from the other passengers who were waiting. She dumped her bags down and sighed, her body relaxing for the first time all day.

Once her belongings were shuffled under her seat, she glanced around. She breathed a sigh of relief when she saw WHSmith because where there was a WHSmith there were books to read, a chance for her to escape for a while.

The world around her fell silent as she browsed the shelves, reading each title and occasionally picking a book up to read the blurb. Twenty blissful browsing minutes later, Anna had picked two books, both of which she had already read, but both she knew she could get lost in.

The hours flew by as Anna immersed herself in fiction. Now and then, she drew her eyes to the departure board, checking on the status of her train. Halfway through the second book, Anna checked the board again. This time, she gave a little start because the train was now on its last boarding call. Quickly throwing the book into her bag, Anna raced to the platform. The stewards hurried her onto the train and to her seat.

A few frustrated faces greeted her as she sat down. Feeling her face burn, Anna smiled politely and sank into her chair, turning her face from the crowd of irritated passengers.

The train moved out of the station, quickly gathering speed. Anna pulled out her book and began reading again. She felt herself unwind. She didn't have to think about anything or anyone, at least for the time being.

Unsure of how much time had passed, Anna was startled from her imaginary world by the steward, who placed her onboard meal onto the tray in front of her.

Smelling the assortment of cheese made Anna's stomach ache. She was suddenly ravenous. Pouring her little bottle of red wine into her plastic cup, Anna took several sips. The wine was full-bodied, not bad quality considering it was train wine. She let the liquid roll around her mouth, relishing every drop. The food tasted delicious. She savoured every morsel of cheese.

Feeling very relaxed and full, Anna put down her book and looked out of the window, noticing that they had entered France. It didn't take long before Anna began scrolling through the past twenty-four hours in her mind and everything that had transpired. Her eyes filled with tears, but they weren't tears of sadness, they were tears of relief and joy.

With the enthusiasm of her newfound freedom coursing through her veins, she quickly grabbed her phone and began searching for hotels. Anna was happy to be returning to Paris, but she wasn't ready to return to her apartment or to her everyday life just yet. She needed to take some time to figure out the next stage of her journey.

After twenty minutes of scrolling through the many rental listings in Paris, Anna found what she was looking for. An apartment in the 16th arrondissement. It was a little above her usual price range for a holiday rental, but she wanted to treat herself. Lord knows she'd been through enough recently to warrant a little extravagance.

The apartment was available immediately and for the foreseeable future. She contacted the landlord directly and was delighted to book it for the next week with the option of extending her stay.

She sent a quick email briefly explaining her change of plans to Kim. Her PA was certain to find it strange that Anna had decided to take a holiday instead of returning to work, which she would most definitely have done in different circumstances. However, Anna was sure that peace and quiet was the right thing for her. She would explain everything to Kim in her own good time.

The sun had long set when the train finally arrived in Paris Gare du Nord. Anna was a little more organised this time. She had already packed away her book and phone and was waiting in line to disembark.

Once she had finally exited the train, Anna headed for the Metro. Without even thinking, she headed for the number 4 line. It was only after standing on the platform waiting for several minutes that she suddenly realised she was in completely the wrong place. Exasperated with her carelessness, she quickly changed direction and headed to the correct metro.

The day was slowly creeping up on her. Fatigue was setting in and all Anna could think about was laying her head on a comfy pillow.

"Only two more stops," Anna murmured to herself as she leaned against the metro doors. The section of the train was relatively quiet. A few people sat listening to music over their headphones. Anna grinned. It felt like a lifetime ago that she herself travelled the underground listening to music, blocking out the surrounding noise. Tonight, though, all she wanted to do was to hear the city. It comforted her.

The walk from the Metro to Anna's new — albeit temporary residence — was short. She was unfamiliar with this area, but a quick look on her phone pointed her in the right direction.

The street was brightly lit with tall ornate street lamps. The pathway was almost as bumpy as the cobbled road, which made wheeling her suitcase unnecessarily difficult. Especially after a day of travelling.

Anna checked each building for the correct number. She didn't want to make a mistake and end up walking for any longer than was necessary. Her body was aching.

A friendly doorman met Anna; he greeted her with a very warm smile and pointed her to the concierge. They completed the paperwork for the short let quickly, which was a relief. Anna could barely keep her eyes open. Sleep was calling her.

Once Anna had the key and door code, she set off towards the little elevator without hesitation. The bell boy had taken her bags, leaving Anna with just her shoulder bag. She slumped against the back of the elevator after she'd punched the button for the fourth floor. After the short ride up, she shuffled down the corridor and punched in the six-digit code to the apartment. She found her bags set neatly inside the door and the lights turned on.

Desperate to sleep, Anna searched for the bedroom, barely taking in her surroundings. There was only one door left after Anna had found the kitchen and bathroom. The bed was enormous, far too large for just one person, but she didn't care. She threw herself face down and buried her head in the pillow, exhaled, and quickly fell asleep.

* * *

Feeling the light pierce through her closed eyes, Anna raised her hand to shield her face. In the race to sleep, she hadn't checked that the shutters had been closed. The sun glared through the window, lighting up the room and Anna.

Propping herself up with the many pillows on the bed, she looked around, adjusting to her new surroundings. The bedroom was magnificent, big, and bright. The décor was minimalist, a few carefully chosen ornaments dressed the oak furniture. The air smelled sweet, perfumed but not chemical.

Glancing around, Anna saw a large vase of fresh flowers sitting on a beautiful dining room table just outside the bedroom door. Smiling widely to herself, she pulled herself up from the bed and headed to the bathroom. She could just remember where it was from her brief exploration of the apartment the night before.

After wearing her clothes for the best part of thirty-six hours, Anna needed to clean herself up. She needed to wash away the past.

Just like the bedroom, the bathroom was exquisite. Marble covered every inch of the walls and floor. The chrome fixtures gleamed brilliantly under the spotlights.

Throwing all of her clothes to the floor, Anna climbed into the shower. The hot water caressed her body, soothing her tired muscles. Feeling relaxed, she closed her eyes, hoping for a familiar dream to invade her mind. The fantasy she had found shocking to begin with, but the fantasy she now longed for, the stranger, the woman from the train station.

However, before she could immerse herself any deeper, Anna was interrupted by the doorbell. Grabbing the bathrobe that was hanging at the end of the shower, Anna stumbled to the door.

A young man was waiting patiently with a tray of pastries and coffee. Seeing the confused look on Anna's face, he quickly explained that the breakfast had been sent on behalf of the owner as a welcome gift. So far, her day was off to an excellent start.

The pastries were divine. Anna felt sad the moment she'd finished them. She wished the young man would return with more. Knowing that scenario was unlikely, Anna took the pot of coffee to a small table and chairs that sat by one of the large windows that faced the street Anna had walked down the previous evening.

She opened the window and breathed deeply. Paris wasn't known for its clean air, but Anna didn't care. She loved it, all of it. The coffee seemed to breathe some life back into her; caffeine had always been a close friend.

Sipping slowly from her cup, Anna surveyed the surrounding buildings. They all seemed very similar to each other. Directly opposite her stood a beautiful building with stunning architecture.

Peering out of the window, Anna looked down at the building's entrance. Once again, it shared similarities to the lobby Anna had walked through last night. Although she could see that the building she was looking at seemed grander. The floor was marble and she could just make out the rows of golden mailboxes that lined the walls. The doorman was also dressed a little better; he was wearing an expensive-looking uniform.

Letting her eyes wander up and across the different windows, Anna's attention was drawn to the window opposite. It was open, revealing a small insight into the room behind it and to the occupant.

Some sort of equipment was leaning against the farthest wall. The furniture was the same as the apartment she was in, which got her wondering. Maybe her landlord owned several properties on the street?

As she pondered, a figure whipped across the window, startling her. Anna was sure the figure that had just darted by was a woman, a very naked woman. Anna felt her heartbeat quicken. A now familiar feeling crept into her stomach. Her excitement built at the thought of seeing the figure again.

With bated breath, Anna sunk a little lower into her chair, hoping that she wouldn't be caught spying. A few minutes passed with no sign of anyone in the apartment. Just as Anna was about to leave her position at the table, the woman came back into view. Disappointingly, she was fully dressed and facing away from the window, therefore halting Ann's attempt at putting a face to the beautiful body.

Suddenly, Anna's phone vibrated loudly. The buzz echoed through the room. She'd forgotten it was on silent and the unexpected noise made her jump. Fumbling with the phone, her face rapidly heated. Glancing over at the apartment, she felt sure that her sudden movement would have caught the attention of the woman in the suit until she remembered she'd been facing away from the open window.

Breathing a sigh of relief and trying to steady her heart rate, Anna answered the phone. "Kim, is there a problem?" Her voice was a little shakier than usual.

"I'm so sorry to disturb you. I just need to know if you will be back by the twentieth?"

"Erm, yes, that shouldn't be a problem." She had no idea if it would be a problem or not. She hadn't looked at her calendar in a few days and so much had happened since she was last at work.

"Okay, great, I'll write it in your diary–"

"I'll text the exact date I will be in the office," Anna interjected before Kim could say another word. "Speak soon." She felt mean for being so short with Kim. It wasn't fair and she would apologise — later.

For now, though, Anna needed to be alone. She needed time to sort through her complicated feelings. She also needed to recover from the very nice and very naked torso that had just sent her libido into hyperdrive.

Chapter Seven

How is it possible for my dream job to turn into such a nightmare? After a few stunned moments, Sam looked at Helene, who hadn't taken her eye off Sam since she'd dropped the bombshell that she had been in a relationship with Lauren.

"I..." Sam stuttered, words failing her. Helene continued to look at her intensely. "I'm sorry, I just can't," Sam whispered.

"Sam..." Helene began. Understanding that it wasn't their professional relationship Sam was referring to.

"No, I'm sorry, Helene. I can't spend another moment near that woman. I can't have her in my life again," Sam croaked. There was no situation that Sam could see where she could deal with Lauren all over again.

Helene lowered her head. Sam recognised the defeated look on her face. After a few seconds, Helene sat up straight, her head held high. "I understand. Please know that I am very sorry for causing you pain. That was never my intention."

Sam reached for her hand. "I know."

"I don't want this to ruin your time here, Sam. You have exciting work to do."

"I won't work with her."

"Of course not," Helene replied without hesitation. "I *will* make sure that Lauren doesn't come anywhere near you whilst you are in Paris." Helene's anger at Lauren was clear in her voice.

"Thank you." Sam felt the weight of the evening's events settle on her like a lead balloon. She was exhausted. "I need some sleep," she continued, not able to look at Helene any longer.

"Of course" Helene nodded, excusing herself, leaving Sam alone. It was clear to Sam that her relationship with Helene had to remain just that: a friendship and no more. She had no desire to be mixed up with anyone that had a link to Lauren or Jo.

With a deep sigh, she headed to the bedroom, noting that the bed remained in a mess from the night before. "How the hell did this turn to shit within forty-eight hours?" It felt good voicing her despair out loud.

Slumped on the end of the bed, she knew she wouldn't be able to sleep until she had spoken to Charlie. She needed her best friend to tell her what to do next.

"Sam, you sly dog, tell me how it went with your French lover."

Silence.

"Helloooo, Sam, have you butt dialled me? Heeeellooo," Charlie chimed.

"I'm here." That's all that Sam could manage before a waterfall of tears came cascading down her face.

"Sam, sweetie, what's happened?" Charlie blurted, shocked by the outburst of tears over the phone. Sam let the tears fall. She couldn't find the words. Charlie remained silent, waiting until she could speak.

"Lauren is here." It was all she could manage. There was more silence.

"Honey, tell me what has happened."

Sam took a deep breath and explained what had happened when she returned to the office that evening. She continued to explain how she had run away and the conversation that followed with Helene at the apartment.

"Okay, Sam, I know all you want to do now is break down, but you will not do that. You're going to go take a shower, climb into bed and sleep. Tomorrow will be better, I promise."

Sam sat and listened. She knew Charlie was right. She couldn't let the life she had been gradually building up be pulled down to a pile of rubble. Not again, and especially not by Lauren.

That was easier said than done, though. Her mind was desperately trying to get her to toughen up, but her heart felt as if it was breaking all over again.

"Sam, honey, are you still there?"

"I'm here. Just taking a minute." Sam sighed deeply, her exhaustion overwhelming her. "I'm going to take a shower and go to bed."

"Good, I'll speak to you tomorrow," Charlie replied. "I love you, Sam."

"Love you too, Charlie," Sam sniffed. She felt a little comfort knowing that Charlie loved her and that no matter what happened in her romantic life, that would never change.

After sliding her phone onto the table, Sam felt as if she had to muster all her remaining energy just to lift herself to her feet. She headed to the bathroom and turned on the shower. She stood under the hot water, dropping her head down and allowing herself one last cry.

A few minutes later, she held her head up, telling herself that she was okay, she was strong and she would deal with this. Her internal pep talk worked a little. Climbing into bed, she let the darkness take her into a dream-filled sleep.

She was in her old apartment. She could see Jo at the end of the corridor, beckoning Sam to follow. Sam glided towards Jo, unable to stop herself from moving. She entered the room where Jo had disappeared. She looked around. Jo was sitting on the bed, Lauren on her right and Helene on her left.

Sam stood rooted to the floor as she watched Jo take Lauren by the throat and roughly kiss her, Jo never taking her eyes off of Sam. Jo turned to Helene and took her by the throat, as she had done with Lauren. Sam couldn't move, she couldn't speak, but she could feel tears running down her face.

Jo looked Sam dead in the eye. A wicked smile spread across her face as she stood and walked towards Sam, her hand extended towards Sam's throat. Sam struggled as she tried desperately to move away. The thought of Jo touching her repulsed Sam to the very core of her being, but it didn't matter what she did, she couldn't move.

Sam held her breath, waiting to be taken by Jo. She waited with her eyes squeezed shut, waited and waited. The touch never came. With her eyes still closed, Sam could tell that the scene had changed. Her senses were engaged by a wonderful smell of almonds and cherries.

Sam opened her eyes. She was still in the room. Jo was in front of her with her outstretched arm, but she was frozen, no longer advancing. Sam felt hands on her shoulders. They dropped down and wrapped around her torso. She was being held.

She could feel lips brush by her left ear and a voice, so soft it was like a melody, a tonic for her fear and anxiety. Sam waited, her breath stolen by this strange presence behind her, holding her and making her feel so safe. "I have you, Sam," the voice whispered. "I have you."

Sam felt all the stress, all the fear, melt away. She saw Jo dissolve. The room washed away until the only thing left was Sam and her protector.

Sam's eyes fluttered opened. Her dream had hit her like a train. It had felt so real. After the breakup with Jo, she was no stranger to nightmares, but this time was so different. She felt no anxiety, no pain, only the echo of the voice that had wrapped her up and protected her from the torture she was going through.

Sam breathed out heavily, trying to get a sense of how she felt. Everything that had happened the night before flooded back, but she didn't feel overwhelmed with emotion. She felt calm, in control.

Well, that's a first.

Shoving a couple of pillows behind her, she propped herself up against the headboard, trying to make sense of her thoughts and the feelings swirling round her head. However, before she had any chance to analyse anything, she was disturbed by the abrupt cry of the doorbell.

Wanting nothing more than to be left alone, Sam slipped down the bed and covered her head with the duvet. Her foolproof plan was thwarted by the person who was leaning on the bell. The relentless noise was excruciating, leaving Sam no choice but to climb out of bed and murder whoever it was on the other side of the door.

"Christ almighty," Sam shouted, "I'm coming." Who the hell was here at 6:15 a.m.?

Sam stopped before she reached for the handle. *What if it's Lauren? No, Helene wouldn't have given her my address.* A sliver of anxiety crept its way into Sam's mind, flashing back to the first half of her nightmare, where she was helpless against Jo.

A voice came from the other side of the door, a voice that was muffled but one that Sam was so happy to hear. "Sam, it's me. Open up," Charlie called.

Sam wrenched the door open to see Charlie leaning against the frame, looking tired and anxious. "What are you doing here?" Sam almost yelled.

"What do you think I'm doing here, dumbass?" Charlie rolled her eyes before walking into the apartment.

"But…" Sam was lost for words.

"Listen, I spoke to John last night. I don't care if you disagree, because what Lauren did was beyond unprofessional. She got away with it last time and I won't let it happen again," Charlie rambled, not allowing Sam to get a word in. "I filled him in on the entire story, every detail, so he could grasp the sheer audacity of the bitch," Charlie continued as she dropped her suitcase and heaved off her coat, letting it drop to the floor. Sam stood there, dumbstruck.

91

"John didn't muck about, I'll tell you that much. He was straight on to the office in Paris and before I knew it, he'd summoned Lauren back to London. I wouldn't want to be her right now!" Charlie mused. "Are you going to give me some lovin' or what?" she shot at Sam, a grin on her face as she watched Sam try to make sense of the last five minutes. Sam took a breath and flung herself at Charlie, wrapping her up in a bone-crushing hug. "Jesus wept," Charlie spluttered, strangled by Sam's body.

"I'm just so happy you are here," Sam cried.

"Alright, alright, I need to breathe, woman," Charlie grumbled.

Sam let her go and stood there with a huge smile plastered on her face.

"Well, I have to admit I'm a tad surprised to see you in such good shape after the way you sounded last night," Charlie chuckled, surveying Sam warily.

"Yeah, I'm surprised at myself, to be honest."

"So why aren't you a sad, crying bag of shit wallowing in bed right now?" Charlie enquired with a raised eyebrow.

"I had a weird dream," Sam answered. "C'mon, I'll make us some breakfast and tell you about it." Sam led Charlie through to the kitchen. It was evident that Charlie was shocked by how wonderful the apartment was because her eyes feverishly scanned the area in wonder. "Nice, right?"

"Too bloody right it is," Charlie agreed.

Sam let Charlie wonder and peruse as she laid out breakfast. Croissant and Pain au Chocolat followed by toast and coffee. "Holy shit, that looks good." Charlie was almost drooling at the sight of the food. "I'm starving." She scooped up a croissant, shoving it in her mouth.

Sam chuckled, then did exactly the same thing. "So tell me about this dream." Sam obliged, recounting the dream in as much detail as she could. "You know what that means, don't you?"

"Nope, no idea," Sam replied truthfully. The dream had made her feel different, but it confused the hell out of her.

"It was your mind showing you how much stronger you have become since the whole Jo incident happened," Charlie stated, as if it was a fact and not just her opinion. "Remember when you first had nightmares?" She didn't wait for a response. "You had no control, no power or strength. You were heartbroken, but not anymore," she continued. "Last night you took control," Charlie finished, beaming a smile at Sam.

"Do you really think so?" Sam wasn't feeling as confident as her best friend.

"I'm positive. I'm so proud of you." Charlie reached over and squeezed Sam's hand.

Sam sat at the table, staring out of the long window. "I recognised the voice, the one that helped me," she mumbled mainly to herself.

"Who was it?"

"I'm not sure, but I know I have heard it before. I couldn't forget a voice like that." Sam let her eyes close as she remembered the soft angelic tone that had whispered in her ear. A small shiver ran down her back.

"Well, whoever it was, I'm super happy that they helped you. Maybe this is the turning point you've been waiting for."

"Maybe," Sam smiled. "How can I continue working with Helene, though?"

"Listen, you had a one-night fling with her, that's it. I presume you clarified the situation with her before all this happened?"

"Yeah, we said we would be professional. We had planned to see each other again, but not now, not after last night," Sam sighed.

"Maybe that's all it was ever meant to be, a quickie to set you straight, so to speak," Charlie chuckled. "You needed someone to push you forward, but I don't think that means it has to be something serious. You have some stuff to work out before you're ready for that, I think."

93

Charlie was spot on. She wasn't looking for something serious, not just yet. Helene wasn't "the one" but she had been someone who had helped Sam look to the future instead of the past. She'd also been an amazing friend.

"It's astounding what a good shag can do, isn't it?" Charlie grinned.

"You were doing so well, Char! Really doing a grand job at being a serious adult for all of ten minutes," Sam laughed, rolling her eyes as Charlie chuckled. "You didn't tell me how you ended up here, though."

"Right, yeah. So it turns out that John is a really cool guy. He was more than happy to let me come over to make sure you were okay. He seems to *actually* give a shit about his employees! Who knew?" Charlie smiled.

"So, how long are you over for?"

"Well, I didn't get a deadline, but I think you need me to stay in this glorious city for a few days, right?" Charlie smirked.

"Oh god, absolutely. I really need your support for at least four days, maybe five," Sam sighed dramatically, as if she would crumble without Charlie by her side. Sam couldn't wait to hang out with her bestie for a few days.

They polished off the rest of the pastries and refilled their coffee cups, both women taking in the grandeur of their surroundings. "Who would have guessed that we would be sitting here right now?" Sam mused.

"Who would have thought it would take a trip to France and a good bonk, to get you over the mountain of despair you've been stuck up for a year?" Charlie shot back comically.

"True," Sam laughed.

The sun had risen considerably since Charlie had arrived. A beam shone through the open window onto Sam's face. The blinding light made Sam wince and then made her jolt into action. "Shit, what time is it?" she barked.

"7:45, why?"

"I have to get ready for work. I wanted to be in by eight, but that's not going to happen now," Sam huffed.

94

"Chill out, go get ready whilst I sort out the breakfast stuff and then we can head out. I don't get why you get so strung out about the time." Charlie rolled her eyes.

"You know I don't enjoy being late."

"Who said you had to be in at 8 a.m.?" Charlie mocked because she knew full well that Sam had made that timeline up all by herself.

"Well, nobody, but that's not the point." Huffing again, Sam got to her feet and headed to the bathroom, grumbling along the way.

Charlie just smiled as she watched Sam leave the room. Pulling herself up from the chair, Charlie began removing the debris of their breakfast from the table. After she was satisfied that the place looked tidy, she hauled her suitcase to the bedroom. "I'm sleeping with you, by the way," she shouted, hoping that Sam could hear her.

"Well, obviously," Sam called back.

Several minutes later, Charlie heard the shower shut off and the bathroom door open. Sam sauntered into the room, naked. "Hey, sexy."

"Oh shut up, I forgot my towel in the bedroom."

Towelling her hair dry, Sam was distracted by the buzzing of her phone that sat on the table in the living room.

Without thinking, she ran to where her phone sat and straight past her open window with not a stitch of clothing on her.

As she picked up her phone, she thought she glimpsed somebody looking at her from across the street. Not wanting to stick around, she ran back to the bedroom.

"Have you lost your mind?" Charlie barked. "Sam, it's one thing for me to see you in the buff. I'm used to it. Flashing half of Paris is a bit much, though."

"Why are you shouting at me?" Sam laughed. Charlie was looking at her as if she'd just committed a crime. "I did not just flash all of Paris. That's a tad dramatic, don't you think?"

"You've got your windows open, Sam. Any old perv could look in."

Sam flashed to the person she thought she had seen looking into her apartment. "Alright, I may have just given some unfortunate soul an eyeful across the street." She tried not to blush at the thought of a stranger seeing her bits.

"See, now you're going to have some creep leering through your window every five minutes to see if he can get a repeat performance. Honestly, Sam, I can't leave you for five minutes."

"She."

"She?"

"Yes, I think whoever got a look was a woman."

Funnily, that bit of information gave Charlie pause. "Okay, that's a little better than a pervy bloke looking at you, but you might not be so lucky next time. Her husband or boyfriend could be there."

"Char, that is the first time I have walked through this apartment naked." Not the complete truth. She had strolled to the kitchen naked after her night with Helene, but Charlie didn't need to know that otherwise she'd never let the subject drop. "I was distracted by my phone and forgot I was naked, that's all." Sam had to bite her lip to stop herself from laughing.

"Are you laughing right now?" Charlie shot.

"Well, I'm trying not to, Char, but you're being ridiculous."

"You won't be saying that when you've got a hoard of skeevy men with binoculars angling for a look." Charlie huffed.

That was enough to make Sam crack. She couldn't stop her laughter from bursting out. "Oh Charlie, you really are the best. I promise I will stop giving strip shows to my neighbours, okay?" Sam wiped a tear away from her eyes.

"Okay... good. I just want you to be careful. I'm not here to back you up if you get into trouble."

Sam's laughter died down. Yes, Charlie was being over the top, but she knew it came from a place of love and she now understood that Charlie was probably missing her as much as she missed Charlie. Being away from each other wasn't easy. Sam pulled on her robe and went over to her friend. "You don't have to worry about me."

"Yes, I do, and I will." Charlie sighed. "Did you get a good look?"

"At what?"

"The woman in the window."

"Not at all, just a quick glimpse, but..." Sam paused, gazing into thin air, lost in thought. *It couldn't have been her. Could it?*

"But...?" Charlie stared at Sam, waiting for her to finish her sentence.

"No, never mind," Sam finished, taking a second to look down at her phone, forgetting that the naked dash into the living room was to answer the text she'd received.

Chapter Eight

A week had passed since Anna had taken up residence in her rented apartment. Seven days of lying around trying to untangle her thoughts and feelings. One hundred and sixty-eight hours of getting absolutely nowhere.

So far Anna had read through a dozen books, eaten takeout and watched some daytime TV. This mini holiday had *not* done what she'd hoped. She'd thought that some quality alone time was all that she needed to get some answers for herself. She'd been wrong.

Huffing out a breath of irritation, she picked up her phone and scrolled to Frédéric's name. Her fingers hovered over the call button. Usually, her brother would be the first port of call for any problem or crisis no matter how small, but this time was different.

Frédéric was her person, her closest confident but after so many years of keeping these particular feelings at bay, she couldn't be sure how her little brother would react. Steeling herself, she finally hit the call button. After a few seconds, the call connected. "Anna," Frédéric sang.

"Freddy, can you meet me? I need to talk." She'd forgone her usual greeting. She needed him now.

Frédéric picked up on her urgency without pause. "Tell me where you are. I am on my way."

"I've sent you the address. Merci, Freddy."

"Okay, j'arrive," he said before disconnecting.

Now she had to work out how she was going to explain everything to Frédéric. She presumed it would come as a shock to him. She could only pray that he would understand.

Anna sat at the little table by the window, unconsciously fiddling with her dainty wristwatch. The clock on the wall seemed to go at a snail's pace. Anna peered out of the window now and then to see if she could see her brother. Not knowing which part of Paris Frédéric would come from, there was no way to know how long she would have to wait.

Fifty minutes passed and Anna could feel beads of sweat forming between her shoulder blades. The waiting had allowed her anxiety to skyrocket. "Maybe this is a terrible idea," she voiced out loud as she paced around the living room, unable to sit still any longer.

Just as she was about to send a text to her brother cancelling, the bell rang to signal Frédéric's arrival. Anna stilled herself against the arm of the sofa. She took a long deep breath in before moving to the door.

Frédéric was red faced and windswept. He had a look of great concern carved across his face. His soft features pulled together as he studied her, searching for any signs of visible injury or pain. Anna stood stock still, staring at him. She couldn't get the words to surface.

A tear streaked down her face. Frédéric bolted towards her, pulling her into a tight bear hug. He kicked the door shut behind them.

"Anna, what the hell is going on?" he mumbled with his face buried into her shoulder. Anna continued to cry. It was as if the floodgates hadn't just been opened, but had been ripped off their hinges entirely.

Minutes passed as Anna let the tears flow. Frédéric hadn't moved a muscle. He simply held her until she finally felt herself breathing normally. Everything seemed a little easier now.

"I'm sorry, Freddy, I didn't mean to drag you away from work."

"You didn't pull me from anything that is as important as you," Frédéric replied, squeezing her a little tighter.

Anna pulled herself free and smoothed down her T-shirt. She needed to regain some composure if she was going to get through this conversation.

"Come and sit." She gestured for him to follow her to the little table by the window. Frédéric complied without a word. He just watched and waited for Anna to speak.

"I broke up with James," Anna began. Her breath steadied, and she felt a little more confident. "It hadn't been working between us for a long time, maybe ever," she continued, determined to say what she needed to before Frédéric could reply. "I came back from England early. I'm sorry I didn't tell you Freddy, but I thought I needed some time to figure it out by myself."

"And did you figure it out?"

Anna let out a long breath, her shoulders slumping. "No, well, maybe, I'm not sure. I need to talk it all through with you, I think. I can't get out of my head."

"Okay, but what is it exactly you need to figure out? Do you regret leaving James?"

"No! God no. That's the one thing I am certain I did right."

"Okay," Freddy said slowly, waiting for Anna to fill in the gaps.

Anna cleared her throat. She was ready. "James and I weren't compatible, that's clear, but I think that… it's not just James that isn't compatible… I think it's me and all men," she stuttered.

Looking Frédéric square in the eyes, she waited patiently for his response. She watched as Frédéric realised what she was getting at. His face relaxed, and a smile crept onto his face. "I think I understand," he said, reaching over and taking Anna's hand.

"You do?"

"Have you said it out loud yet?"

Anna looked a little puzzled before she clicked. "No, no, I haven't because it's only at this moment that I think I'm brave enough to say it," she choked, fresh tears spilling down her cheeks.

Frédéric squeezed her hand lovingly. "Do you want to say it?" he probed, being careful not to push too hard.

Anna took a deep breath in and nodded. Slowly letting her lungs deflate, she smiled. "Frédéric, I'm gay."

As if a plug had been pulled, all Anna's feelings of dread, confusion and apprehension drained away. Just saying the words aloud had free'd her. She smiled and let out a nervous laugh.

Frédéric pulled her from the chair and wrapped his arms around her. "Now you have said it. Do you think you could tell me the complete story? Because I don't think this is something that has just been on your mind since last week."

Anna nodded before she raised her index finger, signalling him to wait as she went to the kitchen to grab a bottle of wine. This conversation needed alcohol.

With a full bottle of red and two glasses in hand, Anna returned to the living room. Frédéric had shed his coat and scarf. Anna settled the bottle on the table and poured them both a generous glass.

After taking a big gulp of her wine, Anna relaxed into the sofa next to him. She wasn't sure where to start.

How long have I had these feelings?

"I don't know where to start. If I'm completely honest with myself, I knew I felt something different when I was at university." Anna gathered her next words. Frédéric sat quietly, listening intensely.

"The thing is, I never thought too much about it back then. I was too busy with my education. I just wanted you guys to be proud of me, so I worked hard."

"You did Anna, you know we are all proud of you," Frédéric said honestly.

"I have never been with a woman. I haven't even kissed one, but I had a dance." Anna felt a little heat rise up her neck at the memory.

"It must have been one hell of a dance," Frédéric chuckled as he watched Anna stare out of the window, clearly reliving it all over again.

"Hmmm, it was."

"So, who was the lucky lady?"

"I do not know. We were blindfolded." Frédéric blushed at the new information, obviously unsure where this story was going. Anna saw his face and quickly interjected. "Nothing like that!" she chuckled nervously. This was a tough conversation to have with anyone, let alone her little brother.

"When I studied for a year in the UK, I must admit that I noticed several women. However, there was one I don't think I will ever forget." Anna's heart had picked up speed. She hadn't thought about that night in a long time, but she would never forget it.

"I was invited to several parties. Most of them ended in ridiculous drinking games. You know how the English are!" she mused. Frédéric gave a brief nod of agreement.

"Well, at one of those parties, there was this game where we had to drink shots, then dance blindfolded to several songs. The best dancer won." Anna explained briefly, realising how juvenile it sounded.

"It was the silliest game I have ever played, but actually quite fun. Everyone enjoyed it. However, the last dance was a slow song. Before I knew what was happening, someone had pulled me close. It was a woman." Anna felt herself blush. She could almost feel the woman against her skin again. "I can't describe it, Frédéric. It was the most sensual dance I have ever had. I felt this connection that was so strong it took my breath away!"

"So you didn't find out who it was after the dance had finished?"

"No, I ran out as soon as the song finished. Freddy, it was one thing noticing a few women, but feeling what I did that night took me completely by surprise. It scared the living daylights out of me."

Frédéric nodded his head. He was the most understanding man Anna knew. "So... after that night, you didn't think anymore about your feelings?"

"Of course I did, but I wasn't ready to fully embrace it. I was too frightened."

Frédéric scooted himself on the sofa so he was sitting by Anna's side. "Oh Anna, I'm so sorry you carried this alone. You were always looking after me, making sure I was doing well. I never stopped to notice if you were struggling with something."

"Freddy, there wasn't anything to notice. Once I buried the feelings away, I submerged myself in my studies and then my work. By the time I met James, I'd gotten comfortable with my life as it was. James was easy, he was comfortable. I know now that I shouldn't have settled," Anna sighed. Guilt washed over her as she spoke. James had deserved better, hell she had deserved better, too.

"I hope you know now that I'm here for you. Every step of the way," Frédéric smiled, pulling Anna into another gargantuan hug.

"I can't believe I was ever worried about talking to you," Anna chuckled.

"I can understand Anna, there are too many instances of people coming out to their families believing they knew how they were going to react, only to have their lives smashed to pieces."

"How did you become so wise?" Anna squeezed his face with her hands.

103

"I have some experience in the matter," He replied with sadness in his eyes.

"What do you mean?"

"Lucie's cousin came out a few months ago. His parents did not react well. It has been a sobering time."

"Lucie?" She wasn't familiar with the name.

"Oh. Mon. Dieu! I never got round to telling you about her the last time we met," He laughed.

"Ooh, ton amoureuse," Anna declared, remembering their conversation that was cut short last week.

"Oui, mon amoureuse," he gushed, smiling from ear to ear. "But now isn't the time either, Anna. Today is about you. It isn't often you need me and I will not let you down now."

"Freddy, you have never let me down," she stated.

"So will you tell mum and dad?"

Anna sucked in a breath. In all the excitement of telling Frédéric, she had quite forgotten about her parents. Frédéric saw her panic. "You don't have to tell them anything, Anna. Only do it when you feel ready. There is no rush, okay?"

Anna nodded. Today had taken a lot out of her, and the thought of doing it all over again was daunting. "I will tell them. I think I just need a couple of days to prepare myself. I'll go back to work on Monday, so maybe I could visit them this weekend. Would you come with me?"

"Absolutely, Anna." Frédéric nodded with such enthusiasm he looked like a bobble head.

* * *

Two days after she had spoken to Frédéric, Anna packed her weekend bag, ready to visit her parents. She'd spent the rest of the afternoon with her brother, talking about her feelings, talking about Lucie and pretty much anything and everything that they could think of. Having such an intense and in-depth catch-up with Frédéric had proved to be both taxing and enlightening.

104

After Frédéric had left Anna alone, she began planning how she would approach such an important subject with her parents. Anna was extremely close with Frédéric and she liked to think that they were close as a family unit but she couldn't be confident that her parents would be okay with her sexual orientation, especially after being with James and never giving away any clue that she may indeed be attracted to women.

Anna disliked talking to her parents about her love life and now, thinking about it, she could understand why. Her mum always pushed her on matters of the heart, but how could Anna speak of such things? Especially when she wasn't able to be honest about what her heart had really wanted in the first place.

A little guilt crept over her as she remembered all the times that she had snapped at her mum for asking about James or how their relationship was going.

For two days, Anna had become more and more anxious. She tried to write her feelings down on paper. She even tried to plan a speech for her parents, but no matter how much she tried, the words failed her. Frustrated, she'd messaged Frédéric many times over the past forty-eight hours. He'd tried his best to calm her, but nothing really worked.

Standing on the platform waiting for her brother to show up, Anna fiddled with her wristwatch again. She desperately tried to focus on her breathing and heart rate, pleading with her body to calm down.

Staying calm was proving to be near impossible though because in just under an hour she would be in front of her mum and dad, opening herself up to them like never before.

Frédéric was late. Again. No surprise, really. Over the years, Anna had suggested plenty of ways that he could better organise himself so that he could arrive on time. He had taken *none* of her thoughts on board at all.

Anna had got used to his tardiness, but today she felt her patience slip. This was too important, and she needed her brother by her side.

105

Just as she let an agitated breath out, she spotted him jogging through the crowd, his scarf dragging behind as usual. "I'm sorry, really I am. I had an alarm set and everything, but somehow I muted it." He looked flustered and genuinely sorry.

Anna couldn't stay mad at him; after all, he was doing her a huge service by going to their parents' with her. He had also been the best brother she could have wished for over the past couple of days, so she let it go. In fact, she would never complain about his tardiness again.

She grabbed his hand and gave it a loving squeeze. "It's fine. I'm just so nervous" The announcement for boarding crackled overhead. With a deep breath in and a look of encouragement from Frédéric, she grabbed her bag and headed for their carriage.

The journey was only forty-five minutes, just long enough to get settled and order a quick drink from the onboard drinks service. She downed her tiny bottle of gin in one gulp, forgoing the plastic cup and ice she had been given.

"Are you okay?" Frédéric looked at her with worry in his eyes.

"No, but I will be. No matter how this plays out, I know it's the right time and the right thing for me." Anna's breathing normalised. Her words were true, she would be ok.

They sat in companionable silence for the rest of the journey. Anna felt the train slow. She squeezed her eyes shut, readying herself. They both looked out of the window as the small village station came into view and the platform slid next to their train.

Anna spotted her dad instantly. He was a tall man, with shocking red hair and a prominent belly. Anna had inherited her father's height but her mother's colouring. She was also thin like her mother, too, which had always been a blessing. She could eat what she liked without having to exercise daily.

Frédéric was very similar to their father. His hair was more blond than red, but anytime he tried to grow out a beard it was beautifully laced with rich orange hair. The only problem was that his beard never quite filled out and was always too patchy to look good.

The train pulled to a stop, neither of them moved for a few minutes. Anna needed a bit more time to find her feet. Once most of the passengers had disembarked, they rallied their possessions. They stepped off the train and were greeted by a wonderful warm breeze. The air was so much clearer than in Paris and Anna always appreciated it.

Before she could take another step, her dad's impressive form was in front of her, leading her into a tight hug. After several minutes of hugs and kisses, they piled into her father's Renault and set off on their twenty-minute drive to her parents' cottage.

Anna sat in the back of the car, grateful that Frédéric was chatting away to her dad about his newest project. She had to concentrate on keeping herself from vomiting or possibly passing out. She watched as the familiar country lanes whizzed by.

Straightening herself up in the back seat, Anna squared her shoulders as they drove up the gravel driveway. Her mum was waiting by the open cottage door wearing her trusty apron that was covered in flour. No doubt there was a pie baking in the oven.

As soon as Anna had exited the car, her mother took her by the shoulders and gave her kisses on each cheek. "Coucou, maman."

"Darling, how are you? It feels like forever since you were here." Before Anna could come up with an excuse as to her absence, she saw her mum searching over her shoulder as if looking for someone. "No, James?"

"No, let's go in," Anna snapped, not wanting her mum to push the subject. She could see the hurt flash across her mother's face as she registered Anna's sharp tone. Anna dropped her head as she followed her mum into the kitchen. She knew she should apologise. It wasn't right to talk to her mum like that.

They spent a few minutes catching up with light conversation before Anna excused herself to the room she would stay in. The bed was made to hotel standards, each corner pristine. Anna smirked. Her mum had probably been up early cleaning and preparing for their arrival.

She threw her bag on the bed, followed by herself. Lying on her back, she turned her head to the window. The photo frame hanging on the wall caught her eye. It was a picture of her and James. Anna heaved herself off the bed and stood in front of the picture, analysing the image. They were both smiling, but she could see neither smile reached their eyes.

I've wasted so much time!

That realisation was why Anna decided she needed to talk to her parents immediately. Her original plan had been to wait until Sunday lunch, knowing that she would hop on a train back to Paris soon after. It was her escape plan if her parents reacted badly.

However, now, after seeing all the wasted time framed and hanging on the wall, she couldn't wait a moment longer. She had to start living her life—the one she had forsaken when she'd settled for *easy* instead of what was *true*—regardless of the consequences she may face.

Anna entered the kitchen; her dad was sitting in his usual seat trying to complete a crossword. Frédéric sat on his left, skimming through the week's TV guide. As usual, Anna's mother was busy cooking; it looked as if she had planned to feed the French Army with the amount of food piled around on the kitchen surfaces.

Anna's stomach rolled, her nerves were completely fried. She stopped at the cupboard that was packed with wine glasses, picked four out, and set them on the table. "It's a bit early for wine, dear," her mother commented.

"Maman, can you sit for a minute? I have something I need to talk to you about." Anna's mum stopped chopping the carrots that were spread over the large chopping board. She threw a surprised glance over at her husband and then back at Anna before settling in the last seat at the kitchen table.

"Oh, you're doing this now?" Frédéric whispered, sitting up straight, waiting for Anna to continue.

"Is everything okay, dear?" Her mum quizzed, concern flashing in her eyes.

"Yes… uh, well, no… I mean, yes, I'm fine. I'm not ill or anything." Anna stumbled over every word. She noticed a slight pressure on her arm. She looked down to find Frédéric's hand holding her forearm. He was reassuring her. "Okay, first thing. I want to say, sorry maman, I shouldn't have snapped at you when we arrived." Anna saw her mum's eyebrows rise in surprise at her apology.

"No need to say sorry, love, already forgotten," she smiled.

"No, I was wrong to talk to you like that. The fact is… is that James and I have parted ways."

Her mum looked at her and then at her father with what can only be described as relief. "Oh, well…" Her voice was far too light for such a serious thing. "He wasn't the one for you, dear."

Anna had to take a second to process what her mum had just said. "You're not upset? But I thought you really liked him?"

"Oh, don't get me wrong, James is a lovely man. He just wasn't the one for you, Anna."

"Riiight…" Anna elongated the word, giving her a few extra milliseconds to get herself back on track. The hardest part was still to come, although she was happy that she didn't have to waste her time arguing over James. "Anyway, it's not just about James. I have something else to tell you." Anna's breath hitched. It was now or never. Her parents were waiting patiently for her to continue. Anna cleared her throat and rolled her neck. "Maman, Papa… I'm gay." She had done it, the words had made it past her lips. Heat was rising up her neck. She stared at her parents, holding her breath.

"Right… well, I wasn't expecting that, love," her father chuckled nervously. Anna studied him, checking for any signs of anger or hurt, but she couldn't see any. Her gaze shot to her mother, who let out a tremendous sigh. *Oh no!*

Her mum dropped her shoulders, "Oh, Anna, what am I supposed to do? I don't know any lesbians, love. How am I supposed to set you up now!?" Anna's laugh was completely involuntary. She was in shock.

Before she knew what was happening, her mother had risen from her seat, rounded the table and was holding Anna like she had when she was a child.

Anna's laughter quickly turned into sobs as she let her mum envelop her. Seconds later, Frédéric and her father had joined the hug. In all her life, she had never been as happy as she was at that very moment.

Chapter Nine

Sam lounged on the large comfy sofa, blissfully content. Her week hadn't started out as planned, given all the drama that had occurred with Lauren and Helene. Her saving grace had been Charlie's unexpected arrival. The world didn't seem such a scary place now. Charlie had eked out a full week in Paris and even though she would leave the next day, Sam couldn't help but smile.

Showing Charlie the Paris offices had been exciting and a little nerve-wracking. It had taken a few awkward conversations between Sam and Helene before they were able to move past the whole "Lauren" debacle. Charlie had absolutely loved talking to Sébastien, and he'd even offered a second tour of Paris sans tourists so that she could enjoy it just like Sam had on her first day.

Exploring Paris with Charlie allowed Sam to get hundreds of new shots. They seemed to walk for days. Charlie had spent a considerable amount of that time moaning about walking, especially when they'd visited Montmartre Basilique, which consisted of an endless flow of concrete staircases that led to the summit.

In Sam's opinion, the hike had been more than worth it. The view of Paris from the Basilique was breathtaking. Charlie had *not* been as enthusiastic and spent the entire trip grumbling. Charlie's mood — and occasional grumpy outbursts — only made Sam laugh at her dramatic friend.

They spent their evenings visiting different cafes and restaurants. Sam was sure she had never eaten so much food before in her life, but as Charlie kept reminding her, they were quote "living their best life".

On several occasions, Charlie had tried to convince Sam to seek out the nearest lesbian bar, which was easier said than done. Considering the size of Paris, it was woefully lacking on the gay scene side of things.

Regardless, that didn't matter. Sam wasn't ready to date. Her little dalliance with Helene and its complete failure only made Sam feel the need to keep her distance from women and dating for a while longer.

Sam definitely felt stronger within herself now. The whole Jo saga had stopped being so painful, she'd stopped feeling the loss so strongly. Charlie put that down to "the damn good shag" she'd had with Helene, which Sam couldn't deny.

Maybe that's what she'd needed to move forward, but that didn't mean she was ready to date. A fact of which Charlie strongly disagreed with but had respected eventually when Sam had got a little firm with her.

Stretching herself off the couch, Sam plodded over to her little table by the window. The weather had been superb, and she had even caught a little colour, which for Sam and her pale ass skin was a miracle in itself. For most of the week, she'd left the windows open to let the gentle breeze waft through the apartment. Charlie was in the bedroom packing, singing along to her favourite tunes she had playing on her phone.

Sam had taken the afternoon off, or to be honest, she was skiving from the office. She knew Helene wouldn't say anything and that she would probably let Sam get away with worse, considering how things had turned out between them.

Flicking through her phone, she mindlessly scrolled through her social media accounts. Normally she didn't post, but she had uploaded a couple of selfies that she'd snapped with Charlie in front of the Eiffel Tower and other monuments.

She was so unaware of her surroundings that she didn't see or hear Charlie standing right next to her. With a prod in the shoulder, she almost flew out of the seat in surprise. "Jesus Christ!!" she yelled.

"Whoa there, lassie," Charlie laughed. "Are you alright?" she continued, now bent over laughing at Sam, who was clutching her chest as if her heart might jump out of it.

Breathing heavily, Sam sat back at the table, eyeballing Charlie. "Why did you sneak up on me? You know I hate it when you do that."

"Keep your knickers on, woman, it's me who should be pissed. I've been calling you for five minutes and you've been ignoring me."

"I didn't hear you," Sam replied, her anger dissipating. Now feeling embarrassed about her overreaction.

"Well, no shit, Sherlock," Charlie grinned. She pulled out the chair next to Sam and sat down, her features changing from amused to borderline serious. Sam noticed and squirmed in her seat. She knew this look, and she didn't like where it was going to lead.

Sure enough, before she could say anything, Charlie spoke, her tone serious. "Before I go, I need to talk to you." She paused, gauging Sam's reaction. Sam just sat and stared. Once Charlie realised she wasn't about to hightail it out of the room, she continued. "First, let me say how proud of you I am. I know that having Paris sprung on you was difficult, taking you out of your comfort zone. But you came, and you conquered." She let out a bark of laughter. Sam looked confused.

"What do you mean 'came and conquered'? I'm no way near the conquering stage yet," Sam quizzed.

113

"I mean, you came out here and promptly humped a local," she grinned. Sam felt her face go beetroot.

"I'm not sure that's something to be proud of," Sam murmured, looking down at her lap. Charlie's stare was making her uncomfortable.

"Oh, but it is my dear friend. It is because even though I joke, you sleeping with Helene meant so much more than a one-night stand, considering everything you've gone through over the past year."

"If you say so." It was the only thing Sam could think to say.

"I know talking about this sort of thing makes you uncomfortable, mate." Charlie leaned over to squeeze Sam's arm. "Which is why I wrote you a letter."

"A letter."

"Yes, a letter, you know, it's a bit of paper with writing on it," Charlie shot back, rolling her eyes.

Sam sat for a second, gathering her thoughts. "You have never once written a letter to me or any other person in the world."

"Well, no, but it's the only way I can get you to hear me without feeling like I'm lecturing you," Charlie replied, frustrated.

"I always listen to you," Sam argued.

"No, Sam, you don't, you don't hear me. So I have written you a letter, and I left it by the bed. I won't force you to read it, but I hope you do."

"Well, what's it about?" Sam grumbled. She didn't like this conversation at all.

"Read it and find out. That's all I am going to say about it." She gave a nod of finality before getting up and heading to the kitchen.

Sam sat a little shell-shocked. She had thought Charlie was going to give her another one of her lectures about getting back out into the dating world, but obviously not.

Charlie returned with a pizza takeout menu as if she'd said nothing out of the ordinary at all. "Pepperoni sound good?"

"Um, yeah... fine... whatever you want," Sam replied quietly.

114

They ate their food in silence. Sam couldn't quite muster up the enthusiasm to play hostess. Charlie seemed happy enough to let Sam wallow a little. She didn't push, but she didn't shrink away either.

They shared a few drinks and a large pizza. Finally, after the third beer, their conversation started to flow. They began sharing their favourite memories of the past week and discussed which restaurant was their favourite. By the end of the evening, the earlier conversation had been forgotten.

* * *

The morning sun shone through the apartment. Charlie had been up since six, making sure she had all her belongings ready to go. The car that Helene had sent was due to arrive at eight sharp.

Sam stood by the window, looking out onto the street and the building opposite. She already missed her best friend. She wasn't sure when she would see her again.

"I'm not dying, Sam," Charlie chortled when she saw Sam's bereft look.

"It's been awesome having you here, Char, I'm gonna miss you." She pulled Charlie into a deep hug.

"My job is done, mate, you're good to go. No holding you back, Sammy." Charlie smiled, her cheek wedged against Sam's. "You are gonna rock this project." She squeezed Sam as tight as she could.

"Thanks, Char." Sam squeezed her back. The sound of the doorbell broke them apart. Sam wasn't sure why she felt so emotional about Charlie leaving. It wasn't the first time they'd been apart.

Charlie collected her bags and headed to the door. She turned to Sam and gave her a wink. "See you around, woman." And then she was gone. Sam headed to the window to watch her leave. The way Charlie had said goodbye felt a little too final.

Sam let out a deep breath. She stood with her back to the window and cast her gaze around the apartment. Without Charlie by her side, everything felt too much, Paris felt like too much.

Sam saw the letter as soon as she entered the bedroom. Without hesitation, she swooped down and grabbed it, tearing it open. Curiosity had gotten the better of her. What could Charlie possibly have to say that she hadn't heard before?

Sam,

I know this is lame, but I don't know how else to get you to listen. You know how much I love and support you and I hope you know that I have tried my hardest to give you love and support whilst you went through the breakup with Jo.

Now it's time for me to say some things that I should have said years ago. The last thing I want is for you to be pissed at me. I know I can get under your skin when I push you about dating again. I'm sorry about that. I just want to see you happy again. No fuck that, I mean I want to see you happy again, obviously, but what I really want is my best friend back. I haven't seen her in a decade!!!

Jo cheating on you was not the worst period in your life! You didn't see it, but I did. Jo began changing you from the very start. You think she was the love of your life, but you are dead wrong, on that I am certain.

The Sam I met all those years ago was so sure of herself, but not in an arsehole kinda way. That Sam was never scared to take chances, to love and live life to the max. That Sam knew she was a friggin' rock star behind a camera and was not shy about putting herself out there. That Sam disappeared the night she met Jo!!!

That woman systematically tore you down. She took your confidence and your spirit and manipulated them over the entirety of your relationship. There were several occasions that I tried to talk to you about the way she was treating you, but she'd done such a good job of screwing you up that you just couldn't see anything but her. Once I realised I could lose you as a friend if I pushed you too hard or Jo realised I was onto her, I did the only thing I could think of and stepped back.

116

I watched for years as my best buddy, my gay hero, wilted away, losing everything that made her so wonderful.

I doubt very much that Lauren was Jo's first indiscretion. I think that once she had finally tamed you; she got bored and moved on to others. I understand you will probably hate me for saying all this, but what I have I got to lose? I had hoped that once she was out of your life, you would eventually get over her and I would get my mate back. Now I realise Jo did a better job of breaking you than I realised.

I'm so sorry I couldn't keep you away from her! I'm so sorry that she preyed on you and I couldn't stop it. Please, Sam, please understand your worth. You are a ray of light in this world, a ray of light that had a huge shadow cast over it for far too long.

You are ready to shine again, honey. Please take this letter in the way I intended it, with only love and support for you! Start loving yourself. Start healing properly.

Jo leaving was the best day of your life and I pray to all things good in the universe that you will come to see it as the best day of your life too. Start healing by finding your way back, the real you! Become the best version of yourself, my gay hero! I love you, Sammy. You are my family. I'm always here, ALWAYS.

Charlie xx

Sam must have read the letter five times. She just couldn't process what Charlie had said. She read the words *wilted away*. *Such a good job of screwing you up* and *Jo began changing you from the very start*, over and over, until they seemed to be seared into her brain.

Sam hadn't known that Charlie had felt this way. She tried her hardest to recall a time that Charlie had tried to warn her away from Jo. The truth of the matter was that Charlie was right. When Sam met Jo, she had been swept off her feet. Jo made her feel like the most special woman in the world, and Sam knew she had fallen for Jo right off the bat. She wouldn't have heard a bad word said against her, not even from Charlie.

117

Sam slowly lowered the letter to her side, letting it slip from her fingers. She felt numb. Was Charlie right? had she been manipulated as Charlie had written?

A heavy weight settled on her chest. Trying to push past her misery, Sam headed to the bathroom. She needed a damn hot shower to burn and wash the words away.

Flipping on the light and she leaned against the worktop, staring into the mirror above the sink. She stood there, staring at her own reflection.

Have I really been changed that much? she thought as she studied her face, trying to look deep within herself.

Sam let her mind wander back to a time before Jo. She remembered how much fun she had, how carefree she always felt and how sure she had been in her ability to make art with her camera. Sam pictured herself getting ready for parties with Charlie, always knowing she would capture the attention of women easily with her confidence and charm. Could she say the same now?

Sam ran a hand through her hair. Sandy-coloured hair that once shined and bounced now fell limp and lifeless, scraped back into a tame ponytail. Her blue eyes, that had once sparkled with joy, now stared back at her dully.

The sight in front of her was too much. Sam dropped her eyes from the mirror as a tear fell down her face, hitting the worktop. "What happened to me?" she whispered out loud. Shaking her head in disbelief, she stripped and stepped under the water.

After a very long and soothing shower, Sam lay on the sofa, wrapped in her fluffy dressing gown. Her mind was going a hundred miles a minute. The reality that Charlie could be right about the last ten years of her life was unbelievable. She couldn't wrap her head around it. There was only one person who she needed to call, one person who would get her through this.

The call connected after the third ring. "My darling, how are you? Are you taking Paris by storm already?" Sandy chimed, ecstatic to hear from her daughter. The silence lasted for several seconds. Sam did not know how to begin. "Sam, love, are you alright?" Sandy enquired, the cheer stripped from her voice.

"Mum, I need to ask you something and I need you, to be honest."

"Well, of course, love."

"Did I change when I was with Jo? I mean, did I... did I stop being me?" Sam stuttered, the emotion overwhelming her again. Sam heard her mum take a sharp breath in. *That can't be good!*

A beat or two went by before Sandy answered. "Yes, my darling, you changed." Sam's breath hitched, tears swam in her eyes. "I must admit that I didn't see it straight the way, but over time, you shied away. You stopped going out with friends. Stopped doing anything that Jo disapproved of, which my darling seemed to be everything." Sandy sighed as she continued, "I spoke to Charlie on a couple of occasions, times when I was worried. Charlie told me she'd tried to talk to you, but it was no good."

Silence.

"Sam, are you still there?"

"I... I'm still here."

"I just wanted you to be happy, Sam. You were a grown adult making your own choices, and I wanted to support you, love."

"I know," Sam whispered. "Charlie wrote me a letter. Can I read it to you?"

"Of course."

Sam cleared her throat and began reading. Hearing the words aloud seemed to cause her more pain than when she'd read them silently to herself. The words were painful because they were true.

"How do you feel about what Charlie said?"

"I don't know. I don't know how to feel," Sam answered honestly. "I've read it so many times, and after reading it to you out loud, I think Charlie's right. I think I am lost, Mum." Sandy remained silent. "I was so devastated because I thought Jo was the love of my life. But even I thought I would start to feel better about it after all this time, but I just haven't been able to move on," Sam continued.

The words were pouring from her and she couldn't stop, even if she wanted to. "I'm so ashamed that I let this happen. I lost ten years of my life, Mum." Her tears of sadness were being replaced with tears of anger. "All of my twenties gone!" she was almost shouting now. "All the goals and dreams I had in uni, gone! Gone because I let myself get sucked into something that wasn't even real. She never loved me, she just used me for her own sick games and I fell for it. I feel like such an idiot." She was panting hard down the phone, waiting for her mum to speak.

"Do you feel better now, love?"

Sam controlled her breathing and checked in with herself — a trick that Sandy had taught her when she was younger. On reflection, she was feeling better. She'd needed to vent. The weight on her chest eased. "Yeah... yes, I felt better."

"Good...now my girl, tell me what you are going to do? You may have lost time to that woman, but you still have the rest of your life to live. As far as I see it, you have two choices: either you stay angry at the situation, at the past, or you let it go, stop spending your precious time thinking about what could have been. So, I'll ask you again, what are you going to do?" Sandy quizzed.

"I'm going to look forward... I... I'm going to work on loving myself again, I... I'm going to remember who I am and what I'm capable of. I'm going to know my worth and... I'm going to make art in Paris," Sam declared, her voice strong and her resolve steadfast.

"You are going to shine, my darling."

Sam stood with the phone to her ear, looking out of the window. It had become her favourite place to be. As she watched the world go by, a reassuring feeling settled over her. Paris was going to help her heal, help her move forward to become the person and photographer she always wanted to be.

Chapter Ten

Anna blinked rapidly. Her neck felt sore from spending hours in an awkward position. She had fallen asleep on the couch again. It wasn't the first time since she'd begun renting the swanky apartment and she was sure it wouldn't be the last. She'd arrived home late from her weekend with her family and simply couldn't make it to the bedroom.

It was past ten o'clock when she finally woke. She couldn't remember a time when she had stayed in bed that long. Other than when she was ill, Anna always rose early, which was strange because she was a terrible morning person.

Usually the slightest sound would wake her, but not last night. Last night, she'd fallen into the deepest sleep she'd ever had. There could have been a pneumatic drill going off next to her head and she wouldn't have stirred.

She'd spent a wonderful Sunday with her family, eating and drinking in the luscious garden at the back of the cottage. The weather had suited her mood, being bright and warm all day. They'd all had such a good time that Anna and Frédéric had taken the last train home to Paris, instead of the one they'd originally planned to take just after lunch.

Anna pulled herself up to a sitting position, stretching out her long limbs. Her phone pinged, an email notification popped up on the screen. As much as she had tried to disconnect herself, she knew it was time to get back to her life. She reached for the phone, presuming the email would be work-related. It wasn't. It was from James.

Hi Anna, just wanted to make sure you are ok. I came back a little earlier than planned and noticed you haven't been home. I think it's best that I move out as soon as possible, so I've collected some of my things. I'm going to stay with a friend until I decide on my next move.

Please keep the apartment, you always liked the place more than me. I'll message you once I'm settled. I'll organise some movers to get my bigger items in a few days. I hope that in the future we could be friends. No reason to part on bad terms. I don't think either of us is to blame. Just the way life is, I suppose.

Anyway, hope you're doing ok.

Speak Soon

James

Anna let out a sigh. She didn't want any animosity between them. Friends could be an option, but she wasn't sure *he* would want that after she had told him she was gay. As much as James was a nice guy, she wondered if her sexual orientation would hurt his ego. *Do I have to tell him?*

They weren't a couple anymore; did he really need to know? She tabled the idea for now. There was only one person left she felt needed to know, and that was Kim.

Anna had been a little curt with her PA the last time they'd spoken, and she hadn't deserved it. Kim was so much more than an assistant, she was a friend. It seemed Anna was doing a lot of apologising lately. Living in the closet had made her a bit of a bitch.

Throwing her phone down, she prepared herself to go to work. She hadn't told Kim when she would be back. She still had plenty of holiday days saved up from years of overworking, but the need to stay hidden away had vanished the moment she had spoken the three words that had terrified her to her parents.

Anna wanted her routine back, although she would still stay in her fancy rental for another few weeks. She'd extended her lease a few days prior to visiting her parents. That gave her time to decide what she wanted regarding the apartment she'd shared with James. She wasn't sure if it suited her anymore.

Showered and dressed, Anna looked at herself in the mirror. It was the first time that she had ever dressed down for work. Her black jeans were fitted and clung to her toned legs; the white V-neck T-shirt was form-fitting, accentuating her subtle curves. Her hair had grown out a little and was hanging below her shoulders in soft waves.

Pleased with how she looked, she threw her phone in her bag and headed out the door. Putting her sunglasses on and her earphones in; she selected an upbeat playlist and started walking. There was no way she was getting on the stuffy metro today. The route to her office would be long, but she didn't care. She wanted to feel the sun on her face. She wanted to look around the city as she walked, something she hadn't done in a long time. There was no rush, not today.

Thirty minutes of walking in the sweltering heat forced Anna to stop at a small bar. She needed a drink and some shade. The bar had a terrace situated out back with six little tables covered by umbrellas. The cold metal of the chair felt delicious on her skin as she leaned back.

A few minutes passed before a waitress stepped under Anna's umbrella. She was cute. Anna couldn't help but notice. Blonde hair whipped into a messy bun, subtle eye makeup framed her deep blue eyes.

Anna could feel herself staring. She cleared her throat and ordered a glass of sparkling water. Stabbing Anna's order into the small handheld computer she was carrying, the waitress left, giving Anna a marvellous view of her tight arse.

"Putain," Anna muttered to herself. "Get a grip on yourself," she exclaimed, a little louder than she expected. Was this how it was going to be from now on? Every time she saw a beautiful woman, she would become an ogling mess. Her body seemed to have a mind of its own. Her clit certainly did.

Squeezing her thighs shut, she accepted the water from the waitress, who had returned quicker than Anna expected with a warm smile. Anna downed the water as quickly as she could and left. Earbuds back in, Anna lengthened her stride to get her heartbeat going; she had to work off her sudden burst of sexual frustration somehow.

She rounded the corner of the street where Tower Publishing was located. A little smile crossed her face. She was happy to be back. Swinging the door open, she headed to her office. Anna saw the instant that Kim clocked her presence and noted the flash of surprise and concern on her face.

Kim was on her feet in seconds, clutching her notepad and making a beeline for Anna. "Anna, what are you doing here?" Kim stuttered.

"It's nice to see you, too," Anna joked.

"No... I... obviously it's great to see you, but I wasn't expecting you in."

"That's because I didn't tell you when I would be back, Kim." She began fingering the papers strewn on her desk, trying to see if anything was of great importance.

Kim opened and closed her mouth several times, not sure how to proceed. "I should have tidied your desk," Kim suddenly blurted, her face still marred with concern.

Anna couldn't let Kim suffer anymore. It wasn't fair. "Relax Kim, please, it's my fault. I should have messaged you."

Kim's shoulders seemed to drop and relax a little. "Is everything okay?"

124

"Can you set up a dinner for this evening, you pick the restaurant? Make it for two."

"Oh. Yes, of course," Kim spluttered, scribbling down Anna's request on her notepad. Which was unnecessary, as Kim had a memory like an elephant. She was clearly nervous about Anna's sudden reappearance. "Um, I don't have you booked to meet anyone."

"No, I don't have a meeting. I'm hoping you will join me for dinner. Pick anywhere you like, my treat."

"Right... Okay." Kim looked utterly bewildered. In all the time they had worked together, they had never gone out to dinner. The odd lunch now and then, but nothing outside of office hours.

"I'll set it up and email you the details, then." Kim gave Anna a sharp nod before retreating to her desk. Anna hoped Kim wasn't going to sit and worry about her sudden dinner invitation, but Anna certainly didn't want to discuss her private business in the office.

Sure enough, five minutes later Anna received an email giving her the time and place for their meal. Anna's office walls were made of glass so she could see out onto the main floor. Kim's desk was just outside to her right. She looked up, catching Kim's attention. She gave an enthusiastic thumbs-up, acknowledging her email. Kim gave her a nervous smile in return.

The day seemed to fly by. Everyone went about his or her business as usual. Kim was the only one acting a little strange; she kept shooting Anna nervous looks. Anna smiled back, trying to convey that everything was okay.

The sky outside was still bright when her colleagues began filtering out of the building, heading home to their loved ones. Anna hoped that would be her one day. A light tap on her door snapped her out of her thoughts. "Are you ready? Our reservation is in fifteen minutes."

"Yes, let's go," Anna replied, putting her bag over her shoulder, gesturing to Kim to lead the way out.

Ten minutes later, they were seated by the window of Kim's favourite pizzeria. Anna knew it was her favourite because it was the only place Kim would order from if they worked late and because Kim never stopped raving about the place to anyone who would listen.

After a few minutes of awkward silence, Kim looked like she was fit to burst. "Are you firing me?" she almost squealed.

Anna's eyes became the size of saucers as she watched Kim become overwhelmed with panic. "Of course not! Why on earth would I fire you?" Kim was looking at her with wild eyes. Anna felt terrible. "I promise you, Kim, you will always have a job with me," she added, hoping to ease Kim's anxiety.

It seemed to work. Kim visibly relaxed. "Okay, so what's wrong?"

"Well, nothing is wrong, per se. I would like to talk to you about something... personal."

Kim looked at her with quizzical eyes. "You can talk to me about anything, Anna. We are friends after all." Kim smiled brightly, her demeanour back to her bouncy self, which was a relief.

"Yes... yes, of course we are. It's just I find it difficult to talk about private matters." A blush had started to creep up her neck. "So, I ended things with James," she continued, hoping Kim wouldn't interrupt. She didn't. "It wasn't right for either of us and in the end; it just wasn't fair to continue on the way we were." Kim sat patiently, giving a little nod of her head in understanding.

"Well, that's not really what I wanted to talk to you about... I... I was able to take a little time for myself after London and well, there is no other way to say it, so here goes... I'm gay, Kim." God, was she going to spend the rest of her life outing herself? she really didn't like the thought of it, far too stressful.

Kim's expression gave nothing away. After a few moments, she reached over and squeezed Anna's arm. "Thank you for sharing that with me, Anna. I'm really honoured you felt

126

comfortable enough with me to do so." Kim smiled, her eyes full of love for her friend.

Anna blew out a breath. "Shall we order and get a drink?"

"Absolutely." Kim turned to signal the waiter that they were ready to order. Two bottles of beer were put on the table. Kim insisted you could only drink beer with pizza. They lifted their bottles and clinked. Anna drank half the bottle in one go. She needed it.

"So what's next?"

"What do you mean?"

"I mean, when are you going to look for a lady?" Kim waggled her eyebrows.

"Oh well, not sure I'm quite ready for that."

"Nonsense, of course you're ready. You've just done the hard part. Now you get to enjoy yourself," Kim continued, a cheeky grin plastered on her face.

Anna rolled her eyes. "I've only just come out, Kim. Maybe I need a little more than ten minutes processing time before I look for a partner," she chuckled.

"A partner? So you want to settle down?"

Anna hadn't really thought about it, but, yes, that's exactly what she wanted. "Yes, eventually, I don't have the time or the interest to play around."

"Well, I'm pretty sure that in order for you to find a partner and settle down, you actually have to go looking for someone. They won't just fall in your lap," Kim quipped. "I can be your wing woman," she added, clearly over the moon with her own idea. Kim was practically vibrating in her seat at the thought of it.

Anna held up her hand. "Slow down." It did little to calm Kim.

"Oh, come on. We could have a girl's night on the town. We've never done that!" Kim pleaded.

Was Anna really considering it? Could she put herself out there so quickly? Kim's excitement was infectious. After all, this was the reason she had braved coming out to her family and friends.

Anna chewed on her bottom lip, "Okay… I'll go out with you." Kim started bouncing in her seat, clapping her hands in excitement. "But only if you calm down," Anna quickly added.

Kim giggled and stopped bouncing. "This weekend, I can come over to yours beforehand and we can have a few cheeky drinks, if you like?"

"Yes, okay, I'd like to show off the apartment I've been renting, anyway. It's very swanky," Anna grinned. She was actually looking forward to it, even if she felt the weight of anxiety settle in her stomach. Kim gave a squeal of excitement before swallowing the rest of her beer.

The rest of the evening was delightful, full of laughter and playful banter. By the end of the meal, they had planned for their night out. Kim would come by Anna's at eight on Saturday to get ready, and then they would head out into the city. Kim had been more than happy to take the reins organising the bars they would visit, which suited Anna just fine; she didn't want to overthink it all. Best to let Kim handle that.

* * *

The rest of the work week flew by. Kim and Anna had eaten lunch together nearly every day. By the time Friday rolled around, Anna was feeling nervous about the weekend plan, but it was a good nervous.

Her anxiety and dread had been left behind days ago. Now she could almost taste the possibilities that lay ahead. The possibility of meeting a woman, even just the possibility of sharing a drink with an amiable lady, was good enough for now.

The day before, Anna had nipped back to her old apartment to grab some much needed clothes. It hadn't been an easy trip. There was so much history between her and James. No matter how it had ended, they'd shared a life together, and the apartment was an uncomfortable reminder.

128

Anna had quickly decided she wouldn't return there to live. She needed a fresh start. All those decisions could wait for now though, because in a few hours she was going to her first gay bar.

The buzzer sounded at eight o'clock sharp. Kim was nothing but punctual. Anna threw open the door with a wicked grin. She may or may not have started a bottle of wine in anticipation.

Kim looked great, dressy, but still casual. Her platinum-blonde hair cascaded down her back in ringlets. Her short body looked fabulous in the form-fitting polka dot knee-length dress she wore. Even with her stilettos — which were ridiculously high — she was still much smaller than Anna.

"You look wonderful!" Anna cheered, leaning in to give her a two-cheek kiss.

"Why thank you," Kim replied, giving a mock curtsy. "You, on the other hand, are in a dressing gown," she giggled. It seemed that Kim had also partaken in a little pre-gay bar drinking herself.

"I know, I'm sorry." Anna walked from the entrance door to her bedroom. "Grab a drink and I'll be with you in five minutes."

Anna heard Kim clinking glasses and pouring the wine she had started earlier in the evening. Kim slinked into Anna's room, almost giddy with excitement. She handed Anna her wine. "Tchin, Tchin." They gently knocked glasses.

"Okay, two minutes and I'm ready."

Kim had parked herself on the bed, taking in the beauty of Anna's apartment. "This place is wonderful," she exclaimed, already slurring her words a little.

"It's a dream," Anna shouted through the bathroom door.

Before Kim could reply, Anna walked into the bedroom. Kim stared at her with wide eyes, causing Anna to stop mid-step. "Do I look okay? You're staring at me funny." She could feel her cheeks growing warm under Kim's stare.

"Holy shit, Anna. You. Are. A. Fox!" Kim squealed, jumping from the bed and grabbing Anna's arms, forcing her into a twirl. "I mean, wow!"

129

Anna's face was burning. She rarely got complimented on her attire. She pulled herself from Kim's grip, a nervous smile on her face. The only thing she needed was her earrings.

Kim beckoned her over to the mirror. She walked over to the mirror, not sure what the purpose was. "Anna, look at yourself, seriously. Looking like this, you should have no doubts at all that you are going to get some serious attention tonight."

Anna took a minute to look. She'd decided on three-inch heels, tight straight-cut dark navy jeans that hugged her arse perfectly and a black satin strappy tank. Her hair brushed against her skin in subtle curls and after several YouTube videos, she'd also mastered smokey eye makeup. Kim was right. She looked good. She gave herself a little smile and turned away from her reflection. "Drink time!" She wiggled her eyebrows devilishly.

The taxi arrived just before nine to whisk them away. Kim explained she had found a couple of bars to try out. The car journey was quick, the first bar being only a five-minute drive. Kim noticed Anna was becoming quite nervous. She was entangling her fingers over and over. "Anna, calm down, love."

Anna stilled her hands and looked at her friend. "I'm nervous," she murmured.

"Listen, you have nothing to be worried about. Tonight is just a little exploration. You do not have to do anything but have a drink with me. There is no expectation of anything else, okay?"

Anna saw the sincerity in Kim's eyes. She took a deep breath and slowly exhaled as the car pulled up to the first bar. "You ready?" Kim held on to Anna's hand. Anna gave a quick nod before walking to the bar entrance.

The outside had neon signs lighting up the street. Anna could hear the music pumping loudly, the glass in the door vibrated from the bass. Kim took the lead and headed to the bar. Anna kept her eyes firmly on her friend.

The space was far from packed, but there was a nice-sized crowd. The place wasn't huge, but allowed for a few small tables to litter the edges of the room and a small dance floor at the back by the DJ stand. Kim collected their drinks and ushered Anna to one of the little tables. "Doing okay?"

"Yes, fine. I think I need a couple more drinks, though," she chuckled.

"Good job I ordered a few shots then, isn't it?" Kim grinned, arching her eyebrow. Sure enough, the barwoman approached with a tray of six shots. "Down the hatch." Kim threw the first shot down her throat, followed by a second in quick succession. Anna followed suit. The alcohol burned all the way down, but it felt good.

They quickly chased off the rest of the tray and let the buzz of the alcohol settle in. Anna was relaxed; the beat of the music was making her body move by itself. They chatted amongst themselves for a good half hour until the DJ turned the music up even higher. "Ready to dance?" Kim shouted.

"Why not?" They made their way to the dance floor, not too far from the table, so they could keep an eye on their belongings. Anna let the music flow through her. She felt absolutely free.

Anna perused the room as they danced. There was a complete mix of people. Some seemed coupled up, many were in friendship groups. There was the odd person on their own, but either way, everyone was having fun.

It was after the fourth song that Anna noticed Kim's eyes widen slightly. Something had caught her attention over Anna's shoulder. Just as Anna was about to follow her gaze, she felt a body press ever so softly up against hers. The unknown person began moving in time to Anna's rhythm. Anna shot a look at Kim, who raised her eyebrows, questioning if Anna felt comfortable. Anna gave a subtle nod. *What could it hurt?* This was the reason she had come out. To experience women.

She danced with her back to the person for a few beats before turning around to fully connect with her dance partner. The woman was tall with short brown hair swept back neatly. She wore black jeans and a white tank top. The music was so loud that any attempt at conversation was futile, so they danced silently, smiling at each other.

131

The music changed, and the woman came in closer. She wrapped her long arms around Anna's waist, grinding into her. As much as she was having fun, Anna was no way near ready to go any further.

Kim must have sensed Anna's body language change because, in an instant, Kim danced herself into Anna's personal space, giving the other woman a little wink as she shimmied herself between them and began dancing with Anna back towards their table. The woman didn't seem very upset and, within a couple of seconds, was pressed up against another patron.

"Thanks," Anna shouted, giving Kim a little shoulder bump.

"Wingwoman Kim at your service," she laughed. "You ready to go to the next bar?"

"Let's do it."

The night air was chilly when they exited the bar. Anna focused solely on Kim as she pushed her way through the small crowd that had gathered by the door.

Rushing towards a cab that had just been vacated, Anna accidentally brushed the shoulder of a woman on her phone. She smelled delicious.

Unfortunately, Anna only had a split second to gaze back at the woman who had her back to them because Kim was hurrying her along. *Shame I didn't get to dance with you!* Anna thought as she climbed into the car.

Chapter Eleven

"Sixteen......Seventeen......Eighteen......Nineteen......Twenty, oof" Sam exhaled as she face-planted the ground with her entire body falling limp. She tried to suck in as much air as possible. How had she become so out of shape? During high school and college, Sam had been an avid sports player; she was at home on a football field and tennis court.

Her mum loathed fitness of any kind, so she presumed she must have inherited her love of it from her dad. She often felt sad that she had never got to share her passion with the person who made up one-half of who she was.

By the time she'd got into uni, Sam had dropped her commitments regarding football and tennis because she knew it would be too much to juggle whilst studying. She simply couldn't find the time. Sam did, however, fit in her workout routines and even though she thought it a little self-braggy, she was in damn fine shape back then.

Then Jo happened. As with everything else she enjoyed, Sam had given up that part of her life when Jo complained it took up too much of her time. Of course, Sam hadn't realised what was happening back then, but after the past few days, she quickly realised it was just another part of herself that she had given up on Jo's behest.

Not anymore, though. Sam couldn't get back the time she had lost, but she could damn well start again and that was why she was now hyperventilating on the solid oak floor of her Paris apartment.

The day after she had spoken to her mum, she'd woken up with purpose. The purpose was to get herself back to her former self, better if she could manage it. Exercise had also been the best way for Sam to work through her feelings. It always helped clear her mind, reset her emotions and help her think things through and find answers.

Sam had an excellent memory of her former workout schedule, which she had been trying to replicate, but it had been so much harder than she realised. Instead of breezing through her 50 squats, 50 crunches and 50 press ups, she had managed to only complete half of that. With her lungs burning, she could already feel her muscles protesting. She was going to be in a world of pain tomorrow.

Undeterred, she scraped herself off the floor and grabbed her bottle of water that stood by the couch. Her mouth felt as if she had been stuck in the Sahara for a week. Half a litre later, she felt a little more human.

"Okay, need to adjust the routine," she panted. Nothing was going to ruin her newfound determination. She spent the next half an hour rewriting her schedule, picking exercises that helped build muscle but incorporated cardio, too.

The results were very pleasing. She had a full week's schedule planned. She smiled at her work. Speaking of work, she needed to get a move on if she was going to make it into the editing suites before it got busy. She threw off her workout gear and headed for the shower. Her muscles needed some TLC.

The shower took longer than she had planned, the hot water soothed her body and she was loath to get out. Her phone buzzed, leaving Sam no choice but to step out of the comforting embrace of the hot water.

Charlie's face was lighting up her screen. It would be the first time they had spoken since Charlie had left Paris. She gave a little smile at her best friend's goofy face, a picture Charlie had taken of herself without telling Sam that she'd saved it as her profile picture; she was pulling a ridiculous face.

"Hey, Char."

"Hey, Sammy, you okay?"

Sam knew Charlie had intentionally given her some space over the past few days. Sam also knew from Charlie's voice that she was worried Sam was angry with her about the letter.

"I'm better than I've been in a long time, mate. Thank you for helping me get there." Sam did *not* intend to let her best friend suffer through the conversation. Yes, she'd been surprised, or more like shocked, when she had first read Charlie's brutally truthful letter regarding Jo and everything that had happened, but she had never been angry at her. Charlie only ever did things out of love. Sam always trusted that.

"You're not mad?"

"Not at you, Char, never at you. At myself, definitely, but I'm working to change that."

"I'm so proud of you, Sam, you're a legend," Charlie laughed.

"Thanks, couldn't do it without you and Mum. I called her after I read your letter. I was just as surprised to learn she felt the same way as you did about it all. Was a shock to the system, but a shock I needed."

"Sorry, Sammy, I hope you don't feel like we were ganging up on you. That was never the intention."

"Not at all. I just needed to hear it straight," Sam sighed. After a beat of silence, she shifted the conversation. She was done with misery and sadness. "Guess what I did this morning?"

"Umm, do I really want to know?" Charlie chuckled. "You didn't bang another local, did you?" she barked.

"No, I did not! God, you always go straight to sex, don't you?" Sam laughed.

135

"Well, yeah, sex is amazing. Nothing wrong with that." Sam could hear Charlie's smile.

"Anyway, no, it wasn't anything sexy, but it left me panting and gasping for air," Sam teased.

"Oh, Christ, you haven't got yourself into some weird fetish, have you?"

"Ha! No such luck. I did a workout session and I think I turned all my muscles to spaghetti. I'm not sure I can lift my camera bag."

"Hell yeah, Sammy, get on it," Charlie cheered. Sam couldn't help but laugh. "God, do you remember all the ladies you pulled just by wearing a tank top that showed off your physique?"

"I'm not doing it to pull women, Char, and what are we, eighteen again? My days of 'pulling' are done. I want to meet someone nice, looking a little more long-term."

"Are you ready to date?" Charlie gasped. She had been trying for so long to get Sam out and about, but with no success.

"I've got a lot of work to do on myself, but I'm not counting it out any longer. I always wanted to settle down, even in uni. It was you and the others that made me out to be some sort of lesbian Casanova," she laughed.

"Oh mate, you earned that name. The funniest thing about it was that you didn't even know how bloody charming you were. You could get the ladies to drop their knickers with just a smile," Charlie chuckled. "The fact that you *weren't* trying to be a Casanova was the reason you were so successful at it. It was epic to watch. I was so jealous of your confidence, mate!"

"You had zero reasons to be jealous. If memory served, you did okay for yourself too."

"Yeah... I suppose, still never as good as you." Sam hated hearing Charlie self-deprecate. Since the whole shit show with Jo, Charlie had stepped up; she had grown in confidence to help Sam in the wake of her broken relationship.

Charlie had struggled with her confidence when they had first met. Her parents had taken a hands-off approach where raising their daughter was concerned, and it had affected her

136

self-belief and self-worth because she'd never got any reassurances from her parents throughout her childhood.

"Stop it. Uni was years ago. You are the strongest and most confident woman I know. You have nobody to be jealous of, do you hear?"

Charlie sucked in a breath. "Sorry mate, not sure why I went down that rabbit hole."

"Any chance you had a call from your parents?"

"How'd you guess?" Her voice was laced with sadness.

"Because that's the only time you feel shitty towards yourself."

Charlie had been her rock for the past ten years. It was time Sam pulled her head out of her own arse and became the best friend Charlie needed. She hated the thought that Charlie had shelved her own issues and she really hated the thought that Charlie had felt she couldn't confide in Sam because she didn't want to cause *her* any more upset.

"They said nothing out of the ordinary. They never do. I just don't understand why they had me. Why bring me into the world and then ignore me for thirty years?"

"I, for one, am thrilled they brought you into this world. They might be a 10 on the shittiest parent scale, but you have me and Mum, always!" Sam hoped Charlie could hear how sincere she was.

"I know Sammy. I don't know why I still let them get to me like this."

"Because you're their kid Char, it's only natural you want them to take an interest in your life."

Charlie let out a deep sigh before sucking in a deep breath. "Fuck 'em, that's enough of that. Christ, the convo's turned a little too deep for a Wednesday morning," Charlie chuckled, sounding a little more like her cheerful self.

"You ain't wrong, mate. Feel like I need a stiff drink now."

"Well, it must be five somewhere in the world."

"I wish… I gotta be an adult and go to work," Sam whined for effect.

137

"Yeah, adulting is bollocks," Charlie whined back. "What's on the books today?"

"Editing, editing, and more editing. I have so many photos I need to have a clear out. Start doing some weeding." Her mind wandered to the two SD cards full of photos. She was going to have a long couple of weeks. She loved it.

"Sounds like you're gonna have a blast. I'll let you get off. I need to head out soon, too. Will you text me later?" her voice more timid than normal. She was obviously still feeling a little vulnerable.

"Absolutely. Catch you later," Sam chirped before cutting the call.

* * *

The screen was blurring in front of Sam's eyes. She wasn't sure how long she'd been staring at the image in front of her. The editing suite had been busy for most of the day, but now she was the only one left burning the midnight oil.

She hadn't been wrong when she thought the next few weeks were going to keep her busy. How she'd taken so many photos was beyond her. She sifted through them slowly; she wanted to look at each photo carefully to see if it hit the mark, fit into the project and her vision.

Sam always made multiple backups of all the photos she took; sometimes she liked to look back at her work, not the work that was perfect but the missteps, the imperfect shots. She could always learn from her mistakes.

As she was organising the pictures, she made a separate file for the photos of her and Charlie that they'd taken. They were mostly silly, but some of them would be great on Sam's wall at home.

Pushing her chair away from the desk; she rolled her head, trying to ease some discomfort she had from staying in one place too long. She swivelled around to take in some scenery. The street lamps were glowing, highlighting the street below and the offices opposite.

As she scanned the building in front of her, she noticed one light remained. Sam knew it would be Helene's office lamp. Before she could second guess herself, she saved her work, shut down the computer and headed out of the building.

Usually, she would text Henry to pick her up straight away and take her back to the apartment, but not tonight. Tonight, she needed to make amends.

Crossing the street, she entered the empty offices. She needed to clear the air properly with Helene. "Knock, knock." She gently tapped on the closed door that led to Helene's office. She rolled her eyes at herself for actually saying, "Knock, knock." *What a twat!*

"Come in," Helene called quietly.

"Hi," Sam smiled.

"Sam, everything okay?"

"Yeah, fine, no problem. Wondered if I could have a word?"

"Of course." Helene gestured for Sam to sit.

"So... There's been a lot going on in the short time that I have been here." Helene straightened her back, giving Sam her undivided attention. Sam pressed on. "First, I want to apologise. I kind of binned you off after the whole Lauren saga."

"Binned me off? I don't understand that phrase." Helene looked confused.

"Right... sorry. I mean, I reacted badly to the situation and then disappeared on you. I know you didn't know who Lauren was to me. In the short time I've known you, I understand you wouldn't have done something like that on purpose. You've been nothing but kind and professional."

"Not completely professional, Sam. I slept with you on the same day you arrived." Helene blushed, diverting her eyes from Sam.

"That was consensual. It was nothing to do with work," Sam replied. "I don't want to get into all the details, but let's just say I've had a few home truths told to me recently, and it's helped

139

me a lot." Helene continued to look at Sam, waiting for her to continue. "I can't be in a romantic relationship with you. That hasn't changed, but I really want us to be friends, Helene. I think we really get on, and my past with Lauren shouldn't stop us from building a friendship." Sam shifted in her chair. Deep conversations made her uncomfortable. "So… do you think we could start again, as friends?"

"I would like that a lot, Sam," Helene smiled brightly, her shoulders relaxing as she leaned back in her chair.

Sam beamed at her. "Great, phew, that got a little tense," she laughed. Helene chuckled alongside her, happy that the tension had dissipated.

"How's the project?"

Sam was glad to move on to a lighter topic. "It's going really well. I didn't realise how many pictures I'd taken over the last week. I'm spending some time picking out the best ones. It's going to take some time before I can whittle them down to the ones I want to use."

"What have you shot so far?"

"Mostly landscape and architecture. I think…" Sam hesitated, not sure if she should say what was on her mind.

"Think what?"

"I think I'm going to scrap the whole model idea," Sam replied, trying to sound confident in her decision.

"Oh, why is that?"

"The project is to capture Paris, the truest version of Paris that I can find. Using staged models doesn't fit. Capturing people in their natural state is the way to proceed. No staging, no lies."

"It's your project, Sam. I trust your creative decisions. Do what you feel is best."

"Thanks," Sam beamed again. "I'm going to head home. Sleep is required."

"Good idea. I'll follow you out. It's been a long day." Helene rolled her chair back and collected her things. They left the offices together and waited for their drivers.

140

"Do you want to go for a drink this weekend? I think we could both do with blowing off a little steam." Sam hoped that Helene would grab at the chance to hang out as friends.

"You know what? That would be great. How about we go out on Saturday night? There is a bar I quite like, and it's full of club members."

This was the first time in ages Sam considered going to a gay bar. The idea was a welcome one. She missed being around her people.

"Deal, text me the address and I'll meet you there."

"Done. See you tomorrow, Sam."

"Night Helene."

Today had been a good day.

* * *

Thursday and Friday whizzed by in a blur of coffee and editing. Sam had made a slight dent in her mountain of photos, but there was still a long way to go. She was happy that she'd had lunch with Helene on both days. They slipped into easy conversation. It felt comfortable between them again, which was a relief.

Sam spent most of Saturday scouring her clothes, hoping to find something wearable for her debut out onto the Paris gay scene. No such luck. All her clothes were only suitable for work.

Rolling her eyes, she faced the fact that she would have to go shopping. "Bollocks!" she shouted. Sam had never been the type of person who enjoyed milling around shops. Well, only one thing for it, she needed a friend.

> **Sam:** *Helene SOS!!!!*
> **Helene:** *What's wrong?*
> **Sam:** *I have nothing for tonight.*
> **Helene:** *For god's sake, I thought you had a genuine emergency!!*
> **Sam:** *It is, you don't want to be seen with me looking like a tit.*
> **Helene:** *I am strongly rolling my eyes at you right now. I can have something sent over if that would help.*

Sam: *You would be my hero. I hate shopping. Do you need my sizes? I don't do dresses.*
Helene: *Trust me. See you later.*

Sam thrust her hand in the air in triumph. Thank god for Helene.

A couple of hours later, her clothes arrived by messenger. Sam unzipped the garment bag and got ready, giving herself a quick once over in the mirror when she was finished.

Helene had done a grand job. She wore tight black jeans and a white slim-fit shirt, which had a few buttons open, allowing some cleavage to show.

The shirt was paired with a form-fitting waistcoat that shimmered in the light. Sam had made an effort with her hair for a change, deciding against her usual ponytail. After an hour of preening, she finally looked good enough to go out.

The taxi pulled up to the bar. It was covered with enough neon lights to be seen from space. Her phone pinged as she got out of the car. It was a message from Charlie. Well, actually, it was a rude meme because Charlie had the humour of a horny teenage boy.

Sam stepped onto the curb, as she replied. She felt someone brush past her to grab the taxi she had just exited. Sam's eyes drifted back over to the cab just in time to witness the nicest bum she had ever seen climbing into the back seat. Not wanting to be caught staring, she headed into the club. Sam was ready to let her hair down.

* * *

Sunday was spent cursing the world. Sam had really let her hair down, like way down. Vodka seemed to ooze out of her pores. Gross. After a long shower and several cups of coffee later, Sam was able to function at a reasonable level.

Helene: *How are you feeling?*

142

Sam: Like death.

Helene: Me too. Why did we drink so much?

Sam: I don't know, ugh, kill me now.

Helene: Listen, you need to go to a meeting at Tower Publishing in the morning before heading into the office.

Sam: Why?

Helene: Rupert wants the prints made into a book, not sure why, but that's what he has requested.

Sam: Send me the address.

Helene: See you tomorrow. I'm going to vomit now.

Sam chuckled. She was happy she wasn't the only one suffering.

* * *

The trip to Tower Publishing was enjoyable. The area was pleasant, and the architecture was wonderful. Sam couldn't help but whip out her camera for some shots. The commute had been an easy one, with little traffic so early in the morning.

The appointment was set for 8:45 a.m., but she'd arrived ten minutes early. A short woman dashed over within seconds of Sam entering.

"Ms Chambers?" Wow, she was far too enthusiastic for the time of day.

"Erm, yeah."

"Great, wow, nice and early. Anna will love that."

"Right...so er, who is Anna?" Sam's brain was not firing on all cylinders.

"You'll work with her on the book. Has no one filled you in?"

"Well, not really. I was only told yesterday about the meeting." Sam hoped she didn't come across as unprofessional.

"Oh… well, never mind. Anna will fill you in on all the details. I'm Kim, I'm Anna's assistant. Would you like a coffee?"

"Thanks, black, no sugar, please."

"Take a seat there and I'll let Anna know you're here."

Before Sam could reply, the woman had dashed off at an alarming speed. Sam took a few deep breaths. No worries, she could rock this meeting, even though she was completely flummoxed by what it was going to involve. As far as she was concerned, she just took the pictures. Job done. Rupert and John obviously had different ideas.

The assistant — Kim, that's her name, right!? — came whizzing back over. "Anna is ready for you now. Follow me."

Sam did as she was told and was ushered into an office. There was a tall, dark-haired woman perusing shelves that were at the back of her desk. Sam cleared her throat and then nearly choked on her own spit when the woman turned around.

Sam definitely knew that face. *Holy shit!*

Chapter Twelve

"Merde!" That's how Anna reacted when she received an email from Marcus on Sunday. She was hungover, and the last thing she wanted to think about was work.

No choice now. The email detailed a meeting that had been wedged in early the following morning. Anna already had plenty to do, and she knew that there were other people in the office that could take it for her, but Marcus had insisted it had to be Anna.

> **Anna:** *Kim, did you see the email from Marcus?*
> **Kim:** *No, I can't open my eyes yet. Everything hurts.*
> **Anna:** *No choice. It's been set for tomorrow morning.*
> **Kim:** *Ugh, give me five to have a look.*

Anna leaned her head back against the headboard of the bed. *Why, why, why did I drink so much?*

Anna was never any good the morning after drinking. Her hangovers were atrocious, which is why she rarely drank more than a glass of wine on the weekend. The night had been a lot of fun though, which almost made the pain worth it. Almost.

Her phone dinged.

Kim: It shouldn't be a long meeting. I have rearranged a couple of things. Did you read the details of the email?
Anna: Not really.
Kim: Didn't think so. You will meet a photographer. Rupert Downes is commissioning a book of photography. The subject will be Paris. It's an initial meeting to start the process, nothing too major.
Anna: Wonderful, just what I need on a Monday morning. A Parisian photographer.
Kim: They're not all bad.
Anna: Really?
Kim: Ok fine, probably another pretentious artiste, but it will be short.
Anna: I have very little choice in the matter. See you tomorrow and thank you for last night.
Kim: See you tomorrow and it was my pleasure.

* * *

Anna arrived at the office early. If she was going to have to suffer through this meeting, she needed to get some work done first. She hated starting her day disorganised, especially when she had done such a good job of preparing herself for the week ahead.

It was also an irritation when Marcus allowed his silent partner to push his agenda. John Spencer calling in a favour would be the only reason that Marcus would be so insistent on a last-minute meeting and that Anna had to be the one to take it.

Kim arrived only fifteen minutes after Anna. "Morning," she chirped as she leant on Anna's door frame.

"It is indeed," Anna replied moodily.

"Oh, you're not still sulking, are you?" Kim tutted.

"Yes, I am," Anna stated. She had every right to sulk.

"You have half an hour until the photographer arrives and I bet you have already crossed a lot off your to-do list."

"That's not the point," Anna grumbled.

Kim gave a little chuckle. "Alright, I'll let you sulk for another five minutes and then we power stand, okay?" It wasn't really a question, but more of a soft order. Anna could agree with those terms.

Five minutes later, Kim slid into the room and cleared her throat. "Ready?" Anna nodded before standing. She brought her hands to her hips and stood tall like a superhero. Kim mirrored her actions. Kim had told Anna that it was a proven way to make you feel in control and powerful, hence why it was called "The Superhero" pose.

The first time they had done it, Anna had felt ridiculous, but she had to admit that it worked. Now, anytime Anna was sulking or felt as if she had no say in a matter, Kim would do the pose with her for five minutes. She really was the best assistant.

"And time," Kim called, smiling. Anna couldn't help but smile back. The pose had worked its magic again. She felt much better.

Kim gave her a knowing wink and headed to her desk. Anna stretched her body. She needed to loosen up. Not ready to settle behind her desk again, she turned and scanned through her books. It was soothing.

Kim popped her head in the door. "The photographer is early. Her name is Sam Chambers. Are you ready to see her?"

"Yes, let's get it over with," Anna replied, not even turning around to answer. *Sam Chambers doesn't sound very French.*

A few moments later, she heard someone clear their throat. Anna spun round to greet her guest and nearly fell over when she saw who was standing in front of her. Her perfect stranger, the woman from the station, wide-eyed and staring back at her.

147

Anna felt as if all the air in the room had been sucked out. She stood frozen to the spot as she tried to process what was happening. *This isn't possible.*

It had only been a couple of seconds at most, but Anna was becoming acutely aware that she hadn't said a word. She just stared. It was her perfect stranger, or as she now knew, Sam Chambers, who shattered the awkward silence first.

"I know you!" she blurted.

Anna sucked in some much needed air before she passed out. "The station." It was the only words she could form.

"The station," Sam mirrored. "You were with that arsehole who pulled a hit and run on me."

Anna could feel her face becoming red. She had completely forgotten about the incident. All she could recall was Sam's beautiful face and that delicious dream. "Oh my god, I am so sorry for that. James, my boyfriend... sorry ex-boyfriend, was in a hideous mood that day. I am truly sorry you got the brunt of it, literally." Anna hoped that Sam could hear how horrid she felt about it.

"It wasn't your fault," Sam muttered, looking sheepish. Was Sam blushing?

It took a second to compose herself. She needed to get it together. She was a professional, after all. "Sorry, I haven't even introduced myself." Taking a step towards Sam, she held out her hand for a shake.

"Right, yeah, sorry, I didn't introduce myself either. I'm Sam Chambers."

"Anna Holland."

"That doesn't sound like a very French name."

Anna chuckled, "That's because it isn't. My parents are English, but I was born in France."

"Sorry, that was rude, wasn't it?

"Not at all. I always get asked. Shall we take a seat so we can begin?" Her usual confidence had returned. "You want to create a book, so I am led to believe?"

"I don't want to create a book, my employer does. Honestly, I didn't know about it until yesterday."

"Okay… your employer wants to create a book of your photographs. Is that correct?"

"Yes, I was commissioned a few weeks ago to capture the 'true' Paris for Rupert Downes. I'd never heard of him, but he's some big shot, apparently."

Anna had to smother a little laugh as she watched Sam's face fall in horror at being a little too candid about her boss.

Anna hoped she could save Sam from feeling embarrassed by pushing forward with the conversation. "I will need to see all the photographs that you want to put into the book. I think it's a good idea if I contact Mr Downes, to find out what exactly he wants. Is that okay with you?"

"Absolutely. I'm still in the process of picking them out. It's going to take me a while to edit them all."

"That's fine, I would like to see any photos that you have already though, it doesn't matter if they aren't edited, I just need to get a feel for your work so we can get a better idea of the style of book we want to create, and I want to make sure they are in line with what Mr Downes wants."

"Sure. I can do that. How do you want to view them? I don't feel comfortable sending them. I would prefer to either come here with the originals or for you to come to me."

God, I would love to come for you!

Anna mentally slapped herself. Her adolescent horny alter ego was back to pay a visit then. "Kim will give you my details. We can arrange something when you are ready."

"Sure, I'll call you." Sam stood to leave.

"Anytime," Anna called after her with a raised eyebrow. Anna was flirting, well, trying to at least. She hoped Sam had caught on to it. She saw a grin form on Sam's face before she left. "Bon sang," Anna muttered. She let out a steady breath, a nervous energy was dancing on her skin.

"What are you smiling about?" Kim pulled Anna's attention back to her office.

"Nothing… it was a good meeting, that's all. Nice and short."

Kim took a step into the room, closing the door behind her, gracefully sitting in the chair that Sam had used, resting her diary on her lap. She looked at Anna and waited. "Really, that's all you're going to say?"

"What do you mean?"

"You know I can see into your office, right?" Kim grinned.

"And?"

"So you know I saw your face when you turned around to greet Ms Chambers."

"There was nothing wrong with my face."

Kim scoffed. "Anna?"

No more hiding, Anna had promised herself. "Fine… I sort of already met her… well, not met her, but saw her at the train station in London."

"That doesn't explain why you went ghostly white and then blushed furiously. I don't react like that when I've seen someone before in a public space," Kim smirked.

Anna chewed her lip for a minute. Could she really tell Kim about the dream? Wouldn't she seem completely crazy? "Fine, but it's not going to make any sense."

"Try me."

"The night before I went to England with James, I had a dream. I had… I had a sex dream and Sam was the woman in it."

Kim looked confused. "So you have met her before then, I mean before the day in the station?"

"No, not at all."

"You must have. I read an article once that said our brains can't create faces in dreams if we have never seen them before. So at some point, you must have come across her."

Anna was the one looking confused now. She racked her brain thinking of any instance that she may have encountered Sam. "Are you sure that's accurate?" She couldn't for the life of her think where she had met Sam before, prior to the station.

"Google it."

150

Anna did just that, she googled and read. Kim was right. It wasn't possible for her to have created Sam in her dream. What did that mean? Surely it meant only one thing. Sam Chambers had been in Anna's life at some point, and Anna was determined to find out when.

* * *

Anna found no evidence that she knew Sam previously. She had spent most of her day searching through her personal stash of records that she kept for most of her past projects; she also scoured through her extensive list of contacts hoping someone would jog her memory. No luck. Sam Chambers was a mystery, a sexy, beautiful mystery.

Anna's mood soured over the course of the next few days. Work was piling up, but she couldn't seem to focus on it. She'd also got snappy with people, not something she was proud of. After years of bottling up her emotions, snapping had become her go-to method of venting her frustration.

After Anna had taken a verbal swipe at Kim for not bringing her a client file quick enough, she knew she had pushed it too far. Kim stood in her office, arms folded and anger searing across her face. "That's enough, Anna," she barked. "What is the matter? I know it's not me. Your mood is atrocious."

Anna momentarily thought about reprimanding her assistant until she checked herself. Kim was not the problem; it was Anna that had been the worst recently. She dropped her head in defeat. "I'm so sorry, Kim, you certainly didn't deserve the way I spoke to you," she sighed.

"No. I did not, and neither has anyone else in the office." Kim took a seat opposite her forlorn boss.

"I can't concentrate on anything. It's ridiculous. Every time I try to work, my brain focuses entirely on Sam Chambers."

Kim studied Anna's face for a few seconds. "It's been a couple of days since the meeting. Why don't you call her and set up an

151

appointment to look at some photos? Then maybe, oh, I don't know, talk to her, ask her if she remembers you."

"She's going to think I'm a raving lunatic if I tell her about the dream," Anna blurted.

"I didn't say you had to tell her about the bloody sex dream, doll. I said talk to her, get to know her. Maybe she will be able to fill in the blanks?" Anna didn't look convinced. "Can I ask why this is such a big deal? Why do you need to know?"

"I'm not sure. I just need to know. I find it incredible that I had this dream, then saw her at the station and now I'm working with her. What would you think if you were in my position?"

"Honestly… no idea. I must admit, the situation is intriguing."

"And entirely frustrating." Kim looked as if she was about to ask something, but obviously thought better of it. "What?"

Kim hesitated. "Well, is it at all possible that you are just super attracted to her, which is why you're being a tad obsessive over the details of where you know her from?"

"Well, of course, I'm attracted to her. I had a sex dream about her, for Christ's sake." Anna had blurted that a little louder than expected. Her face started burning as she noticed a few colleagues peer over in her direction. They had obviously heard her outburst.

Kim bit down on her lip, trying to suppress a laugh. "Anna, relax, no one cares. Call her, set up a meeting, and take it from there. Okay?"

Anna pinched the bridge of her nose before giving Kim a quick nod. "Can you get me her contact info?"

"Right away, boss," Kim winked before heading to her desk.

Kim was back in a flash with a sticky note containing Sam's number. Anna cleared her throat, pulled back her shoulders and rolled her neck; anyone would have thought she was preparing for a fight, not a simple phone call to arrange a meeting. It felt bigger than that, though. Anna was wildly attracted to this woman, and she desperately wanted to unravel the mystery of Sam Chambers.

152

The phone rang for several seconds before the recognisable blip of the call connecting. "Hello?" came Sam's delicious voice. Anna rolled her eyes internally at herself.

"Ms Chambers, it's Anna Holland from Tower Publishing."

"Oh, hi."

"Thank you for taking my call. I was hoping we could set up a meeting to look at some of your work?" Anna used her best — look how professional I am — voice.

"Sure, although as I said, I'm a long way from being done."

"No problem. A few pictures would really help me understand the direction I need to take."

"Great, okay… where do you want me, my place or yours?" Anna audibly took in a sharp breath; her mind had steamrolled into a vision of Sam in her bedroom. "Sorry, that sounded… nevermind. Anyway, what I meant was your office or mine?" Anna could feel Sam blush over the phone. Maybe it matched her own.

"I can come to you. Would this evening work? What is the latest time to arrive? I don't want to keep you at work longer than necessary."

"Tonight's great. Honestly, anytime that suits you, I'm here late every evening at the minute. If you send me a message when you arrive, I'll meet you out front."

"Wonderful, let's say seven o'clock, then?"

"Great, see you later."

"Bye," Anna said softly, as if she were talking to a lover. She pressed the end button before banging the phone against her head. Why in god's name did she say "Bye" like that? All soft and breathy. Sam was going to think she was unhinged at this rate.

* * *

Anna set off towards the metro, her route planned. It would take her a good half hour to get to the address listed on her phone. The time would give Anna a chance to calm herself down.

153

After the relatively quick chat with Sam and her embarrassing "Bye" when they had finished, Anna knew she had to get into the right frame of mind to work on the book.

Regardless of the mystery that was Sam — or Anna's attraction to her — she had to do her job. Somehow, Anna needed to separate the book from the mystery.

Tonight's meeting was about the book, all business. Anna decided that she would "feel out" the situation before she made a move to get to know Sam on a personal level.

All the time these thoughts were ruminating, Anna had chuckled at the absurdity of it all. It had only been a few weeks ago that she had been in a relationship with James, travelled to England, broken it off with James, moved herself to a posh apartment and then come out to her entire family. Anna clearly didn't do things by half.

A quick glance at her phone signalled it was already seven. She was going to be late. Anna picked up her pace. She was only a few hundred metres away, but she detested being tardy.

In the distance, she could see Sam leant up against the railings just outside the building. Sam had a smile stretched across her face. It seemed to go from ear to ear. Anna couldn't help but mirror it.

"Glad you made it." Sam wore a lazy grin. Merde, this was going to be a difficult meeting. All Anna could think about was grabbing Sam by her white button-down shirt and kissing her into oblivion.

"I'm very sorry I'm late."

"You're bang on time."

"I usually like to get to meetings a little earlier," Anna explained.

"Oh, well, no need to do that on my account," Sam grinned again.

Did Sam have any idea what that grin was doing to her? Anna could stand there all evening looking at this woman. She was charming without realising it and just downright gorgeous.

154

Hoping that Sam hadn't caught on that she'd been staring for one too many seconds, Anna gestured to the building they were in front of. "Shall we?"

"Yeah... let's do it." Sam pushed herself off the rail and headed to the main entrance.

Anna followed Sam inside, which turned out to be a very impressive space. Everything seemed new and top of the line. They climbed some stairs and headed to the end of the corridor. Sam pushed on a large wooden door to reveal the most sophisticated editing suite Anna had ever seen.

"Impressive, right?" Sam shoved her hands in her pockets and slowly circled the room, allowing Anna time to take it in.

"Very!" Anna nodded.

"I was pretty blown away the first time I saw it, too. The suites at Bright Lights, that's the company I work for in England, are good, but not at this level."

Anna watched Sam tuck herself behind a desk furthest away from the door. It had long windows behind it and Anna could envision Sam editing away before swivelling round to take in the city. "Excellent view," Anna commented, looking out onto the street.

"Exactly why I grabbed this desk," Sam chuckled. "So, I have a few shots for you, but keep in mind they are the raw file, so no editing." Anna nodded and gestured to the chair next to Sam. "Get comfy." Sam clicked away on the computer, loading up her pictures. Anna slid into the chair, trying to roll it subtly away from Sam. She didn't need to be sitting on her knee. It was already hard enough to concentrate.

Sam pulled up the photos and leaned back. They were beautiful. Sam had captured something so raw, so unapologetically truthful. "These are wonderful," Anna whispered as she continued to be transfixed by the images.

"Oh... uh... thanks," Sam mumbled.

"I can already see the book in my mind. I know exactly how to proceed. Your photos are exactly what Mr Downes was looking for. We had a brief phone conversation after our

155

meeting. He wants a book that isn't just the usual book for tourists." Anna was confident Sam's work would speak for itself. She wouldn't need to fluff it out or use the design to strengthen it. The photographs were going to be more than enough.

Anna sat back; she looked at Sam and saw that she had blushed. "You are very talented." Sam's blush deepened.

"Thanks," Sam replied with a weak smile. Anna could see that Sam wasn't used to her work being complimented — or, more likely, Sam felt uncomfortable receiving compliments in general — which seemed utterly absurd.

Not wanting to make Sam feel uncomfortable, she changed the subject. "How did you end up working here?" Okay, not strictly within her guidelines of a business-only meeting, but she genuinely wanted to learn more.

Anna watched as Sam straightened herself. It was as if a wave of confidence had suddenly rolled over her. She swivelled slightly so she was fully facing Anna. Her eyes had a twinkle in them that almost took Anna's breath away. "How about I take you out for a drink, and I'll answer all of your questions?"

Anna's heartbeat picked up, she could feel it in her ears. Sam was flirting, no doubt about it. Business meeting or not, Anna's body had decided for her. She rolled back her chair and stood up. "Let's go!" She turned on her heel and headed to the door. She hoped Sam would see it as a sexy power move, but in reality, Anna just needed to hide her Cheshire Cat smile.

Anna was going for a drink with her perfect stranger.

Chapter Thirteen

Well, this was an interesting turn of events; Sam never would have thought she'd have the ovaries to invite Anna for a drink. Not after their first meeting. Sam thought she'd handled the meeting pretty well, considering the shock of seeing Anna standing in front of her.

She wasn't entirely sure why it had affected her so much. Sure, she'd noticed Anna at St Pancras, but it had only been a passing glance and nothing more. She had noticed in those few seconds that Anna was a beautiful woman, of course, but that didn't explain why she felt so shocked to be seeing her again.

There was the instance when she thought she had also seen Anna looking through her window when Charlie had visited, but Sam had quickly written that off because she hadn't got a clear look at the figure across the street at all. She'd put it down to wishful thinking.

After the meeting, Sam had left Tower Publishing with a racing heart. Having the chance to spend more time with Anna was exciting. Sam could feel a pull toward the beautiful woman; she wanted to learn more, especially since she had discovered rather quickly that the asshat she had been with at the station was now her ex.

It had been a while since Sam had tapped into her gaydar. Back in the good old days of her youth, she was known for having an incredibly accurate gaydar. So much so, her uni mates often put wagers on Sam guessing correctly. Sam wasn't happy that they made a game out of people's identities; she didn't feel comfortable sticking labels on anyone.

Sam had thought about Anna's possible sexual orientation as she'd travelled back to work. There had been definite vibes between them, although it'd been a while since Sam had any serious game, so she could be way off base. Her gut feeling said that Anna was interested.

Normally, Sam's immediate response after a chance meeting like that would be to call Charlie and ask her what to do. This time, though, she felt like it was her chance to take the reins back for herself and be an adult, figure it out by herself, especially now she was feeling some of her old self again. She would wait until she'd met with Anna again before spilling all the details to Charlie.

Sam checked her phone several times after leaving the meeting, hoping that Anna would call to set up another meeting. She had to be patient, though. She couldn't get ahead of herself. She had a job to do, and that had to take priority. She couldn't afford to let another woman sidetrack her. Sam swore she would never lose herself to another person ever again.

The next few days were spent with her nose to the grindstone. Making some real headway by the time she'd received the call from Anna, asking if they could meet.

After they'd disconnected, Sam had felt a flutter in her stomach, the telltale signs of her romantic feelings pushing through her resolve to focus solely on her work. She'd clock-watched the entire afternoon, counting down the minutes until she could meet her special guest.

Anna had been bang on time, even though she thought she was rude for not arriving early. Sam found that amusing and made a little mental note; Anna was a time-sensitive person. It was good to remember the little details when getting to know someone, especially if you wanted to see more of them. It became clear to Sam after a few minutes of talking to Anna that she *definitely* wanted to spend more time with her and that's why she'd asked Anna for a drink.

Sam watched as Anna strode towards the door after accepting her invitation. She couldn't help it. The pencil skirt Anna was wearing hugged her deliciously, and her legs were indescribably sexy, long and toned. Sam checked to make sure she wasn't dribbling before snapping herself out of her fantasy-filled head and pursuing Anna out the door.

"Anywhere, in particular, you want to go?"

"Honestly, no. I don't know the area. I only see the offices most days."

"Well, let's just walk and see what we find. This is Paris, after all. There is a café or restaurant every twenty metres." Anna smiled sweetly and all Sam could do was stare at those perfect lips.

"Great idea," Sam grinned once she'd managed to tear her eyes away from Anna's face.

Anna strolled down the street with Sam trailing half a step behind. They remained silent for a little while. Sam didn't feel as if it was awkward. She understood they were both just getting their footing. Anna eventually broke the silence. "How are you finding Paris?"

"So far, so good. Thankfully, Seb, a guy I work with, took me under his wing early on. He is an *incredible* tour guide. He's the reason I could crack on with the project so quickly. I've done a bit of sightseeing for myself last week when my friend visited, but apart from that, it's been a routine of travelling from my apartment to work and vice versa."

"How long have you been here?"

"A couple of weeks. In fact, the day we saw each other in the station was the day I was coming here to start work." Sam eyed Anna as she spoke. "Where were you going, if you don't mind me asking?"

"Oh, I was there to attend James' sister's wedding."

"Was it nice?" Sam was trying to keep the conversation flowing, hoping she could get Anna to spill some details about herself without thinking she was trying too hard.

"I hope it was. I never got as far as the ceremony. James and I broke up just before."

"Oh shit, I'm sorry. I shouldn't have asked."

"I didn't have to answer, so it's not your fault. I didn't think you were being nosy."

"Okay… good. And I am sorry about your breakup. That can't have been fun."

"No, but it was necessary. It should have happened a while ago," Anna sighed.

A few more moments of silence passed between them again. Sam hoped she hadn't made Anna feel sad. She didn't want that to be the tone of the evening. Sam pointed across the road. "There's a bar over there." It wasn't big, but it seemed to attract plenty of people.

"Excellent, I knew we wouldn't struggle to find somewhere," Anna smiled.

They crossed the street and sat at one of the vacant tables outside. Sam picked up the menu, pretending to be in deep thought about her choice of drink. She needed a second to steady herself. The fluttering feeling had returned with a vengeance. Anna sat close to her and Sam could practically breathe her in. Almonds and cherries. *Interesting*.

The waiter zipped over, ready to take their order. Anna took a Mojito from the cocktail list. Sam usually drank lager, but tonight she wanted to try something a little different. Her go-to drink in uni had been rum and coke. It had been years since she'd drank it, so she ordered a double Captain Morgan spiced variety with Diet Coke.

160

"Do you have cocktails often?" It was a good talking point. Maybe Sam could find out a few likes and dislikes.

"Actually no, normally I stick with wine, but I fancied a change."

"Me, too. I'm usually a beer drinker, but I used to love a good rum and coke."

"If you loved it, then why did you stop drinking it?"

She was forward, straight to the point. Sam liked that in woman. "Not sure, really," Sam lied.

She had stopped drinking it because Jo had complained every time she'd ordered it. Jo had said she was ordering something complicated, and it always took longer for them to receive their drinks. It was a crock of shit, but, after a while, Sam had started ordering a bottle of lager just to keep the peace.

"Well, I'm happy you are having a drink you enjoy now." Anna smiled again. Sam could get used to seeing that smile.

The waiter delivered their drinks after a couple of minutes. "Will you ladies be eating tonight?"

Sam and Anna shared a look, both of them unsure what the other was thinking. Sam hadn't planned to ask Anna for a drink, let alone a meal, but the chance was being presented to her on a silver platter. "I haven't eaten yet, have you?"

"No, I haven't."

"Want to have dinner with me then?"

"I'd love to," Anna beamed.

Sam watched Anna as she conversed in rapid French with the waiter. She presumed she'd confirmed that they were staying for food. After a few seconds, Anna drew her attention back to Sam. "We need to follow him inside to a table." Sam nodded and followed close behind Anna into the restaurant.

Inside, there were a few small tables. They were all softly lit by dainty candles. It reminded Sam of the restaurant she'd been to with Helene — meaning that it looked super romantic. Sam swallowed hard. If Anna was having the same thoughts as Sam, she wasn't showing it. Maybe Sam was just being oversensitive. Maybe all French restaurants were like this?

161

They were seated at the back of the restaurant. "This is nice." *Jeez, Sam, you're really killing it with your conversational skills, aren't you?*

"It's quite romantic." Anna was looking around the room. Sam felt a slight panic. She didn't want Anna to think she had an agenda for the evening.

"We can go somewhere else if you like?" Anna's eye shot to hers with what can only be described as glaring disappointment.

"Do you want to go?"

"No! I just didn't want you to feel uncomfortable."

"Why would I be uncomfortable?"

"Well… you thought it was too romantic."

"I didn't say *too* romantic, I just said romantic." Anna blushed.

"Oh… right, so you're okay with it being romantic then?" Sam queried. She internally gut-punched herself for sounding like a lovesick teenager.

"I don't mind at all." Anna dropped her eyes to the menu on the table. Sam felt the smile on her face grow wide.

Sam looked directly at Anna. "That makes two of us, then." Anna lifted her gaze back to Sam, her eyes darker. That was all the confirmation Sam needed. There was no way on earth that Anna didn't know what was happening between them. They each took several sips of their drinks, all the time keeping eye contact.

They were interrupted by the waiter, who asked if they were ready to order. They weren't. They'd been too busy sussing each other out. Neither of them had paid attention to the food on offer. Anna spoke rapidly to the waiter again. He smiled and left. "I asked him to give us a few minutes."

"Great." Sam perused the menu — which had been translated to English on the back, thank Christ.

"Any idea what you are going to have?" The burger options looked pretty good. Sam wondered what Anna would go for. Was she a salad kind of woman? It was more than possible with her figure.

"I'm having the Burger Royale," Anna added before Sam could answer. Not a salad girl then.

"I'm going to have the Chicken Supreme."

"I hesitated between that and the Royale," Anna commented as she continued to look at all the different options.

"I'll tell you what. You get the Royale, I'll get the Supreme and we can share."

"Sharing food, that's interesting."

"Interesting how?"

"Few people like to share food in my experience."

"Well, I think it depends on the person you're sharing with."

Their eyes were locked on each other again. Sam saw Anna drop her gaze briefly to Sam's lips before speaking. "Indeed," Anna whispered. Christ on a bike, Sam was in trouble.

They ordered their burgers and made easy small talk. Anna politely excused herself to the bathroom, giving Sam a little time to check-in with herself.

The evening was shaping up to being a very similar situation to the one she found herself in with Helene on her first evening in Paris. Sam already knew that she didn't want this night to be like that. She didn't want it to be a one-night stand where they barely knew each other.

Sam didn't regret her short fling with Helene. Their night together had given her a confidence boost, taking her out of her comfort zone, which she had hidden in for far too long. It was different with Anna, though. Sam felt drawn to her, but not just physically. It felt like there was something much stronger pulling her towards Anna, something she couldn't explain.

That thought gave Sam pause. It had only been a few days since she'd promised herself that she wouldn't get lost in another person. She hadn't completely found her way back from the last time.

Being around Anna didn't feel like it did when she was with Jo, but in reality, Sam had known Anna only for a few days. She had spent a handful of hours in her company. Sam couldn't be one hundred percent sure that Anna was safe for her, not yet.

So, Sam had no choice but to slow things down. It was better for everyone if they took their time. She had to stop getting ahead of herself. There had been some minor flirting, but Sam couldn't let it escalate, not just yet. Hopefully, Anna would want to have a few more dinners or drinks with her. They could do the old fashion thing of actually dating.

Sam needed to find out where Anna stood in all this. It was all well and good Sam coming up with a list of dos and don'ts, but she couldn't make that decision for Anna, too. Sam thought of how she was going to handle the situation. Sam had always prided herself on open honesty with people. That's how Sandy had raised her.

Sam watched Anna return to the table. *My god, she's stunning.* She quickly drew her lips to her glass to stop her mouth from falling to the floor. It was time to take the bull by the horns. "So, how bizarre is it we saw each other in St Pancras?" Sam chuckled. She was going for light-hearted.

"Very. It certainly took me by surprise when you walked into my office." Anna nibbled her lip as if she wanted to say something more.

"Something on your mind?"

"Well… it's a little more strange for me than you think," Anna began, "I think if I say what is actually on my mind, you will think I'm slightly bizarre."

"Oh well, now you have to tell me," Sam chuckled, again trying to keep it light.

"I'm not sure I'm ready to tell you. Maybe the next time."

"You want there to be a next time?"

"Of course… I mean, we have to have several more meetings for the book."

Okay, this was the part where Sam needed some clarification because she hadn't been hallucinating. Anna had been flirting, but if that was all it was and she wanted to keep it strictly about the book, Sam needed to know.

"Can I ask you something? It might make you uncomfortable if I've read the situation wrong."

"Of course."

"Is this strictly business for you?"

"What do you mean?"

"I can only speak for myself, but this evening has felt more like a date than a meeting." Sam paused, trying to read Anna's body language. The good thing was that she hadn't stood up and slung her drink in Sam's face, so that was a bonus. Sam ploughed through. "I personally would like it to be a date. I'm attracted to you and would like to get to know you better outside of a business capacity."

Anna shifted in her seat slightly. "That's quite forward of you."

"I hope you're not upset. I prefer to be honest about things. I don't like miscommunications," Sam replied earnestly.

"Yes, I would like this to be a date, too. However, in the name of honesty, you should know that I only came out a couple of weeks ago. This is very new to me." Anna gave her a small smile.

Sam leaned over and rested her hand on Anna's, which was sitting on the table. "Congratulations. There's no pressure. I thought we could talk some more and get to know each other, that's all."

Anna released a breath that she had been clearly holding in since she'd made her confession. "That sounds perfect," she beamed.

"Maybe I can get you to tell me what you were going to say earlier?" Sam retracted her hand. No need to make it awkward.

"Oh, no, that's going to have to be for another time," Anna winked.

"Okay, I can wait."

* * *

The food had been delicious, and the company had been even better. Once they had finished their meal, they took themselves back to the little table outside to have their espresso. The night was clear, and the stars were peeking through.

165

They'd spent several hours chatting about everything — well, almost everything. Sam had kept the whole Jo situation under wraps for now. Delving into past partners wasn't a first date topic. She'd done a decent job of deflecting questions about her previous relationship, giving only the bare minimum amount of information.

They'd chatted about their jobs and their families. Sam told Anna all about Charlie and her surprise promotion from John. Anna already knew John and explained the relationship between their two companies. It came as a shock that there was another thing that linked them together.

They had flirted, but mildly. Sam didn't want to come across as a smooth talker, she didn't want Anna to get the wrong impression of her. It still to this day made Sam uncomfortable to be referred to as a "Ladies' woman" or "Heartbreaker" or "Smooth talker" or "Casanova." It made her feel gross.

Once they finished their coffee, Sam proposed they walk a little. Paris was beautiful at night. They walked side by side, bumping shoulders now and then. Sam enjoyed the brief contact and the warmth that Anna radiated. As time wore on, Sam realised Anna had a slight shiver running over her body. "You're cold." It wasn't a question.

"A little."

"I'll call my driver." Sam pulled out her phone and sent a message to Henry.

"A driver, wow, that's impressive," Anna smirked.

Sam grinned back. "That's Rupert chucking his money away."

"I can't complain." Anna bumped Sam's shoulder again.

"He will be here in a few minutes."

"Wonderful. It's nice not to have to use the metro at this time of night." Anna toed the floor. Sam thought she seemed suddenly shy.

It was coming to the end of their first date. Usually, Sam would swoop in for a kiss, but not tonight. She wanted Anna to be fully in control of their physical closeness. However, she didn't want Anna to have any misconception that she hadn't enjoyed herself.

That being said, Sam leant in and gave her a light kiss on the cheek. "I've had a really lovely night, Anna."

Anna leaned in, turning her head slightly. "Me, too."

Sam would have given her left kidney to plant one on those delicious lips right then, but she resisted, instead she smiled and retreated to a safe distance. Before they could say any more, their car pulled up. "It is an efficient service," Anna chuckled.

"The best," Sam laughed. She opened the door and waited for Anna to climb in the back.

Although Sam was reining it in tonight, she wasn't a nun, so she didn't feel too bad about following Anna's backside with her eyes as she got into the car. Sam rolled her eyes at the sky. "Universe, give me strength."

Chapter Fourteen

Anna settled back in the car seat. It was a far cry from her usual mode of transport. Thank god for Sam and her very rich boss.

After securing her seat belt, she reeled off her apartment address. For some strange reason, the driver asked if she was sure that was the correct address. Sam was also giving her an indecipherable look.

Anna flicked her gaze from Sam to the driver a few times. "Is everything okay?"

After a beat, Sam looked at her driver and told him to drive to the address Anna had given him. "How long have you lived there?"

"I rented it when I returned from England. After James and I went our separate ways, I thought it better to have a break. I've extended my stay for a while because it's wonderful. A big step up from the little apartment I shared with James." She couldn't shake the feeling something had changed between her and Sam since getting in the car.

Sam nodded and then turned to look out of her window. She was deep in thought. The silence made Anna uncomfortable. She just hoped that Sam would tell her if she had done something wrong.

Following Sam's lead, Anna turned to gaze at the scenery whipping past. It wasn't too late in the evening, so there were still plenty of people sitting outside cafes and restaurants chatting with friends and loved ones.

Anna wished she could turn back time to when she had been sitting with Sam laughing and chatting, getting to know each other. They were getting on so well, Anna had especially enjoyed the mild flirting and meaningful looks. That seemed to be a distant memory now as they sat in awkward silence.

The car pulled up to the curb opposite her building. Anna turned to Sam, ready to say goodnight, but Sam had thanked her driver and was exiting the car. What the hell was going on? Surely Sam didn't think she was being invited up to her place, not after one date and not after Sam had assured her they would take it slow.

Puzzled, Anna climbed out of the car and shut the door. She stared at Sam, hoping to get an explanation as to what was happening. Sam shoved her hands in her pockets and studied her feet. "Tonight was fun."

"Yes, it was... but... I'm sorry if you misunderstood something. It's just I'm not ready to invite you in." Anna hoped Sam wouldn't feel rejected.

"I wasn't expecting an invitation. I'm going back to my place."

"Right... okay then... I'll call you soon." Anna began walking backwards toward her building, her eyes still firmly on Sam.

"Yeah, I look forward to it." Sam turned round to the building behind her. Anna stopped in the middle of the road. *What the hell is she doing?*

"Night," Sam called before yanking the door open and disappearing inside.

Anna stood rooted to the spot for several seconds. *What is happening right now?*

Finally regaining control of her body, she forced herself into her apartment building. Her mind was going a thousand miles

169

a second. Just as she cracked open her door, she felt her phone buzz.

Sam: So we're neighbours as well ;)

Anna regarded the text, her brow pinched tight as she finally understood Sam's odd behaviour. Was it possible? Were they really neighbours? She closed the door softly behind her, still staring at her phone. She didn't really know how to respond.

Sam seemed to be everywhere in her life. She was in her past and present. The big question was; would Sam be a part of her future too?

Anna's fingers hovered over the keyboard of her phone. She wanted to say something meaningful or even flirty, but words were failing her. A second buzz showed Sam had messaged again.

Sam: Go to your window.

Anna dropped her coat to the floor, along with her bag. Her pulse spiked. She was nervous all over again, and this time she knew why. If Sam lived in the apartment Anna thought she did, she knew she had already seen more of Sam than Sam realised.

The thought made her feel uneasy. It had been okay when she had caught an eyeful of the naked torso across the street when the naked torso was just an anonymous woman, but if it turned out to be Sam, well, that was a different matter.

Anna drew herself to her full height before rounding the corner and heading to her window. Long opaque voile curtains that hung down the full length of each windowpane obscured the view. Anna could only see a dim light of the apartment directly across from her, but in that moment, she knew who she would encounter when she opened the window and looked across the street.

She opened the window and stared at the person opposite her. Sam. They both stood silently for several seconds, simply

170

looking at each other. Sam deposited her mobile into her back pocket before shoving her hands into her front pockets. Anna recognised it as one of Sam's "tells" when she was nervous.

"Hi," Sam breathed.

"Hello again."

Sam shifted gently. "Neighbours, eh?"

Anna gave a little giggle. Sam was adorable when she was nervous. "It seems so."

The sight of Sam was doing things to Anna, decadent things. Her breathing became faster as she raked her eyes over Sam's gorgeous body. The air between them was charged. It wouldn't surprise Anna if she saw sparks flying between them. That's how electrified the moment felt. For whatever reason, she and Sam were being thrown together once again.

The last few weeks had been the biggest of Anna's existence. She had taken charge of her life, no longer satisfied with settling. All she'd wanted was to live as her authentic self. It had been a long journey to get to where she was — a journey that she thought she had done alone, but the realisation that Sam had been there in some way or another for each step made Anna pause.

Why was she holding back? Why was she taking things slowly with a woman that was beautiful, interesting and a constant presence in her life?

Goddamn it, she'd wanted Sam from the moment she'd seen her in that station. No, since she'd had that magnificent dream. If life was determined to throw Sam in her path, then why shouldn't she embrace it? Embrace Sam.

Her mind was made up. Sam would be hers tonight. Forget slow, forget everything. Anna knew in her heart that Sam was meant to be the one to show her the way. Anna fixed her gaze on Sam's eyes; she wanted to make sure she had her full attention. Slowly, she brought her hands to her shirt. She slipped the first button free, followed by the second. Anna saw Sam's eyes widen, her posture grow tall. She definitely had the Englishwoman's attention now.

Her fingers worked swiftly until she reached the last button. Anna could feel Sam's anticipation pulsing off her in waves. Gently, she pulled the shirt from her skirt and let it fall from her shoulders.

The cold air felt good on her skin. Anna was more than pleased that she had worn her matching white lace lingerie set. Her nipples grew hard under the fabric. She took a beat before she turned her back to Sam. Drawing her hands up her back; she unclasped her bra. Sam let out a gasp as her bra fell to the floor.

Anna turned her attention to the small zip at the back of her pencil skirt. Slowly, she lowered it. Before she got to the bottom, she turned her head and looked at Sam over her shoulder. Sam had stepped forward, right to the edge of her window. Anna could see her nostrils had flared, she could see that Sam was beyond aroused. Anna was ready.

"I'm going to bed. Are you joining me?" Her pencil skirt fell to the floor, revealing her matching white lace thong.

Anna hadn't even finished her sentence before she saw Sam make a beeline for the door. Smiling widely, she strolled over to her door and peered through the little spy hole. Sam must have sprinted the entire distance because Anna had only stood there for a few moments before the door down the corridor that led to the building's stairs was ripped open.

Taking a deep breath, Anna opened her door. It was a risk. A neighbour could walk out at any moment and see her in nothing but a lace thong. However, it was worth it when she saw Sam falter in her step. Anna's heart felt as if it would beat out of her chest. The pure desire coursing through her body stopped any doubt or anxiety from surfacing.

Sam barrelled towards her like a woman possessed. It made Anna feel proud that she could elicit such a reaction in another person. She had never felt so powerful, so sexy.

Anna braced herself for Sam's body to collide with hers. She instinctively took a step back as Sam stepped over the threshold. Sam's pupils were completely blown open. Only deep pools of black stared back at her.

Sam snaked her hand around Anna's neck before pulling her close and crushing their lips together. Anna closed her eyes. It was ecstasy. She heard the door slam shut. Presumably, Sam had kicked it with her foot because the rest of her was firmly pressed against Anna.

She felt herself being guided backwards. Her back hit the wall with a soft thud. Electricity shot through every nerve in her body. Sam was warm, commanding, and strong.

Anna grazed her tongue along the bottom of Sam's lip. She wasn't asking permission, she just needed to taste. Sam welcomed Anna deep into her mouth. Sam's hand gripped the back of Anna's head firmly, their bodies moving in unison.

Suddenly, she felt Sam retreat. She opened her eyes and saw Sam panting, searching for breath. She was analysing Anna's face. "Are you sure?" Her ragged breath proof of her want. Anna didn't reply, she couldn't form words, she didn't want to talk, to think, to pick apart this moment. This moment was for them, for action, for want and desire only.

Anna seized Sam's face with her palms, nodded her consent and drew in her lover. Sam needed no more convincing. She kissed her without hesitation. Anna moved them down the hall. They stopped and started as they made their way to the bedroom. Every second their lips were apart felt like a lifetime.

Anna wanted Sam all over her, caressing her very soul. She pushed Sam away slightly as her legs bumped the back of the bed. "You are wearing too much," she gasped. She wanted — needed — to see Sam's body, to see all of her.

Anna watched as Sam stripped off her clothes, letting each article fall to the floor without care. The sight almost took Anna's breath clean away. Sam was beautiful. Her skin was creamy white with freckles dotted all over her body. Anna saw her muscles tensing as Sam tried to keep control of herself.

Even though she had an idea what Sam would look like under her clothes — from her dream and the quick glance she'd had when Sam had dashed across her window showing her bare torso—the reality of Sam was incomparable to her fantasy; she was sex; she was power; she was all woman.

Anna hooked her thumbs under the sides of her thong and gently slid them down until they pooled on the floor. She took a graceful step to the side, leaving her underwear next to her. She heard Sam take a breath. She knew Sam couldn't wait to touch her. "Take me," Anna whispered.

Sam closed the gap between them. This time when their lips met, it wasn't chaotic, it was slower, more controlled. Anna understood Sam wanted to take her time showing her all the wonders of sleeping with a woman.

Anna let Sam guide her down onto her bed. She watched as Sam took one last long gaze over her body. She watched as Sam slowly lowered herself on top of her. The feeling of Sam's skin on hers was astounding, her body was practically humming with anticipation.

Sam was looking at her, looking deep within her as she brought her thigh to rest in between Anna's. "What do you want, Anna?" Sam's lips hovered a few centimetres from her own.

"I want everything," she breathed. No truer words had ever been said. Anna wanted everything Sam had to give. Her clit tightened as Sam rocked against her. Anna's hips danced to the same tune as they found their rhythm. Anna couldn't take her eyes off of Sam. She saw every feeling that mirrored her own play across Sam's face.

Their breathing was laboured. Anna felt herself slipping into oblivion. Sam dropped her head to Anna's shoulders, unable to focus as her own orgasm built. Anna grabbed Sam's hips and ground them down harder. She could feel Sam's wetness coat her thigh.

"Oh… Oh god, Anna," Sam panted into her shoulder, her teeth grazing Anna's skin.

Anna was ready to climax, she couldn't hold on much longer, "Sam… I–" Anna was lost. Waves of pleasure overtook her. Her body tightened, her vision blurred. All she could do was hold on tight to Sam as she rode out the orgasm that threatened to undo her completely.

Anna felt Sam shake, her body tensing. She felt the muscles of Sam's body go rigid. She heard Sam moan into her hair as she came, long and hard. Their bodies fell limp, Sam laying half on Anna, their breathing erratic.

As cliché as it was to say, Anna had experienced nothing like it in her life. She felt as if she was floating outside her own body. The only thing reminding her she was indeed still on Earth was the delicious weight of Sam draped over her.

Sam moved slightly. Anna shifted her head so she could look at her. It was difficult to decipher the look on Sam's face. Anna hoped she wasn't overthinking it or worse, regretting it because in Anna's eyes they had just shared something deep and emotional, far beyond sex.

She leaned in and claimed Sam's lips. They weren't finished; it was just the beginning for them both. Without hesitation, Anna took the lead, Sam relinquishing control without question.

Anna often thought of her first time with a woman. Would she be good enough? Would she even know where to begin? All those questions vanished in an instant because as she held Sam, as she kissed her and inhaled her, she couldn't think of anything more natural. She knew what she wanted to do and how she wanted to do it.

Anna pushed herself up and over so she was lying on top. She broke away from Sam's lips and travelled to her neck, kissing and tasting. Sam writhed beneath her, sounds of pleasure emanating from her mouth, her head pressed back into the bed. Anna slowly began her descent down Sam's body. She took Sam's nipple into her mouth, her hand caressed the other, pinching and rolling until it was rock hard. Sam moved her hips, rocking, searching for purchase.

As she flicked her tongue back and forth, she felt her own nipples tighten. Everything she was doing to Sam was mirrored in her own body. She spent a few more moments worshipping Sam's breasts until she couldn't stand waiting any longer. She

175

needed to taste Sam. She lowered herself further until her lips brushed the coarse hair at the V of Sam's thighs. Anna gently ushered her legs open wide so she could see all that Sam had to offer.

Anna took a second to take in Sam's exquisite form. Sam was laid bare, vulnerable and wanting. Anna dipped her head in between Sam's legs and kissed her gently on her clit. Sam jerked. She was sensitive to Anna's touch. Slowly and lightly, Anna ran her tongue over the length of Sam's wet folds. Anna could have come on the spot.

"Fuck!" Sam gasped.

Anna hummed in agreement. She swiped her tongue several more times before she took Sam completely into her mouth. Gently, she sucked on Sam's clit. Sam was rocking harder and harder. Anna knew she'd found the spot that Sam responded to the most. She continued to lick and suck. Orbiting Sam's clit with the tip of her tongue. Sam was becoming untethered as her hips writhed and lifted in pleasure.

"Please don't stop," Sam panted as she ran her fingers through Anna's hair "Oh... oh... oh, yes... yes, Anna... I'm coming."

Anna planted her hands on Sam's hips to keep her rooted down. Sam bucked and strained as another orgasm claimed her. Sam screamed, calling out Anna's name. Her body shook like before, her muscles tense. Anna watched in awe. This was all so unbelievably gorgeous. Sam was a goddess.

Anna looked up. Sam had her arm over her head, breathing rapidly. Her chest was red, a slight sheen of sweat covered her skin. Anna gave Sam's pussy a quick kiss before she crawled up the bed to lie next to her lover.

Sam uncovered her eyes and turned to Anna. "I... I don't have any words." A laugh of disbelief escaped her as she spoke.

"That was magnificent," Anna breathed. She felt as if she was coming down off the biggest high of her life.

"Are you okay?"

Anna shook her head in disbelief, her face conveying utter bliss. "I am more than okay," she answered, kissing Sam once again. Sam responded by pulling Anna close to her body. They lay silently in each other's arms, both processing what they had just experienced.

"Would you like a drink?"

"Water please."

Anna untangled herself from Sam. She missed her warmth immediately. Her legs felt unsteady beneath her. She used the walls to help guide her to her kitchen. Taking two glasses, she filled them with water. Her hands trembled. Leaning against the kitchen worktop, she chuckled to herself as she thought of everything that had transpired. She couldn't be happier if she tried. *Wow!!*

Anna took a deep breath in, allowing herself to check-in with her body. Her thighs shook slightly, her skin tingled and her clit felt wonderfully sated, although she could already feel herself aching to be touched again.

Pushing herself off the counter, she walked back to the bedroom. She stopped and leaned against the doorframe. Sam had crawled into the bed. She'd lifted one side of the quilt for Anna. Sam was propped up on her elbow, waiting. Anna strode over and placed Sam's water on the bedside table before rounding the bed and slipping under the covers. She propped herself up to mirror Sam.

"Can I stay?"

"I hoped you would."

Sam beamed at her before leaning in and kissing her delicately. The feeling of Sam's warm body pressed into hers was heavenly.

Anna had never been the type of person to cuddle, well, not until now. Sam nuzzled her nose into Anna's neck, her arm pulling her in close as they settled.

For now, Anna was perfectly happy to just be held. It was the perfect way to end their night. Although Anna was sure that they would come together again before the sun came up.

Chapter Fifteen

The soft glow of sunrise stirred Sam from her sleep. She shifted, feeling Anna's soft skin on her lips. They had fallen asleep holding each other in the early hours of the morning. Sam couldn't—and didn't want to—repress the smile that formed on her face as she recalled the events of the evening before.

Sam had been taken aback when Anna had given the driver her address. She couldn't quite believe what she was hearing. In fact, she thought maybe Anna was joking, being a little suggestive, but she realised that wasn't the case. Not when Sam hadn't mentioned where she lived and also because the look on Anna's face at the reaction of the driver and Sam had been confusion and concern.

Sam hadn't known what to say, and she realised that Anna may have taken her quiet demeanour as a bad thing. She'd been in a state of shock, pure and simple. How could it be that one woman was all around her all the time? The train station, work and now possibly her neighbour? Surely not.

As they had driven into the street where it seemed both of their apartments were located, Sam wondered how she should approach the situation. Should she tell Anna that they lived next to each other? No, Sam wanted to see Anna's face when she figured out what was happening.

Sam had chuckled internally to herself when she saw the look on Anna's face as they'd both exited the car. It was fun playing with her a little, which is why she'd said good night without providing Anna with an explanation and entered her building, leaving Anna looking even more bewildered.

Sam grinned like an idiot when she thought of the next part of her memory. Anna undressing at the window, undressing for her. They'd set boundaries earlier in the night, both of them happy to take it slow. Anna had clearly changed her mind and Sam couldn't have stopped herself even if she'd tried. Why *would* she try? They were adults and Sam already knew that Anna was the type of person who knew her own mind.

Sam had *literally* sprinted over to Anna's apartment. She had nearly tripped over her own feet when Anna had swung the door open wearing only a lace thong, waiting for Sam to take her. In Sam's head, Anna could have been wearing a bin bag and she would still have been the sexiest woman to walk the earth.

They'd made love. There was no doubt about it because saying that they'd had sex in no way did it justice. Sam remembered the feeling of Anna's body the first time she held her close after she had slammed the door and kissed her. Sam had felt a strange sensation wash over her. She remembered that Anna's body pulled into hers was a familiar sensation, as if she'd held her once before.

Sam took in a deep breath. She breathed in Anna, who still slept soundly next to her. She felt completely at peace. They'd made love several times, falling asleep and then finding each other again in the night.

Sam had worried about asking to stay over, she didn't want to overstay her welcome. Especially since it was Anna's first time with a woman and it probably felt a little overwhelming. Anna

179

may have needed some space, but Sam couldn't help herself. She needed to stay as close to Anna for as long as she was allowed.

So, now Sam lay still, holding Anna as she slept. Nothing could disturb them.

Bzzzzz Bzzzzz Bzzzzz

Sam lifted her head. Her phone sounded like a demented wasp buzzing around on the floor. Anna stirred. She rolled over to the other side of the bed in no rush to wake up. Sam smiled. She liked the fact that she was learning new things about Anna, one being that she obviously wasn't a morning person. Not if her grumbling at the noise being made was anything to go by.

Sam slipped out of the bed and frantically searched the bedroom floor. Her clothes were everywhere. Finally, after a few moments, she located the source of the incessant buzzing and switched it off.

Unfortunately, it wasn't the weekend, and Sam couldn't cry off sick. She had too much work to do, and she didn't want to take advantage of Helene's good nature. She had to go into the office.

Sam puffed out a breath of irritation. The only thing she wanted to do today was make love to Anna. She would be quite happy if they never left the bed ever again. She stood for a second, looking at Anna's body splayed out across the bed like a starfish. Sam chuckled again, *so Anna's a bed hog too.* Pulling on her rumpled clothes, she headed to the kitchen.

The layout of the apartment was nearly identical to her own. She found the coffee and set the machine whirring. The smell was intoxicating. Her body felt tired and sore, but in the best possible way.

After a quick scout through the cupboards, Sam found what she was looking for: a brioche loaf, fresh from the day before. She set about cutting it up and toasting it. That was her favourite way to eat it, especially with jam smothered on top. A little more searching wielded a jar of strawberry jam and some butter. Perfect.

180

Sam carried the plate of brioche and a cup of fresh coffee into the bedroom. She rounded the bed to where Anna was and set everything on the bedside table. Sam hated having to wake her when she looked so peaceful, but she thought it best in case Anna overslept.

She gently shifted a mass of brown curls from Anna's face, leaned down and placed a kiss on her temple. Anna didn't move. Sam smiled. She could do this all day if needed. Another kiss, then another until finally, she caught Anna smiling.

"Bonjour." Anna's voice was husky from sleep.

"Hello, sleeping beauty." Sam planted another kiss on her head.

"This is a wonderful way to be woken," Anna smiled, rolling over and shifting herself into a sitting position. The sheet she was wrapped in fell to her waist. Sam sucked in a breath. She wasn't sure how she was going to function properly, especially when all she wanted to do was reach out and take Anna's breasts in her mouth again. Work be damned.

Sam reached for a T-shirt that was at the bottom of the bed and passed it to Anna. "Please cover up, I have to go to work and If I look at those any longer, my boss is going to have to pry me out of here with a crowbar."

Anna giggled. "Are you sure you don't want a little longer with them?" Anna playfully lifted an eyebrow. "It seems my breasts are rather partial to you," she grinned.

Sam moaned loudly before turning her back to Anna. "Dear lord, give me strength."

Anna laughed out loud, "Okay, okay... I'm decent." Sam turned back to face her, visibly disappointed that Anna had indeed covered up. "You can't look at me with sad eyes now. You wanted this," Anna smirked.

Sam enjoyed the back-and-forth playfulness. She sat herself down on the edge of the bed and passed Anna the plate of brioche. "I didn't know how you like it. I hope this is okay?" She suddenly felt nervous. She wanted everything to be perfect.

181

Anna cupped her face and pulled her in for a kiss. It was supposed to be a thank you kiss, but quickly deepened. Sam could feel herself pushing Anna backwards to a reclining position. "I thought you had work," Anna whispered against her lips.

"Christ. You're dangerous to be close to." Leaning in, she nipped Anna's lip.

Anna smiled, her eyes sparkling, "You are just as dangerous for me."

Sam felt as if she was going to combust. "Eat your breakfast. I need to nip back to mine and shower. I'll call you later. That's if you want me to, of course."

"I would be upset if you didn't." Anna bit into the brioche. A glob of jam dripped on her lip. Sam watched as Anna slowly licked it away. Sam looked from her lips to her eyes. Anna had mischief written all over her face.

"No… nope, you're not getting me like that," Sam laughed, tearing herself from the bed.

"I don't know what you mean," Anna replied innocently.

"Oh yes, you do… being all seductive with your tongue."

"Sam, I simply rid myself of some jam," Anna teased.

Sam shook her head. "Uh uh… nope, not falling for it," Sam laughed. She needed to leave, but her body wasn't cooperating. She stood rooted in the middle of the room.

Anna placed the plate back on the nightstand. Shifted herself to her knees and removed her T-shirt. Sam thought her heart might stop. "Are you sure you haven't got five minutes to say a proper goodbye?"

Well, fuck my life. Sam pulled off her clothes and went to Anna. She was going to be a little late, after all.

* * *

Sam gave herself a pat on the back for arriving at work only ten minutes late. After she had given Anna a *proper* goodbye, *twice,*

182

she'd moved like a bat out of hell to shower, change and get to the office.

The editing suite was quiet, which Sam was grateful for. She needed to concentrate, although she wasn't entirely sure if that was going to be possible after the past twenty-four hours. Her mind strayed to Anna constantly.

At one point, she had to physically shake herself, as she tried desperately to shift her focus into work mode. Nothing worked. She was consumed with thoughts of Anna, thoughts of her body and everything she wanted to do to it. Christ, on rollerskates. She needed a cold shower now.

Sam felt her underwear grow damp, and her face flush. She hoped to God no one would come into the editing suite. She wasn't sure she could explain why she was looking so flustered.

It was as if the universe heard her plea and laughed in her face, because thirty seconds later, Seb walked in and plonked himself down in the chair next to Sam. He wasn't in there for social reasons because he quickly logged onto the computer and began editing.

A few moments later, he turned to Sam, "Are you okay? You are very red."

"Yeah... yeah, totally fine, just running a little late."

"Okay good, take a breath. You are a little sweaty."

Sam gave a weak smile. Of course, she was sweaty. She was thinking of Anna naked, writhing underneath her. Just for good measure, her clit chimed in on the action. Sam slammed her thighs together and clenched. She tried to conjure any image that would help calm her down. She could *not*, repeat *not*, get herself off in the middle of the friggin' office, especially not with Seb sitting next to her.

Finally, the universe cut her a break. Sam's phone rang. She snatched it off the desk and quickly excused herself from the room. "Charlie," she exclaimed, a little louder than needed.

"Sam!" Charlie belted back. "Why are you shouting my name?" She laughed. "You know I don't see you in that way, although it's been a while since anyone shouted my name so enthusiastically, so I'll take it."

"Gross," Sam chuckled. "What's up?"

"Nothing, just checking in. I'm allowed to do that, right?"

"Sorry, it's been a little while, hasn't it? I've been neck deep in editing."

"Glad to hear it. You feeling good about everything?"

Sam sighed. She had to talk to Charlie about Anna. She couldn't hold it in. "I met someone," she blurted.

"What do you mean... like you met someone, or you *met* someone?"

"I definitely *met* someone."

"Who?" Charlie screamed in excitement before checking herself, "Sorry... I mean, who have you met, Samantha?"

Sam snorted, "Nice save."

"I'm just so excited for you, mate."

"Her name is Anna. She works at the publishing company that will create Rupert's book."

"Well, fuck a duck...you don't mess around, do you?" Charlie laughed.

"It's not as simple as that, though."

"I'm intrigued," Charlie replied in a quizzical tone. "Tell me more."

"Do you remember me telling you about the woman that I saw in St Pancras?"

"Vaguely."

"Well, it was Anna."

"Anna?"

"Yes. The woman in the station turned out to be Anna. The person I saw in the window across from me, when I was buck naked, also turned out to be Anna. She's my neighbour." Sam waited for Charlie to realise how absurd it all sounded.

"Are you taking the piss?"

"No, I am not," Sam replied seriously. "I walked into the meeting at the publishing house only to be met by Anna. We stood there dumbstruck because we recognised each other from the station. We had a meeting and then a couple of days later we met here to look over a couple of photos; she needed to get a feel for the book. I asked her out.

"This was yesterday, by the way. Anyway, we had dinner, it was great. We both decided that we enjoyed each other's company and would like to get to know each other. Being the lady that I am, I gave her a ride back to her apartment. Lo-and-be-fucking-hold, she lives in the apartment building opposite me." Sam took a breath. She had reeled off all the information on one lung full of air.

"Char?"

"It's fucking fate!" Charlie whispered. "Oh my god, Sammy, this is awesome. I have to tell Sandy she's going to freak."

"Whoa, chill your beans, buddy, no one is telling my mother anything. I cannot handle an hour on the phone listening to her go on about fate and destiny. She will try to do a reading over the phone. You know she will."

"But Sam, this is insane... I mean, what are the odds of you guys meeting like this, having randomly seen each other from afar?"

"It's mental, I get that, but please don't tell Mum. Not until I know it's going somewhere."

"Right, yeah, of course. So, are you seeing her again? Do you want to jump her bones?" Charlie chuckled. Sam fell silent. The memory of Anna undressing filled her mind. "Oh. My. God!" Charlie bellowed. "You fucked her!"

"Stop shouting for Christ's sake. I did not *fuck* her."

"Oh sorry, mate, you went silent, and I just assumed."

"We made love."

It was Charlie's turn to fall quiet. Sam waited with bated breath. "Wow, that's big news, Sammy. You doing okay?"

Sam smiled. She knew Charlie would understand the magnitude of what she had just said. Sam hadn't made love to someone for a very long time. Charlie knew what it meant for Sam to give that part of herself to someone. "I'm doing great. She is wonderful, Charlie."

185

"Did you know it was going to happen?"

"Not at all. We had discussed the idea of taking it slow. Anna has only recently come out, and I didn't want her to feel any pressure. We chatted for hours. It was great. When we got back to our apartments, we said good night and left each other."

"So, how did you end up in bed after that?"

"I won't go into details, Char, that's for me to know. Let's just say Anna changed her mind about the whole taking it slow part and I was happy to go along for the ride."

"Jesus."

"I know. I ended up staying the night in her bed," Sam sighed in contentment.

"You sound good, Sam."

"I feel good. It's really early days and I have a lot of work still to do on myself, but I can't help but feel that Anna is important." Sam heard Charlie sniff. "Char, are you crying?"

"No!"

"Charlie?"

"Okay, maybe a little. It's just been so long since I heard you talk like this. You sound hopeful. I'm just happy for you."

Sam smiled "Thanks, Char."

Charlie cleared her throat. "Right, enough of my blubbering. When are you seeing her again, actually the more important question is, when will I meet her?"

"We've only had one date. Calm down."

"Don't you tell me to calm down, missy! I want to meet the woman who's swept my best mate off her feet."

"I didn't say she swept me off my feet."

"You didn't have to. I can read you like a book." Sam rolled her eyes. "Don't roll your eyes at me either," Charlie added.

Sam bolted upright. "How did you know I rolled my eyes?"

"As I said, I know you."

"Yeah, you do," Sam admitted. "I'll speak to her later, I hope." Sam more than hoped. She hated the idea of not speaking to Anna soon.

"Keep me posted. Now, how's work?"

186

They stayed on the line for a few more minutes whilst Sam filled her in on the project. They chatted about Charlie's work and how her new promotion was going. Before calling off, Sam promised to update Charlie on all things "Anna" related.

Sam looked at her watch and realised how much time she had been talking to Charlie. She was seriously behind. She had to knuckle down and get moving. The only thing keeping her in Paris and close to Anna was this project. The thought crashed down on her like a ton of bricks. What happened when the project was done and Sam was heading back to England?

Sam pushed the feeling deep down. This wasn't the time for worrying, they would take it one step at a time.

* * *

Sam felt like her eyeballs were melting. She couldn't look at her screen for a moment longer. She was happy, though. After she had given herself a talking to, she had pushed through the day without a break to catch up. In fact, she'd done a lot more than she realised.

A few clicks on the computer confirmed that she only had one folder left to sift through. She was more than happy with the photos she had chosen and was really excited to share them with Anna. Ah, Anna. Sam let her mind drift for a moment. Shit, she hadn't called or texted Anna all day. "Well done, dip shit," she blurted.

Sam had been so determined to work that she had forgotten about the world around her, including Anna. She felt awful. Hopefully Anna wouldn't feel like Sam had ghosted her. She ground her teeth in frustration. There was nothing for it. She'd have to grovel. There was no way she was letting someone as wonderful as Anna feel used or forgotten. Sam whipped out her phone.

Sam: *I'm so sorry I haven't spoken to you today.*

187

Sam sent the message and hoped Anna would reply quickly. Her heart soared as she saw the three little dots bouncing on her screen. Anna was replying.

Anna: I guessed you were busy. It's ok, I know you have a lot of work to do.
Sam: Is it really cheesy to tell you I missed you?
Anna: Did you?
Sam: I really did.
Anna: Then it's not cheesy ;)

Sam breathed a sigh of relief. She realised she had been holding her breath in anticipation.

Sam: Can I see you tonight?
Anna: I have a guest over for dinner. Tomorrow evening?

Sam's heart sank. She had to wait another twenty-four to see Anna.
Does she really have a guest or is she upset because I didn't call or message all day?

Sam: Yeah, no problem. Let me know if you're free :)
Anna: I just told you I'm free tomorrow?!

Sam swallowed hard. She was trying to come across as ambivalent. "Idiot, she's not Jo!" The words were out of her mouth before she knew it.

That's why Sam was feeling anxious about Anna's reply. It was an automatic response after being with someone like Jo for ten years. There was no way Jo would have reacted so well if Sam had forgotten to contact her all day. She would've been made to feel guilty, as if she was the worst partner in the world.

Sam took a breath. This was one area of her life that was going to be difficult to correct. Years of manipulation were hard to

188

unpick. She had to remember that Anna was *not* Jo. She was nothing like her.

> **Sam:** *Tomorrow would be great, 8pm good?*
> **Anna:** *I can't wait.*

Satisfied with how her day had begun and ended, Sam closed down her workstation. Maybe if she was lucky, she could sneak a peek at Anna from her apartment. They were neighbours after all.

Chapter Sixteen

There was nothing on the planet that was going to drag Anna away from her apartment. The most beautiful woman — who had given her several mind-blowing orgasms — had woken her up in the most beautiful way. She needed the day to process.

> *Anna: Bonjour, I am working from the apartment today. Could you come over when possible?*
> *Kim: Yes, of course, I will be with you at lunch. Do you need anything?*
> *Anna: No, I have my laptop.*
> *Kim: I'll grab us a sandwich and maybe a couple of chocolate eclairs ;)*
> *Anna: A Bientôt.*

When she'd finally let Sam go to work, after another two rounds of earth-shattering sex. No, not sex, something better. She'd finally dragged her tired body into the shower. She felt deliciously worn out. Her body was protesting with every movement, but Anna didn't care. She revelled in it. Her aching was a reminder of the night she'd just spent with Sam. It had been everything she had hoped for.

Anna waited anxiously for Kim to show up. She was almost bursting out of her skin to spill the beans to her friend. The morning had dragged by; trying to work had proven impossible, because the only goal she'd accomplished was tidying up her email inbox.

Not the most efficient way to pass the time, but her mind refused to entertain any thoughts at all unless they were about Sam, Sam's body, or Sam doing mouthwatering things to Anna. Several times, she had to physically shake her head to snap herself out of her fantasies.

Anna breathed a sigh of relief when the doorbell rang. She almost tripped over herself to answer it. Kim looked a little startled when the door flung open. Her eyes grew a little wider when Anna beamed at her wildly. "Thank god you're here!" She pulled Kim through the door.

"Has something happened?"

Anna laughed maniacally, "Oh, Kim, you have no idea," she grinned. "I will tell you everything, but first you need to know that from the moment you stepped in the door, you stopped being my assistant and I stopped being your boss. This is strictly friendship territory."

"Excellent, I love it. Skiving off work to have a natter sounds delightful. Can we drink?"

"I opened a bottle of red earlier. It's been breathing for long enough. Let's drink and talk."

"Eekkkee," Kim squealed, clapping her hands in excitement. She almost skipped to the kitchen to retrieve the wine. In no time at all, Kim had returned to the living room with two full glasses. She put them on the coffee table and jumped onto the sofa, tucking her legs under her bum. Anyone would have thought she was settling down to watch a movie.

Anna took in a deep breath and prepared herself. "I had a meeting with Sam yesterday evening."

Kim's excitement dulled a little. "Yes, I know. You told me yesterday. That's not new or exciting. I hope there is more to come?"

"There is." Anna nodded reassuringly. She was enjoying the build-up. Kim looked like she was ready to explode.

"Well?" Kim was getting impatient.

"We had dinner afterwards."

Kim had shifted forward in anticipation. "Aaannnnd?"

"I found out where she lives," Anna grinned. Kim's eyes grew wide with excitement, but she kept quiet, knowing Anna still had more to say, "Look out the window." Kim frowned. Clearly that wasn't where she thought the conversation was going, but she complied and looked out the window and across to the apartment building opposite.

Not entirely sure what she was looking for, she turned back to Anna, raising her eyebrows questioningly. "She lives there." Anna pointed at Sam's apartment, giggling as she watched Kim swivel her head from Anna over to Sam's and back again several times.

"She lives there? As in right there?" Kim pointed.

"Yes, right there."

Kim left the sofa and went to the window. Anna wondered if she was trying to spot Sam or any evidence of her through the window.

"She's at work," Anna chuckled.

Kim turned around with a raised eyebrow. "So, did you get to see inside?"

"No, I didn't."

"Well, that's a shame."

"She got to see inside mine, though," Anna smirked.

"Okay, before I get excited, is this story going to end the way I'm praying it ends?" Kim clasped her hands together excitedly.

Anna kept her face neutral. "What do you mean?"

"Anna," Kim squealed. "Did something happen between you, sexy-wise?"

Anna couldn't keep her composure any longer. She smiled from ear to ear as she nodded. "It most certainly did."

Kim exploded in cheers. "Tell me everything!"

Anna was laughing hard at her friend's reaction. It made the whole thing so much better. She loved having a friend to share

192

this monumental news with. Kim scrambled back to the sofa and took a healthy glug of her wine. Anna followed suit.

"How did it happen? How did she end up here? Did she ask to come up? Did she kiss you before coming up or when she was up here?"

"Kim, slow down," Anna laughed. "Stop asking questions and I'll tell you."

"Right, sorry, you go."

Anna adjusted herself in her seat. Kim waited like an excitable puppy. After another slug of wine, Anna launched into the story. She told Kim about their meal, the car ride back, the confusion of it all, and then the seduction.

"So, let me get this straight... so to speak. You stripped and bared all at that window whilst Sam watched?" Anna nodded. "Then she raced over here and you did the nasty all night?" More nodding. "And again this morning?"

"Twice," Anna clarified.

Kim was subconsciously nodding her head with Anna as her mind worked through all the information. Suddenly, she burst from the sofa and launched herself at Anna. "Oh my god!" she screamed, hugging Anna within an inch of her life. Anna laughed loudly. She returned the hug with as much force as she could.

Kim broke away. She took Anna by the shoulders and looked her in the eye; her face turning serious. "Are you okay? Did it go well?"

"Oh, Kim, it was... it was wonderful. We fit together completely, perfectly. Sam was everything I imagined she would be."

Kim was smiling again. "And did she... you know... visit the south of France?"

It took Anna a second to catch on to Kim's meaning. "Kim!" she barked playfully. "What kind of question is that?" she laughed.

"Well?"

"Yes, as a matter of fact, she did visit the region."

193

"And how was it?"

Anna puffed out a breath and fanned her face. "Oh Mon Dieu, Kim, she is talented."

"Put it there." Kim thrust her hand in the air triumphantly, holding it up, waiting for Anna to give her a high-five. Anna happily complied with a chuckle. She felt like a teenager experiencing her first crush.

"So you felt comfortable, through it all?"

"Completely. There was no expectation. We just went with the flow and I have to say, the moment we touched, all the anxieties I had about… you know… about what to do vanished. I may have visited the south of England a few times, too."

Kim grabbed her shoulders again. She was visibly shaking with happiness for her friend. "Oh, Anna, I'm so happy for you."

"I'm happy for me, too."

"So I take it you're seeing her again?"

"Considering she lives just there, yes, I'm sure I will."

Kim rolled her eyes. "You know what I meant."

"Yes I do, sorry, it's quite fun winding you up. I really want to see her again. I want to date her. She made me breakfast in bed, Kim."

* * *

Their boozy lunch quickly turned into a boozy afternoon. It was the first time in her working life that Anna had taken time off, without permission, to spend a personal afternoon with a friend. Kim didn't worry too much about the fact that she was skiving, considering she was doing it with "the boss".

Now and then Anna picked up her phone, hoping to see a message from Sam. It was becoming a bit of an obsession. A few times, she caught Kim's eye, making her blush. Anna had never been the type of person to become overbearing with a partner. Most of the time, it was her partner that vied for her attention and it had always been a source of irritation.

194

James had been the same in the beginning. Their relationship had started through friendship, but Anna remembered James was always the instigator. He had called Anna to arrange their first date and had been the one to follow up the next day.

James had been keen at the beginning, which made Anna feel bad now because she'd never shared his enthusiasm. She felt worse because she was getting a taste of her own medicine now. It had been less than twenty-four hours and she was champing at the bit to talk to Sam again, hoping to arrange another date or, even better, repeat the performance of the night before.

Talking to Kim was a temporary balm, but their conversation couldn't keep Sam from flooding Anna's mind, especially as she was well on her way to being drunk. They needed food to soak up some wine. The last thing Anna wanted was for Sam to call and she be inebriated.

Anna looked at the time and realised — disappointingly — that Sam was probably going to be home late. She knew how much work she still had to do.

It had been difficult waiting all day to hear from her, but Anna knew that she just had to be patient. She couldn't expect Sam to drop everything for her, not after just one — gorgeously sexy and steamy — night. They hadn't even decided what was going to happen between them. Anna already knew that she wanted more, but would Sam feel the same?

Her stomach knotted with worry. It was a natural reaction for her, but one that was desperately unwelcome. Just as she was feeling the panic rise in her chest, her phone chimed. It was Sam. Relief washed over her instantly. Anna berated herself internally for getting worked up.

"I take it by your face that Sam's finally messaged?" Kim slurred.

"Yes, she wanted to know if I would see her tonight."

"And will you?"

"I told her we are having dinner together and that I'm free tomorrow."

"Why on earth did you do that?"

195

"I panicked," Anna blurted. She had indeed panicked. She wanted nothing more than to see Sam. She'd been waiting all day just for a call or message, but for some reason that Anna couldn't fathom her first instinct when Sam asked if they could meet was to back away.

"Panicked? What's there to panic about? The woman had her head between your legs not too long ago. The time to be shy or panicked has well passed," Kim laughed.

"I know… It's silly. Before she messaged, I was getting myself into a bit of a state about what was happening between us. We hardly know each other and I'm sitting here pining. Maybe I should slow it down, really think about what it all means?" Anna was talking to herself more than Kim.

"Whoa… chill out, doll. Honestly, I think this is the wine talking. Let's have a coffee and some food and talk about it, okay?"

Anna nodded, "Good idea."

They ordered pizza and drank copious amounts of water and coffee. It angered Anna that she'd been in a state of bliss since yesterday, yet now she was feeling anxious, letting her old insecurities get in her way.

"You feeling better?" Kim mumbled through a mouth full of pizza.

"Much, but could you save any more questions until you have stopped chewing your food?"

Kim laughed. "Sorry, boss."

Anna took a few calming breaths. "I panicked because I like her. I like her a lot and I'm scared that she won't want the same."

"Have you asked her?"

"Well, no, we did a negligible amount of talking last night and this morning, as you know."

"Yes, yes, you were too busy being taken to heaven repeatedly to stop and have a chat," Kim chuckled. "You just have to talk to her. Maybe she doesn't want the same as you, but then again, maybe she does. From what you have told me, she seems to appreciate honesty."

196

"She is straightforward, she hates miscommunications, she told me that over dinner."

"Well then, that settles it. I'm going home. You're going to message her and get her to come over and then you are going to talk. You will have your answer either way. Don't let your insecurities ruin something before it's even started, love."

"When did you become so wise?" Anna grinned.

"I've always been wise. I'm amazing."

Kim had hit the nail on the head. Anna just had to communicate. Granted, she and Sam didn't know each other well, but they had spent hours over dinner talking about their work and families. Anna knew there was a lot more to learn, but Sam wasn't exactly a stranger. They had clicked. That's why Anna had felt confident enough to sleep with her.

This wasn't the time for Anna to back off, it was her chance to seize something good. Her gut was telling her that Sam *was* that something and now she had to bite the bullet and talk to her.

Anna grabbed her phone and typed. She felt Kim gently touch her arm. "I don't think you need that," Kim grinned, looking over Anna's shoulder. She turned, following Kim's gaze. Sam was home, standing by her window with a shy smile on her face. "Go get her, tiger," Kim whispered before giving her a kiss on the cheek. Anna went to her window and gave Sam a little wave. "Hi."

"Do you want to come over?"

"You have company."

Anna looked towards where Kim had been sitting moments ago. She'd only just realised that Kim had bolted out the door, leaving her free to talk to Sam.

"Kim has gone home. I'm all alone."

Sam smiled widely before turning and heading out of her apartment. Anna took a deep breath; it was going to take all her willpower not to pounce on Sam the minute she was in reach.

"Just talk to her," Anna muttered, gearing herself up for whatever Sam had to say.

She heard a light tapping on the door. Sam must have sprinted again, which caused Anna to chuckle. It felt good to know that Sam seemed just as eager as she was.

"Hi, come in." Anna stepped aside to let Sam pass. She was almost wishing that Sam would take her like she had done last night, but it wasn't to be. Sam passed by and headed to the living room, her hands in her back pockets. *So, she's nervous too.*

"How was your day?" Sam hovered next to the sofa.

"It was good. I worked from the apartment." Anna left out the part where she couldn't work because all she'd done was fantasise about Sam. She also omitted the fact that she had spent the afternoon gossiping like a schoolgirl to her friend about their night of lovemaking.

Sam was looking everywhere but at Anna, her face flushed. "How was your day?" Anna hoped that Sam wasn't about to freak out or tell her that last night had been a mistake.

"Honestly… I had to give myself a verbal smackdown to get anything done. All I could think about was you."

Anna felt a gasp escape her lips. "Really?"

Sam nodded. "Really."

In an instant, Sam was upon Anna, thrusting her hands into her hair, pulling her into a scorching kiss. Anna thought her legs were going to give way. Talking could wait.

Wrapping her arms around Sam's neck, she clung to her. She wanted to be as close as humanly possible to this woman.

Sam let her arms travel down Anna's back, grabbing her arse. In one fluid motion, Sam scooped Anna's legs up, wrapping them around her waist. They kissed deeply as Sam carried her over to the table by the window.

Anna was gently lowered down. She was aching for Sam. Her clit throbbed, as she waited to be touched. She felt Sam slide her hands from her bum to the front of her jeans, quickly releasing the button and lowering the zip. They hadn't said a word, they were completely lost in each other.

Their lips had parted only briefly to suck in some well-needed air. Anna braced her legs around Sam's waist and let her hands

198

drop to the table so she could lift herself, which let Sam slide her jeans and underwear off. Anna couldn't wait any longer. "I need your fingers… now," Anna panted.

She felt Sam's hand tracing along her inner thigh. She was being teased. Sam ripped her mouth away from Anna's lips and hungrily kissed her neck as she brought her hand to Anna's centre. Anna felt herself being filled with Sam's fingers. She threw her head back, allowing herself to feel everything, every sensation, every thrust of Sam's hand. Anna moved her hips in time with Sam's fingers. She wouldn't be able to hold on much longer. "I'm going to come," she gasped.

"Come for me, baby," Sam whispered in her ear.

Anna felt herself tighten. Her orgasm began ripping through her body. "Oh god… oh god, Sam," she moaned.

"That's it, let go."

"Sam… Oh god, oh god, yes. Yeeesssss," Anna screamed before her body went limp, falling forward into Sam.

They stayed clamped together as Anna came down. It took several minutes for her breathing to stabilise. "Are you okay?" Anna nodded her head, which rested on Sam's shoulder. She couldn't form words. "Are you sure?"

Anna finally pulled herself up and looked into Sam's eyes. There were no words, nothing could describe what she had just felt. Words simply weren't enough. Anna continued to look into Sam's eyes, hoping she could convey everything in one look.

Slowly, Anna pushed herself off the table so she was standing in front of Sam, who said nothing. Anna effortlessly turned them, so Sam was pressed up against the edge of the table. Swiftly, she unfastened Sam's trousers and slid them down her legs along with her underwear, never once breaking eye contact.

Dropping to her knees, Anna reached for Sam's right leg, gently lifting it so her knee draped over her left shoulder. She placed both hands on Sam's arse and pulled her fully into her mouth. Anna was ravenous. She was going to feast on Sam.

Bracing herself, Sam grabbed the edge of the table, her eyes boring into Anna as she was devoured repeatedly. She felt Sam's body tremble and convulse as her inevitable climax built deep within. "Oh, fuck," Sam growled. Anna pulled her in tighter, her tongue dancing over her clit as she sucked harder and faster, "Don't stop, right there... right there." Anna had no intention of stopping. She was going to send Sam into the stratosphere if it was the last thing she ever did.

Needing more, Anna pushed two fingers into Sam, thrusting as she licked and sucked. Sam was dripping. Anna's hand was soaked with Sam's pleasure.

"Oh, Christ... Oh, fuck... Anna." Sam came, gripping the back of Anna's head. Anna clutched Sam as she came apart, her body shaking into oblivion. Anna withdrew her mouth slowly, all the time watching Sam as she came back down to earth with ragged breaths.

"Are you okay?"

Sam laughed, "You astound me." Her voice was shaky.

"I know the feeling."

Anna held Sam's hips and lifted herself up. She ran her hand through Sam's hair, knowing full well that she had to tell Sam how she was feeling. Anna was falling and there was no way back. Sam was taking possession of her heart.

Chapter Seventeen

Lying in bed with Anna wrapped in her arms, Sam stared at the ceiling, her mind drifting back to the night before. They'd shared another wonderful night together, exploring each other's bodies, driving each other into blissful euphoria.

Unfortunately, Sam was finding it hard to hang on to the memories; the talk that Anna had started several hours into their lovemaking was at the forefront of her mind.

Sam remembered the very moment that she saw Anna's face turn from hunger and desire to concern and fear. Sam felt her stomach tighten as she replayed their conversation.

"What's wrong?" Sam felt Anna's body stiffen in her embrace.

"I think we need to talk." Anna pulled away from Sam. "What is this? What are we?"

Sam sat for a moment looking at Anna; she wasn't expecting to have this conversation, especially at this moment. She tried desperately to sift through her jumbled thoughts. Of course, she had asked herself the same questions. How could she not?

The circumstances in which they had met were extraordinary. Sam didn't really believe in fate and destiny, but she couldn't help feeling that she and Anna had been put on the same path for a reason, a reason that she didn't understand yet. Sam also knew that they had become close quickly. She felt good with Anna, safe to let down some of her protective walls, but not completely… not all the way.

The fact of the matter was that they had only spent a few days with each other and that surely wasn't enough time to really know someone? Even if her heart *was* telling her, she already knew enough about Anna to know she was someone truly special. How was she supposed to answer such a loaded question when she hadn't had the time to process her own complicated feelings?

The last thing she wanted was to upset Anna or make her pull away from what they had. Yes, making love to Anna was beyond anything Sam had experienced before, but it wasn't just the physical. Anna was smart, funny, caring, and honest. She was beautiful inside and out.

"We're two people getting to know each other."

Anna nodded as she contemplated Sam's answer. "I suppose I wanted to know if this is more than just sex for you?" Sam hated seeing her looking so vulnerable and scared.

"It *is* more than sex for me, Anna."

"I don't want to push you. I just want to make sure we are on the same page."

"I think we are." Sam cupped Anna's chin, pulling her softly towards her. "Anna, I had a bad breakup with someone I was with for a really long time. It's only recently that I understand how much that relationship took from me. Being here in Paris, being with you, is like a fresh start for me, but I have some work to do on myself before I can be fully into something and committed.

"You are fresh out of the closet and that's so wonderful. You can finally figure out who you really are. Both of us are going to need time if we want this," she pointed back and forth between them, "to be something special. And trust me when I tell you, I think we are supposed to be special."

Anna took a deep breath. "Where do we go from here?"

"Tell me what *you* want."

"I want us to keep seeing each other. I want you in my bed still." Anna brushed her fingers across Sam's cheek.

"So let's keep doing what we're doing, no pressure on either of us. How does that sound?"

"I can do that. I need you to know that I like you a lot, Sam, and I think we could be special as well."

"We have to communicate. If you have something on your mind, tell me. You can talk to me about anything. No matter what, we are friends first, and I want you to trust me." They kissed slowly, sealing their new understanding.

Even though they had come to an agreement of sorts, Sam felt nervous. She'd had a fitful night, unable to settle into a deep sleep. Staring at the ceiling hadn't provided her with the answers she was seeking.

Anna shifted in her sleep but didn't stir. Sam wasn't sure how much longer she could stay there. She needed to move, to do something that would shift her addled brain into a more positive space.

As gently as she could, she slipped out of the bed and got dressed, ready to go home. She was going to exercise, sweat away her confusion. After a quick search, she found a pen and paper and wrote a quick note to Anna. Maybe she should wake her and explain how she was feeling, but she couldn't bring herself to do it. Anna looked far too peaceful. Sam put the note next to Anna's phone, bent over, and kissed her temple before leaving.

* * *

"Come on… come on Sam," she shouted at herself as she pushed to finish what had been a gruelling workout session. Her hair was soaked in sweat, as well as her back and practically every

203

other part of her body. She'd pushed herself hard and enjoyed every painful minute of it.

Two weeks had passed since Anna and Sam had had their talk. They'd both felt a little awkward the following evening when they'd met for dinner, but Sam was pleased that they'd manage to slip back into their usual relaxed conversation and playful banter after a couple of drinks. It was safe to say that both of them were consciously keeping topics of discussion light. There had been no mention of their feelings or of the future.

Sam checked in with herself as much as possible. She was feeling good, and she wanted to make sure she was putting her best foot forward. That meant that she had to ask herself some hard questions. Was she willing to go the distance with Anna? If so, what did that look like to her? If not, could she let Anna go but remain friends? All these hard questions but still without solid answers.

She was proud that she'd so far stopped herself from dwelling and overthinking. She could accept that she wasn't in a place yet where she could answer those harder questions, and that was okay. She would take as much time as needed, as long as Anna was willing to wait and vice versa.

Sam was also proud of the progress of the assignment. She was in her stride and she had made some bold choices with a few of her photos, choices that she knew a few weeks ago she wouldn't have made. It was amazing what a little self-assurance and support did to a woman's confidence.

Finding herself alone that evening, Sam mulled over her options. Anna had a dinner date with Kim, and Sam didn't want to impose on their time together. Anna had told Sam that her friendship with Kim had evolved since she had come out.

Sam had met Kim a few times since her first meeting with Anna. She could see why Anna liked the feisty blonde so much. Her bubbly personality and wit were contagious. It was impossible to feel down with Kim around. Sam was happy to see Anna come out of herself a little more each day and she knew Kim had a big part to play in that.

So what was a girl to do on a random Wednesday evening all by her lonesome? She'd tried to call Charlie, but she hadn't answered. The idea of going out didn't really appeal, as she'd worked so much lately that she simply didn't have the energy. Pizza and beer it was then!

Sam was just about to shove a fourth slice into her mouth when she heard her phone blaring out the Skype theme tune. A picture of her mum flashed on her screen. Sam smiled widely. She hadn't spoken to her mum in a few days, and she was eager to find out how her new painting was coming along. She pressed the screen to answer, but what she saw definitely wasn't her mum's sweet face.

"What is that?" she blurted. Her screen was filled with a multi-coloured vagina.

"It's a vagina, dear," Sandy said matter-of-factly from behind said vagina.

"I can see that Mother, why are you showing it to me, for Christ's sake?"

Sam should have been used to this type of behaviour from her mum by now. Sandy had never had a problem sharing some of her most provocative art with Sam, even as a kid. Sandy could never understand why parents were so guarded with their children about the human body; she thought every aspect of the body was beautiful and captivating. Sam, on the other hand, had wished many a time that her mum would conform to the social norm where this subject was concerned.

"It's a part of my new series. I haven't got a name for it yet but I am so excited to paint more. You are my inspiration, darling."

"Well, that's disturbing," Sam deadpanned.

"It's not yours, love," Sandy chuckled.

"I know it's not bloody mine! Sam barked.

Sandy lowered the painting. She was laughing hard. "I didn't mean that yours inspired this particular vagina, you prat." More laughing.

205

Sam scowled, but she couldn't stay serious for long. Her mum's laugh was one that made everyone that heard it giggle along, regardless of the hilarity of the joke.

"So how in god's name am I your inspiration?"

"Strength, my love, you are a strong and beautiful woman. I wanted to celebrate all that you are."

"And a massive vagina is what you came up with?"

"You know, for a lesbian, you have always been averse to looking at vaginas, dear."

"No, Mum, I have been averse to *you* showing me vaginas."

"Sammy, I just don't understand why you find it so upsetting. It's a beautiful and natural thing."

"I couldn't agree more, but that doesn't mean I should be okay with my mum randomly showing them to me."

Sandy rolled her eyes. Sam would never convince her mum that she should at least try to have some boundaries with her daughter. "You should be thankful I didn't share the male version," Sandy chuckled.

"Er... okay.... thanks for not showing me a multi-coloured penis, mum."

"You're welcome, love. Anyway, the reason I called was to see if you're going to be home for Charlie's birthday next month?"

"Maybe you could have led with that and then eased me into the whole vagina painting thing next."

Sandy tutted and rolled her eyes again, choosing to ignore Sam's comment. "So, will you be home?"

Sam felt surprised by the weight she felt in her stomach. Her mum had asked her an innocent question, one that should be easy to answer, but wasn't.

In normal circumstances, Sam would be ecstatic thinking about the time she would get to spend with Charlie on her birthday, but now Sam felt sick—not at the thought of seeing Charlie but at the thought of being back in England. By the time Charlie's birthday rolled around, Sam would likely have finished her project, meaning she no longer needed to stay in Paris with Anna.

"Sam?"

Sam pulled herself from her thoughts. "Sorry, Mum, er, I hadn't thought about it."

"Will you still have a lot of work to do? Are you worried you can't get the time off?"

Sam shook her head. "No, no, actually I'll probably be finished before then, so I'll be coming home, I guess."

"You don't seem thrilled about that, love."

Sam looked away from her mum, deciding if she should tell her about Anna. Of course she should. Not talking about her feelings in the past had led her down the garden path; she didn't have time for that again.

"I've met someone."

"A woman?" Sandy's face softened into a smile.

"Yeah, a woman. It's a bit of a crazy story, right up your street," Sam chuckled.

"Ooh, do tell," Sandy said, far too enthusiastically.

Sam launched into the story without hesitation. She gave her mum every detail bar the amazing sexy ones. She did *not* need those. Once she finished, she sat back and waited for her mum's reaction.

"Well... slap my ass and call me Mildred."

Sam laughed loudly. Her mum never failed to surprise her. "Well, that's a truly horrifying thing to hear. Please don't use that saying again, Mum."

"Sorry, love, I'm just a little shocked. I mean, you have found your cosmic soulmate, my love. Do you know how lucky you are? Oh, Sam, I'm over the moon, darling."

Sam rolled her eyes. She knew her mum would latch onto the whole "soulmate," "fated," "destiny" bollocks.

"Whoa, chill your beans, Mum. You can stop with the 'cosmic' mumbo jumbo right now. Anna is great and yes, the circumstances of our meeting are questionably odd, but that does not mean we are soulmates."

"Say what you will, Sam! You will see," Sandy chirped. "Just promise me you won't dismiss what you have because you live in different countries. Stay open-minded."

"I will, and I will be at home for Charlie's birthday. You know I would never miss it. What are you getting her?" Sam needed to change the subject from Anna.

"You've seen what I'm gifting her."

"You're giving her the vagina, aren't you?" Sam sighed.

"Of course, she'll love it."

"Yeah… she really will," Sam chortled.

* * *

The video call with her mum had been unsettling. She was worried about how quickly her project was nearing its end. Anna and Sam had continued dating, but now Sam could see the flaw in their plan.

The longer they carried on seeing each other, the closer they became, which was all fine and dandy if their end goal was friendship, but Sam knew they were more. They'd slept with each other nearly every night, sharing food, laughs, and intimacy.

Sam felt as if she was at a crossroads. She could either stay the course, continue to spend time with Anna growing closer in every way, or she had to pull the plug. The biggest question was: could she walk away?

The past few weeks had been wonderful in so many ways. From the day that Sam had read Charlie's letter, she had promised herself to work *towards* something instead of living with the past.

Sam was dedicated to her health and well-being now, something that had been neglected for over a decade. Her work was a big part of that, which is why she had steamrolled this assignment. She was focused and determined, and for once, she had pride in her art. Anna was also a big part of her positive

208

outlook too. Sam had been able to open up to Anna in a way that she had feared to do for so long.

Still, she had that niggling voice in the back of her head warning her not to dive in headfirst. Sam knew that's why she couldn't take their relationship further right now. She was still dealing with scars. Maybe she would never be rid of them completely, which terrified her because she hated to think that she wouldn't be able to give herself to someone fully ever again.

* * *

Sam had compiled all the photographs that she wanted to present to Helene for final approval. Helene had made it clear all along that Sam was in sole charge of any decisions, but Sam really wanted Helene's opinion. This was a career changing opportunity, and she wanted to make sure that she was on the right path, even if her gut told her she had smashed it.

Sam knocked lightly on Helene's door; she hadn't set an appointment because she knew she would only get herself worked up if she had to wait. Spontaneity was the best course of action.

"Oui," Helene called.

"Hi, have you got a sec?" Sam couldn't hide the slight quiver in her voice. Her nerves were at an all-time high. This project had become something really important to her, as had Helene's friendship.

As well as the deadline for her relationship with Anna, Sam realised she was also going to be saying goodbye to her new friends when she left for England. After the rocky start with Helene, they'd pushed past any awkwardness and become good friends.

Helene was funny, smart, and kind. They'd spent time working together, Helene always keen to get Sam's opinion and vice versa. They'd gone out a few times, Sam acting as a wingwoman for Helene as she prowled for a woman to take

209

home. Sadness filled her up. In a short time she had made these offices, these people, her family, and now she was going to leave.

"Of course." Helen gestured to the chair in front of her desk.

"I've got ninety percent of my photographs edited and ready to go. I wanted you to take a look at them and give me some feedback." Sam's leg was bobbing up and down with nervous energy.

"Give me the thumb drive and I'll look now. I have half an hour to spare for my favourite photographer," she winked.

Sam passed her the drive and sat back, waiting as patiently as possible whilst Helene loaded her work. Helene's face was unreadable as she clicked through the photos. Finally, after what seemed an eternity, Helene looked from the screen to Sam, who had been holding her breath in anticipation. "Well?"

"I don't know what to say."

Fear gripped at Sam's chest. Had she been wrong about her competence, had she screwed the pooch so badly that Helene was lost for words?

"That bad, huh?" Sam chuckled trying to break her crippling anxiety with humour.

"Sam, your work... it... it's breathtaking." Sam stared at Helene as if she had just grown a third boob. "Sam, you are so talented. Rupert is going to be ecstatic, and so is John, in fact. You should be so proud, I certainly am." Helene rounded her desk and pulled Sam into a bear hug. Sam let out a nervous chuckle. She was still processing Helene's praise. After Helene let her go, she sat back at her desk, ejecting Sam's USB drive and handing it back. "How much more have you left to do?"

"Not much at all, just a few final touches before I send them for printing. I have the photos selected for the book ready to be sent to Anna."

Helene regarded her friend for a moment. "How are you and Anna?" She was looking at Sam as if she was about to break down. Maybe her worries were easier to read than she thought.

"We're good. I mean, we are still seeing each other."

"And with your project coming to a close? How is that sitting with the two of you?"

"We haven't talked about it. I think we are both too scared to face up to it."

"Understandable. Remember that it doesn't have to be the end. You could look at long distance if you think she is worth it."

"It's not a question of her being worth it. It's more to do with it being fair to us both. Anna has so much to discover about herself and I want her to do that, so I'm not sure keeping her tethered to me when I'm not even in the same fucking country is a wise choice, no matter how I'm feeling." It felt good to express what had been rattling around in her brain for weeks.

"You may have a point there. Talk to her, get some clarity for the both of you," Helene smiled warmly, giving Sam's shoulder a little squeeze of support.

Sam left the office. She needed some fresh air, some time alone to think. She knew it wasn't fair to keep them both in limbo any longer. The hardest part was knowing that no matter what she did, she was going to get hurt, and so was Anna.

Chapter Eighteen

Anna sat at her desk. She was in complete shock. The meeting she'd had with Marcus first thing that morning had knocked her sideways. She hadn't been prepared for what he'd had to say at all. She registered the sound of her office door closing and Kim sitting down, looking concerned. "Everything alright, doll?"

"I... I..." Anna couldn't articulate what had happened.

"Anna, talk to me...you're scaring me."

Anna sat staring at her friend, her face pale. "Marcus."

"Marcus? Okay, what about him?" Kim pressed.

"He's leaving," Anna spluttered. "He's retiring."

"Right, so what does that mean for everyone? Are we all out of jobs?"

"No, no one is losing their job, nothing like that."

Kim let out a long breath, letting her fear go with it. "Okay, so why does your face look like that then?"

"He's given it to me," Anna choked. "He's signed over his half of the business to me."

"What!" Kim bellowed, causing every member of the office to look.

Anna took a second before answering. "He called me last night and set up a meeting for this morning. Nothing out of the ordinary." Kim nodded. "So I attended the meeting thinking it was going to be about a deadline or something like that, but the moment I saw his face, I knew something was going on."

"What did his face look like?"

"Peaceful," Anna replied. It was the only word that described his look perfectly. For the first time in years, Marcus looked at peace.

"Right… okay then what?"

"He just came out with it, said he was retiring at the end of the month, said he'd been planning it for a while and that the only thing that was stopping him was finding the right person to take over and–"

"There's taking over the job and then there is being given half a company," Kim interjected.

"I fully agree, which is exactly what I said to him the moment it was out of his mouth. He said that he didn't want to keep his part of the company. He said it held too many memories of Claire. He said that he'd already spoken to John about handing over his half to me and they were in complete agreement.

"Apparently, John doesn't want to take over fully. He wants to remain a silent partner, and he wants to collaborate with someone who is passionate about the job and apparently, that's me. Marcus was adamant."

"Bloody hell, what did you say to him?"

"I said that I was very grateful for the offer, but I felt he was giving me something I didn't deserve."

"What did he say?"

"He said he knew exactly what he was doing and he wouldn't take no for an answer, he said that he knew I was the right person for the job years ago, he just wanted me to learn more and get comfortable in a managerial role. He said he has been moulding me to take over. He also said that owning Tower

213

Publishing had been a dream, but it was time to move on. Apparently, he owns several other companies, which is why he doesn't want me to buy him out. He wants to gift it to me because he thinks that's what Claire would have wanted. Did you know he owned other companies?"

"Nope, not at all."

Replaying the conversation with Kim was helping it all sink in. Anna hadn't thought about the possibility of taking her career any further in years. She certainly hadn't entertained the idea that she was passionate about what she did — yes, she loved it, but passionate? Now, though, the more she thought about Marcus' words, the more she realised he was right.

Anna had attributed her despondency to her job as a lack of interest — or more like she'd become too comfortable — but that wasn't true at all. Anna had been despondent with her whole life and that was because she had been living as someone else, a stranger that she no longer recognised.

She hadn't realised at the time that being closeted had affected every aspect of her life, including her job. At university Anna had dreamed of working in publishing. She had been so excited, but, at some point, her excitement and dreams had been tossed to one side for mediocrity.

"What do you think?"

"Well, I think you would be bloody brilliant quite frankly," Kim chimed.

"Really?"

"Really. Anna, you have changed so much in such a short amount of time. Everyone here can see how much happier you are and that is definitely showing in your work and your love for what you do."

Anna took a few deep breaths. "This is a big step Kim, would you be ready for it too? I presume you wouldn't mind being my personal assistant still?"

"Will I get a raise?" Kim joked.

"Of course."

"Oh… well, I was only joking, but I won't turn it down. The more important question to ask is, are *you* ready?"

"I think I am, yes. I need to have another conversation with Marcus."

"Congratulations my sweet, we need to celebrate. How about a drink this evening, or have you got plans with Sam?"

Sam, shit, Anna hadn't even considered what this would mean for them. Taking over from Marcus meant she was cementing herself permanently in the company, hell it would be her company, meaning any options for her and Sam would be severely limited outside of Paris.

Kim must have read her thoughts. "You need to talk to her, Anna, sooner rather than later."

"Yes, you're right." Anna dropped her head to the desk with an audible thud. For a few minutes, she had been on cloud nine, the future looking so bright until she thought of Sam, which made her come crashing back down to earth like a sack of shit.

As if she had summoned her with the power of thought alone, Anna looked up to see Sam walking towards her office. Kim looked over her shoulder, noticing Sam approaching. She turned to Anna with love in her eyes. "You got this," she winked.

Sam knocked on the door and waited for Kim to answer. "Hi, Kim."

"Hey, doll, Anna's free, go right in." She squeezed Sam's shoulder. Anna shuffled in her seat, preparing herself for what was to come.

"Hi."

"Hey, you."

"I brought over the finished photos for the book."

"Excellent." Anna was kicking herself over her lack of vocabulary.

"Everything okay?"

"Yes, I had some interesting and exciting news. Take a seat." Anna stood and went to her windows. She pulled the privacy blinds down, which she had never done before. She didn't want them to be disturbed. She caught Kim's eye, who gave her a little nod of encouragement.

"I didn't know you had blinds."

"I have never used them; I never saw the point of them, to be honest."

"But now you do?"

Anna pulled her chair so she could sit next to Sam. She took her hand and began explaining about her meeting with Marcus, detailing everything that had been discussed and her decision to take over the company. Sam sat silently, listening until she was finished.

"Wow. That's huge, Anna. I'm so happy for you." She pulled Anna into a heartfelt hug. Anna sank into it, breathing in Sam's wonderful and calming aroma. Once they released each other, Anna sat back in her chair. She began entwining her fingers as she became more nervous.

"What? Talk to me, Anna."

"Taking this job is an enormous step for me. It's such a positive step, but I fear for what it means for us."

"I know. I came here to talk to you, too." Sam looked equally uneasy as Anna. "I'm really close to wrapping up my project. Once that's done, I'll be going home."

"How long?"

"A couple of weeks at most."

Anna's heart plunged. She knew Sam would leave eventually, but it didn't stop her from feeling utterly broken. There was no use. She had to lay it all out there. She couldn't think of a world where she wasn't with Sam. She went to open her mouth, but Sam beat her to the punch.

"I think we should concentrate on staying friends." Those words were like a sledgehammer to the heart. Anna wanted the ground to open up and swallow her. She didn't want to be just friends, but it wasn't only up to her. "Long distance would be brutal on both of us. You mean so much to me, Anna, and I want you to be happy."

Anna was in an emotional freefall. Sam would make her happy. She'd been making her happy since they'd met. How could she say that, though? She knew Sam wasn't ready to commit to something more, and she respected her enough not to push her.

"I don't want to lose you out of my life," Anna choked, tears began filling her eyes.

"Oh, Anna, that's never going to happen. We're in each other's lives forever. There's no doubt in my mind about that." Sam cupped Anna's cheek tenderly.

Anna was overwhelmed with emotion. The feel of Sam's hand on her face warmed her and made her feel safe. She leaned in and kissed Sam with as much passion as she could muster. Sam reciprocated with an equal amount of pressure and want. They pulled away, their lips hovering a centimetre apart. Their breaths coming short and fast.

"How private are these blinds?" Sam panted.

"Very." Anna pulled Sam back into another searing kiss. She felt Sam pulling her up and walking her towards the bookcases that lined the walls behind her desk. Her back hit the shelves with a thud. Sam pressed against her body. Anna felt her underwear become soaked.

"I've wanted to take you up against these bookshelves since the moment I saw you standing by them looking sexy as hell in that first meeting," Sam whispered into her ear.

Anna thought she was going to come on the spot. "Sam," she gasped.

"What do you want, Anna? Tell me."

"Anything, anyway, you want, Sam."

She heard Sam groan in anticipation and desire. Sam began kissing her neck, her hands exploring Anna's body. "Turn around," Sam demanded. Anna turned to face her books. She felt Sam's hand tracing up the back of her thigh, lifting her skirt. She felt the cold air caress her ass as Sam hooked her thumbs under her thong and slid them down to her knees. "Spread for me," Sam panted. Her excitement was palpable.

217

Anna opened her legs, waiting for the inevitable euphoria she was about to experience. She gasped as Sam brushed a hand over her pussy. "You're so wet, baby."

"Now, Sam," Anna demanded. She couldn't wait any longer. She felt two fingers slide inside of her, picking up rhythm. Anna clutched the bookshelves for support. She wasn't sure she could stay upright for much longer.

"Oh god," she whispered.

"Tell me what you need."

"Harder."

"Like this?"

Anna clung to the shelves for dear life. Sam was taking her with masterful precision. Just as she thought it couldn't get any better, she felt Sam bring her other hand around to her front. Sam's nimble fingers began circling her clit. "Mon Dieu," she exhaled as the pleasure built to an almost unbearable level.

Anna couldn't be sure, but she thought for a brief second that Sam paused momentarily. Her thoughts were quickly pushed to one side as she felt herself tighten, the orgasm tearing through her like a raging fire. Anna did her very best to stay quiet as she came, but she wasn't confident that she had pulled it off.

She released her hands, allowing the blood to return to them. She hadn't realised how hard she'd been holding on to the shelves. Anna let her body go slack, the weight of Sam against her as they tried to slow their breathing.

"That was amazing," Sam whispered.

"I agree," Anna chuckled.

"You might have been a little loud." Sam gently bit Anna's earlobe, which sent a shot of desire straight to her clit.

"Let's see if you can do any better. Sit on the desk." Anna felt Sam's body move away from her. She turned to watch Sam casually lean against her desk, waiting. Anna pulled up her underwear slowly. She took her time straightening out her clothes. "Take off your trousers and underwear."

Sam was breathing hard. Anna knew it wouldn't take her long to tip Sam over the edge. Once Sam had removed her trousers

218

and her underwear, she looked at Anna for her next command. "Put your right foot on my chair."

Anna watched Sam get into position. She was completely open, ready and waiting for Anna's mouth. Slowly, Anna walked over and sank to her knees. She sent a gentle breath over Sam's exposed clit. Sam groaned quietly. "Hold on," Anna whispered. Anna grabbed Sam's backside with her hands and plunged into her.

After sleeping together every night, Anna knew Sam loved to come in her mouth. She knew the exact spot that would drive Sam wild. She felt Sam thrust her hips, grabbing the back of Anna's head, tugging at her hair gently. Anna could see she was struggling to stay silent.

Anna was relentless. She sucked Sam's clit over and over before releasing it. She tongued Sam's entrance, which caused her to moan. She was losing the battle to be quiet. She felt Sam tense. It was time to unravel her.

Flattening her tongue, she ran it up the length of Sam's sex. Sam threw her head back as her body quivered. Her release was strong, and Anna adored every second. She stayed in place until Sam had stopped shaking. Satisfied with her work, she gave Sam's clit one last kiss before standing up and wrapping her arms around her lover's neck.

They seemed to both understand that this could be the last time they made love. Anna placed her hands on either side of Sam's head and kissed her, slow and deep. They pulled apart and looked into each other's eyes.

Anna wanted to stay like this forever, but it wasn't to be. They were pulled out of their post-sex haze when she heard knocking on her door. Anna stepped away and adjusted her hair and clothes whilst Sam redressed. Once Anna was sure they were both decent, she opened the door.

Kim grinned. "I hope I'm not interrupting?"

Anna cleared her throat. She could feel her face flush crimson. "No, of course not, we had just finished... the meeting, just finished the meeting."

219

Kim snorted and entered the office. She looked several times from Anna to Sam, who was trying her damndest to look casual.

Anna closed the door behind her and turned to Kim. "Everything alright?"

"Oh, yes, fine, you have a meeting with the team in ten minutes," Kim smiled.

"Of course, thank you for reminding me." Anna tried desperately to sound as normal as possible.

Kim cleared her throat before gesturing to Sam. "Er, you're flying low, pal." Anna looked from Kim to Sam, who was as confused as her. Anna looked back to Kim, who was giggling and looking pointedly at Sam's crotch. Anna shot her gaze back to Sam, who'd also clicked onto Kim's meaning.

"Shit," Sam barked, twisting around so her back was facing them. Anna watched Sam fumble with the zip on her trousers. A fresh wave of heat crashed over her. They had clearly failed at being discreet.

Kim saw Anna's look of mortification. "Relax guys, funnily enough, I felt it was time the team took a well-earned break. They headed out to the café when you began your 'meeting'," she laughed. Neither Anna nor Sam said anything until they caught each other's eye. Anna burst out laughing, followed quickly by Sam.

"I'll get going, text you later?"

"Please do," Anna smiled.

Sam placed a soft kiss on her cheek before leaving. "See you soon, Kim."

"See ya," Kim chimed.

Once Anna was sure that Sam was out of range, she dropped her head into her hands, "Mon Dieu, I am so embarrassed."

"Stop, no one else twigged you were getting randy in your office," Kim chuckled. "You might want to straighten those books though," she added, pointing to the spot where Anna had been pressed.

"Merde." Anna scrambled to the case to tidy up the mess.

She felt Kim place her hand softly on her shoulder. "Anna, seriously calm down. No harm done. Did you talk at all?"

Anna nodded slowly. The effects of their office rendezvous had worn off. The stark reality of their situation hung over her like a dark cloud. She had to let Sam go. She wasn't ready, but she couldn't torture herself by continuing to make love to Sam, knowing it couldn't go any further. She had to accept that Sam would be her friend and nothing more.

"We're going to stay friends. She will probably leave for the UK soon and she wasn't willing to try long distance."

"I'm sorry, doll." Kim wrapped Anna in a hug.

"So am I." Anna sighed.

* * *

Anna sat at the table by the window of her rental. It was time to decide. Her lease was ending, and she hadn't found an apartment. Her new position at Tower Publishing afforded her the luxury to think bigger when it came to the square footage of her next place, but the thought of leaving her current lodgings didn't sit well.

It had been almost three weeks since she and Sam had been together physically. They had both pulled back, trying to make it easier on each other. They still spoke over the phone and sent texts several times a day, usually discussing the progression of the book, which was almost finished, and Sam's photos.

Anna had made a point of only accepting lunch invitations in public places. She still couldn't trust herself when she was near Sam. It was going to be difficult, but Anna wasn't prepared to say goodbye completely. She would be friends with Sam, no matter how badly her heart ached.

She sighed deeply, which seemed to become something of a regular thing now. Fingering through her rental contract, she noticed in the small print that the owner would consider a long rental agreement if the right occupant came along. Anna was on good terms with him and didn't think he would have an issue with her staying on a long-term basis.

The apartment was in a great location for work. She'd explored the area, and already had a favourite bakery and café. The place was a little above her budget, but she wasn't planning on any large outgoings any time soon. Maybe this could be a celebratory gift to herself? The downside would be when Sam left, she feared the apartment would only remind her of her loss.

Her phone buzzed on the table. Frédéric's name flashed on her screen. "Coucou," she chirped, trying to sound upbeat.

"Hey, are you in?"

"Yes, here all day."

"I'm just round the corner. Be there in a minute," he said before cutting the call. Sure enough, the doorbell rang a few minutes later. Anna let her brother in and sank back onto the chair at the table. Frédéric sat opposite, looking at the rental paperwork. "You thinking of staying?"

"I can't decide. It's a great place, a little pricey, but I've really grown to love it."

"What's the problem, then? You look like someone's pissed in your cereal."

Anna grimaced. "I wish you wouldn't blindly repeat what dad says."

Frédéric laughed. "I was trying to cheer you up. Come on, tell me what's wrong?"

"Honestly... I'm worried that once Sam's gone, it will spoil the place for me."

"Ah, the mysterious Sam. I'm surprised you haven't asked me to meet her."

"We have an agreement about that," she reminded him. They wouldn't meet partners unless it was love. Anna was still to meet Frédéric's girlfriend Lucie.

"Yeah, I know what our agreement is and I also know you are completely in love with that woman," He said plainly.

Anna went to protest, but she couldn't muster the energy to do it. He was right. She had fallen for Sam hopelessly, but she wasn't sure she was ready to call it love just yet.

"It doesn't matter. We are staying friends, and that's all."

Frédéric shrugged his shoulders. "If you say so, sis."

"Can we get back to the apartment hunting?" Talking about Sam was just too much right now.

"Sure. Look, if you like the place and you can afford it, then go for it. The building and area are exquisite. I would kill to live around here. It's going to feel crap when Sam leaves, but you can't run away from every place that reminds you of her."

He was right. Again. Anna rolled her eyes internally; it seemed that Frédéric was doing a better job at being the older sibling than she was at the minute.

"You're right, I'll call the owner."

"Great, you should have a housewarming party. I can bring Lucie," He smiled.

"If the owner agrees, then I'll have a little get-together. I would love you to bring Lucie."

"Bon. Lunch?"

"Absolutely. Let me call the owner first and then we'll go."

Ten minutes later, she put the phone down. "I've got a new apartment," she beamed. Frédéric picked her up and twirled her around, laughing. Anna broke out into giggles as she spun.

Yes, her heart might be breaking for what she couldn't have with Sam, but she couldn't ignore the things that she had; close friends, new apartment, better job and, most importantly, a new sense of self.

223

Chapter Nineteen

Sam had prolonged the project as much as possible; she'd stretched out the final edits until she couldn't, in good conscience, continue to waste her time any longer. She'd been chosen for this project to prove herself, which in her opinion she'd done magnificently.

Dawdling now was unprofessional, and she didn't want to take anything away from her pristine work or her reputation. That being said, her heart was aching because she had just sent off the last photographs to be printed. She had officially finished.

All that was left to do was send an email to Helene formally closing the project. She'd written the email half an hour ago but couldn't find it in herself to click send. "Just send it." Her body wasn't cooperating. She squeezed her eyes shut, willing herself to take the plunge. No matter how long she waited, the outcome wouldn't change. Sam was finished with the project, finished with Paris and heartbreakingly finished with Anna.

Sam swivelled her chair to face the window. The sunlight filtered through gaps in the blinds that had been pulled closed to keep the editing suite dark. Considering she was the only one in the room, she didn't see a problem with opening them now.

The street below was busier than usual, with plenty of people flitting between the buildings going about their daily lives, unaware that Sam felt as if her newly built world was crashing down around her.

Nobody could understand the feeling of dread that had settled within her since she last saw Anna and had let her go romantically, friendship being the only possibility that Sam could see, even if it was going to crush them both in the beginning.

Twenty-three days had passed since they had taken each other in Anna's office. They both knew it was the last time they would be like that together.

Sam tried to distance herself as much as possible without causing Anna to feel rejected. They'd spoken a few times, but nowhere near the amount they had when they'd been dating. Sam berated herself for dating Anna in the first place. She was furious with herself for letting them get to a point where all they'd be left with was pain. Sam had known from the beginning that she still had too much baggage to sort through to give Anna what she deserved.

God, she just wanted the dull ache in her chest to go away. She took a few deep breaths, not wanting to let herself overthink and overanalyse. It was part of the "new her." She was adamant that she was going to go forward — well, back to England — with all the positivity she could summon.

She was done living in the past with regrets and insecurities, yet she couldn't bring herself to apply the same focus and determination with Anna. It was like a part of her had been broken and she couldn't figure out how to mend it.

After a few more minutes of looking out over Paris, Sam turned back to the computer and the email that seemed to torment her. With a resigned sigh, she clicked the send button. Now it was official.

* * *

Sam spent the next two days organising herself and saying goodbye to her new colleagues and friends. Helene had planned a night out to say farewell, something Sam was *not* looking forward to.

There were two more days to go before her leaving party and she knew she had to spend her time wisely, meaning she needed to concentrate on packing and getting ready to leave. But no matter how much she tried to focus on the job at hand, she couldn't stop herself gravitating towards the window, hoping to see Anna.

Sam wanted nothing more than to run over and take her in her arms, but she wouldn't let herself do it. She wouldn't open those wounds. After the fifth time of wandering over to the window, Sam caught sight of her. She was setting lunch out for herself on her little table. The sight of her made Sam melt. Her presence, even from afar, was mesmerising and calming.

A pang of guilt washed over her. Sam had promised Anna that she wouldn't disappear from her life. They would be friends no matter what, and yet Sam had *not* been a good friend at all lately. She had distanced herself so much she hadn't even invited Anna to her leaving do. *Shit!* She was ghosting Anna. She had to rectify her mistake immediately.

Sam: *Bonjour :)*

Sam looked from her phone over to Anna's apartment. She saw Anna pick up her phone and type. Sam smiled from ear to ear.

Anna: *Who is this?*

Sam's smile fell from her face. Anna was upset.

226

Anna: I wonder if it's a friend I used to know, Sandy hair, who enjoys taking pictures.

Fuck, fuck, fuck!

Sam: *I'm so sorry Anna, I've been a right melt! You deserve better.*
Anna: *Yes I do!*
Sam: *Will you forgive me?*
Anna: *Depends. Are you going to disappear on me again? You said we would always be friends?*
Sam: *You're right, I have been a shitty friend. I've just been struggling with leaving and I pushed you away.*
Anna: *Why?*
Sam: *Because leaving you is proving harder than I thought.*
Anna: *It's hard on me too.*

Sam sighed heavily. She looked over at Anna, who was looking straight back at her. Sam called Anna's number and pressed the phone to her ear. She saw Anna do the same as the call was connected.

"I miss you," Sam whispered.

"I miss you too, but you can't just disappear like that." Anna's reply was cool, her tone was a little stiff.

"I know. I really am sorry. You mean the world to me. Can you give me another chance?"

"Of course. You pissed me off, but friends always forgive each other."

Sam felt the tension fall away. Yes, the situation sucked major balls, but at least Anna would still be in her life.

"Do you want to come to my leaving party on Friday? Kim, too?"

"I'll be there."

"I'll send you the details."

"Great."

There was a beat of silence. Sam wanted them to go back to normal. She didn't want her last moments with Anna to be strained. "How was your week?" She saw a smile unfold on Anna's face before she delved into the details of her week.

They chatted as if nothing had changed between them. Sam sank into the chair at her table by the window, looking over at Anna as she listened to everything she had to say.

The packing could wait a little longer.

* * *

Friday rolled around quickly. Sam had packed all of her things without too much trouble. She had texted Anna every day without fail. Sometimes they spoke about random things and other times they hit on Sam's departure.

Their most recent text chain was about clothing for the party. Anna wasn't sure how "dressed up" she should be. Sam was in the same boat. Helene hadn't given her any details regarding a dress code. Thankfully, her question was answered when Helene arrived at the apartment with a clothes bag slung over her shoulder.

"Coucou," she chirped before giving Sam a two-cheek kiss.

Sam pointed at the bag. "What's that?"

"It's your outfit for tonight."

"Thank god, I didn't know what to wear. Anna, too."

"I messaged Kim earlier. Don't worry."

"Great," Sam exhaled. That was one less thing to worry about. "So, what did you bring me?"

Helene laid the bag on the sofa before opening it. Sam peered in to see skintight green chino trousers and a form-fitting tank top. Sam knew she was going to look good, especially seeing as her workouts had given her muscle definition on her arms and torso.

"So I take it we're not going to a fancy ass restaurant then?" she chuckled.

"No way. Tonight we are dancing and drinking."

"Fantastique," Sam shouted in the world's worst French accent.

Helene almost snorted with laughter. "Please stick to English."

"Hey, I thought that was pretty good!"

"Oh, Sam, I am going to miss you." They both fell silent. It was a heavy moment. Sam knew this evening was going to be difficult.

"I'll miss you too, but you have to visit and call."

"Of course." Helene threw her arms around Sam. *Wow, this is going to be hard.*

"Okay, give me ten minutes to dress and grab my wallet." Sam needed a few moments to compose herself. With a few calming breaths, Sam put on a brave face. She was determined that her last night out was going to be unforgettable.

They were going to drink and dance and focus on everything that had made her trip to Paris so wonderful.

Anna.

Anna had made her trip unforgettable. Sam couldn't focus on her, though. That would be a mistake. They had formed a close but tentative friendship and one slip tonight could ruin it all. No, Sam had to stay vigilant.

"Ready?" Helene called. Sam had taken longer than necessary to prepare.

"Let's do it." Her feelings didn't match the tone in her voice.

The car was waiting out on the street. Henry smiled softly as they climbed in. Sam was feeling a mixture of things; excitement and nerves being at the top of the list. After tonight, she knew her life was going to change again.

When she had first arrived in Paris, she would never have pictured herself sitting in this car with a wonderful friend like Helene feeling so confident in herself and craving the next adventure.

Sam had been a shell of herself for so long. She had been lost and confused, focusing on all the wrong things and asking herself all the wrong questions, questions that only led her to feel

229

worse about herself. Her heart clenched as she looked over at Helene, who had produced a bottle of champagne from the centre console of the car. She had a wide and infectious smile which made Sam's chest tighten.

Sitting in the car, looking over at her friend, Sam finally felt as if she had shed the weight and misery of her past. She had people around her who lifted her up and supported her. No matter where she was in the world, that could never be taken from her and yes, Sam now believed that she could go and do anything she wanted. Her ambition was limitless, and she had Paris and her friends to thank for it. She was so full of love that she almost broke down.

"Drink!" Helene cheered.

They happily drank and talked as Henry drove them through the streets of Paris. Sam didn't know where they were going and she didn't care. She was too busy soaking up the city one last time.

The car finally pulled up to the curb. Sam peeked out the window and recognised the area immediately. "This is the bar we went to weeks ago," she stated as she followed Helene out of the car.

"It is, but this time it is ours for the night." Helene was almost bouncing in excitement.

"What do you mean, it's ours?"

"I hired the entire bar, courtesy of Rupert," she squealed.

"Fuck me," Sam bellowed.

Helene threw her head back and laughed. "I knew you would say that. You English and your cursing." Shaking her head, she tutted in mock disapproval. Helene slung her arm around Sam and walked her to the door. "Everyone is here. The entire office showed up. You made a big impression on everyone, Ms Chambers."

Sam could feel her face burning. She still wasn't great at taking compliments. "That's... that's incredible," she whispered as she was ushered through the door.

They were greeted by a large crowd of people who cheered as soon as they stepped inside. There was no use even trying to stop the tears. The love and support on show was completely overwhelming.

Taking a step towards the crowd, she allowed herself to be pulled into hugs and kisses by people that she knew well and some that she had only met in passing. All of them were there to wish her well.

After what seemed an age, Sam finally sat at the bar where there was already a line of drinks waiting for her. "Let's get this party started," Helene shouted.

The music grew steadily louder, along with everyone in the bar. "I may have mentioned to the DJ that you love 90s songs, so I think that will be the theme of the night," Helene giggled. She was already on her way to being tipsy.

Sam chuckled along with her, the beat of the music flowing through her body as well as the alcohol she had downed. Sitting at the bar, she began scanning the room. Everyone was having a whale of a time. Her breath caught as she locked eyes with Anna. There in the centre of the dance floor stood the woman that had turned her world upside down and, sure enough, she looked out-of-this-world stunning.

Sam felt her blood rush south; Anna wore black pinstriped trousers that seemed to have been perfectly tailored to her body, a black ribbed tank top that clung to every delicious curve, and, to finish, white suspenders. Her hair was loose and wild around her shoulders; it swayed with every beat of the music.

Fuck me sideways! How the hell was she supposed to get through the evening without getting close to her, especially in those three-inch heels?

Realising that she was ogling, she gave Anna a little wave. *Lame.* Anna smiled before turning back to the crowd dancing. *Do not dance with her!* Sam knew that her aim tonight had to be staying away from Anna. There was no way she could keep it "just friendly" if she got too close.

231

On that decision, she grabbed a drink and started making the rounds, chatting and laughing with her guests. *Good idea, stick to the crowd.* Half an hour had passed and Sam was feeling her throat getting sore from all the talking/shouting — the music was really loud. She searched the dance floor to see if Anna was still there, but she was gone. Sam did, however, see Helene and Seb ripping up the dance floor with very questionable moves.

"What are you doing? This can't be classed as dancing," she laughed as she joined them.

"It's interpretive," Seb bellowed.

Sam clutched her sides, laughing as she continued to watch Helene and Seb dance. *Well, if you can't beat 'em.* Sam threw herself into the music.

Several songs later, she cast her eyes around the room. There was no denying that she was looking for one particular guest. She found her sitting at one of the small tables talking to Kim.

Breaking away from her dance companions, she headed to their table. Sam couldn't dance with Anna, but they were still friends after all, and not saying hello would be wrong.

"Hey, guys." She said casually plonking herself down into the free chair next to Kim.

"Hey, yourself," Kim winked.

"You enjoying yourselves?" Sam looked from Kim to Anna.

"It's wonderful," Anna replied with a soft smile. *God, could she be any more beautiful?*

Sam returned the smile but didn't know what to say because the things that were running through her mind were far from appropriate. Kim sensed the tension and dived into conversation, effectively saving them all from any more polite awkwardness.

Kim was fantastic at filling the silence; she spoke of her boyfriend, work, the weather, and anything else she could think of. Sam could have kissed her. She was a great friend to them both.

They sat chatting for a good twenty minutes before they were interrupted by a tall blonde woman in a black miniskirt, Lena?

Yes, that was her name. Sam couldn't, for the life of her, remember where they had met. Her legs seemed to go on for days. Her hair cascaded down her back in soft layers. The halter neck top she was wearing strained against her ample chest. She was hot.

Everyone stopped and stared as the woman bent down and whispered into Anna's ear. Sam saw her blush. Whatever Lena had said clearly had the desired effect. A pang of jealousy ripped through Sam. She waited with bated breath to see what Anna would do next. Anna looked from Lena to Kim and then to Sam. Sam could see the pain on her face as she decided what to do. It felt as if Anna was waiting for Sam to say something, which she didn't.

No matter how she felt about this woman clearly hitting on Anna, it wasn't Sam's place to stand in the way; she lost that right when she drew a line under their relationship and marked it "friends only."

Anna seemed to understand Sam without a word passing their lips. She saw Anna sigh with disappointment before turning back to Lena. Smiling widely, Anna stood and took Lena's hand, who led her to the dance floor. Lena rested her hands on Anna's hips, drawing her in closer. Sam was transfixed. She couldn't look away, even though the sight was torturing her.

"If you want her, go and get her." Sam jumped at the sound of Kim's voice.

"It's not that easy. I'm leaving on Sunday."

"So what? Why are you torturing yourself? Have one last night together. You both clearly want it."

Could they do that? Have one last night? Hadn't the office been the end? Sam watched as Anna and Lena ground their bodies together in time with the music. Sam couldn't give a flying fuck about the Lena anymore. Her eyes were on Anna and Anna alone.

The second she had spotted her on the dance floor, Sam had wanted nothing more than to whisk her away to bed and make love to her one last time.

From Sunday they would be apart, they'd have no more nights together, no more chances. Who was Sam kidding? She didn't want to be friends with Anna. She wanted her for so much more and maybe just for tonight, she could.

The music changed, and Lena leaned in to talk to Anna. Sam watched vigilantly. Anna gave a little nod, and Lena disappeared to the bar. Anna stood to the side of the dance floor, waiting for her to return with another drink. That's what Sam surmised from their interaction. The time was now or never.

"Kim, tell Helene I left." Without waiting for a reply, she walked with purpose to where Anna was waiting. She approached her from behind, slowly drawing herself into Anna's back. Anna gave a small gasp as they touched. "One last night. Let me have you for one last night," Sam whispered.

Anna turned her head slightly so she could glance over her shoulder at Sam. "Take me to bed." Her voice was soaked in lust. Sam didn't need to hear anything else. She stepped around Anna and took her hand, leading her to the door. Sam was going to make this a night to remember.

* * *

The car ride back to Anna's apartment had been fraught with sexual tension. Sam had struggled to keep her hands from Anna's body. It seemed Anna was struggling with the same problem because her hand had crept several times to the inside of Sam's thigh. Each time Sam had given a small groan in anticipation and each time Anna had squeezed her thigh before withdrawing her hand.

Even though the air was thick between them, they hadn't uttered a single word since leaving the bar; words weren't necessary. They both understood what was happening, and they didn't need to discuss it. No more speeches, no more goodbyes.

234

They entered Anna's apartment and walked to the bedroom hand in hand. Anna turned to Sam, placing her hands on Sam's chest. Sam cupped Anna's cheek, tracing her face with her thumb. She brought her free hand around Anna's waist, pulling her in. The kiss was slow and deep, their tongues met but didn't do battle. They caressed and danced in sync, tasting and exploring. They sank into each other, neither leading but working as one.

They kissed until they ran out of air. Pulling back, their eyes locked onto each other. They undressed each other slowly, there was no rush. Tonight was about delicacy and passion. Their clothes were left scattered around their feet. Anna stepped backwards, lowering herself onto the bed. Sam watched, her gaze scanning along Anna's body, memorising every beauty mark, every curve.

When she couldn't wait any longer, Sam lowered herself on top of Anna, her thigh pressing into Anna's centre. The move was met with a wanting gasp from Anna. Sam's mouth hovered mere millimetres from Anna's soft lips. She wanted to breathe her in entirely. Anna's eyes sparkled, her pupils dilated. Sam wanted to give Anna everything she desired.

Their bodies moved in perfect rhythm, their eyes never leaving each other. As if they could read each other's minds, they reached down and placed their hands between each other's thighs, increasing the friction. Their breaths became staggered, sweat coated their bodies as they picked up the pace. Sam felt Anna tense, and she knew she was close to coming.

"Oh god," Anna moaned. "Sam, I'm coming."

"Come with me, honey," Sam gasped.

"Oh… oh, yes… yes," Anna moaned loudly. Her entire body shook. Sam pressed herself even closer, finally allowing her own climax to take over. They crashed over the edge together, holding each other, riding out their passion as one.

Their bodies stilled as they came down. Sam sank into the bed, her leg still draped across Anna, her head resting on her shoulder. They lay silent, steadying their breaths. "Will you stay tonight?" Anna whispered.

"Yes."

Anna rolled onto Sam, straddling her hips. She lowered herself so her breasts rubbed against Sam's as she rocked her pelvis. Sam could feel Anna's wetness paint her stomach. She cupped Anna's arse with both hands. Anna sat upright, her back arching as she rocked.

Sam wanted, no *needed,* to taste her. In one smooth motion, Sam momentarily stilled Anna's hips, slid herself down and took Anna into her mouth.

Anna's moan was almost Sam's undoing. She could feel a second orgasm begin to build, and she wasn't even being touched. She clutched Anna's cheeks firmly, thrusting her deeper into her mouth. She ate her entirely.

Anna's movements became wild. She grabbed the headboard with one hand whilst the other massaged and played with her own breasts.

Sam was like a woman possessed. The sight of Anna writhing and moaning only spurred her on. She was going to make Anna come over and over again. It was her mission. Anna was trembling. Her muscles were taut. Sam pressed a little more until Anna dropped forward, screaming in sheer pleasure.

* * *

The room was dark, only the light from the street illuminated their bodies, which were wrapped around each other. They'd made love to each other for hours. Consuming each other repeatedly.

Sam lay awake staring at the ceiling with Anna sleeping soundly on her chest. It had been the perfect night. Sam felt a pang of guilt for abandoning her leaving party without saying goodbye. However, the feeling was fleeting as she felt Anna hold her a little tighter as she slept.

236

The time had finally come. Sam had to go. They'd said all they'd needed to say, they'd shared the perfect goodbye. Sam wanted to preserve this night in her memory for eternity. No matter how much she hurt, she couldn't have asked for a better way for them to part.

Sam kissed the top of Anna's head, breathing in her scent one last time before slipping out of bed and gathering her clothes.

Once dressed, she let herself look for a little longer at Anna laying so beautifully in her bed. "Goodbye, Anna," she whispered and with that, Sam was gone.

Chapter Twenty

Anna knew she was alone in bed before she even opened her eyes. Last night had been perfect, maybe too perfect. Now she was left with the stark reality that Sam was gone. They'd decided not to pursue each other so many times over the past few months, but still they ended up in each other's arms and bed.

Last night felt different, though. They both knew it was their last goodbye, so Anna understood why Sam had left before she had woken. Pulling the pillow from the other side of the bed, Anna took a deep breath and let Sam's lingering scent fill her senses. She had a decision to make; either she could wallow in sadness at the loss of what could have been, or she could hold on to the precious gift they had given each other over the past few weeks and move forward.

Releasing the pillow and therefore Sam, Anna pulled herself into a sitting position, allowing a few more seconds to sit with her feelings. Sam wasn't supposed to leave Paris until tomorrow, but Anna wouldn't be surprised to find that she had taken an earlier train. Anna was under no illusion that she was the only one that felt this pain deeply. Sam would be in the same boat even if she didn't feel as strongly for Anna as she did for Sam.

With one last sigh, Anna voiced the one thing she wished she could've said to Sam before she had left, "I'm going to miss you."

Anna searched for her phone. She needed sustenance, and she needed a friend.

> **Anna:** *Morning! Any chance you want to swing by for a coffee?*
> **Kim:** *Great idea, I need some fresh air, I'm not feeling wonderful right now :(*

Anna chuckled to herself. She wondered how late the party had run after she and Sam had disappeared.

> **Anna:** *Any chance you want to grab the coffee on the way over, croissants too :)*
> **Kim:** *I suppose I could, just for you. See you in twenty.*

Time to get up and ready for the day. Standing in the bedroom, Anna surveyed her kingdom. The thought hit her square in the chest. This apartment was hers for the foreseeable future. For once, she felt she was exactly where she wanted to be.

Kim strolled into the apartment twenty-five minutes later, armed to the teeth with caffeine and baked goods. Anna had given Kim a spare key as soon as she had signed the contract to the apartment. She smiled to herself as she watched Kim saunter about, preparing the little table with plates and cutlery.

The feeling she got watching her best friend warmed her body. It was only a few weeks ago that she would have been locked away in her old apartment, alone, possibly reading, with little chance of venturing out and even less chance of having a friend over. Wow, how things had changed.

"So do we need to talk about it?" Kim slunk into one of the chairs at the table. Anna noted that for the first time in their professional and personal relationship, Kim was not dolled up. She was wearing snug yoga pants and a long oversized sweater, her hair was in a messy top knot and she was wearing no makeup.

"No, we don't." Anna was more than grateful for Kim's unwavering support. She'd never passed judgement, she'd never questioned Anna and Sam's decision to just remain friends, and she'd never made Anna feel ashamed of her inability to stay out of bed with Sam, either.

"Sure?"

"Yeah, I'm sure. We said goodbye, she's gone, and now we both move on. I just hope she doesn't disappear completely." Truthfully, that was the one thing that was still clawing at her. She hoped beyond anything that Sam would keep her word and be her friend. They were too important to each other. What they'd shared was too special to just forget.

"She won't. I'm sure after a day or so, she'll message you." Kim squeezed Anna's forearm gently.

"Yeah, I hope so. Thanks for the coffee, by the way. Can I just say that you look like balls this morning?" Anna laughed. Although Kim looked comfortable, she also looked like a woman who'd drunk far too much the night before.

"I look like balls? Well, that's charming and not a very ladylike thing to say." Kim huffed with fake outrage.

"My father's sayings sometimes are appropriate," Anna grinned.

"Well… I feel like balls if that helps. Why… why… why did I do shots?" Kim grimaced and dropped her head with a bang on the table. "Ow," she mumbled.

Anna couldn't help but laugh. She was so happy to have avoided a hangover. "Drink your coffee and eat your croissant. You'll feel better soon."

They spent a pleasant morning by the window chatting and drinking copious amounts of coffee. Kim eventually resembled a healthy-looking human being after an hour. "How are you

240

feeling about Monday?" Monday was Anna's first official day as "the big boss".

"I'm confident. Marcus has spent a lot of time helping me with the transition. I think everyone in the office is happy and on board. Honestly, I'm looking forward to the challenge."

"You're going to be wonderful. Have you any plans, you know, to change things up?"

"What do you mean?"

"Well, you're taking over from Marcus, who has been at the helm for a long time. Nothing has really changed for years. I just wondered if you had any plans to shake things up a little, you know stamp your mark?"

Anna took a second to think about what Kim had just said. Maybe she was onto something. This was a new beginning for Tower Publishing and she could think of a few things that she had floated by Marcus over the years that he had gracefully refused to look into. He was so set in his ways.

This was her chance to change things up, rock the boat a little. There had been an idea percolating in Anna's mind for a couple of weeks now, and she knew it was the right thing to do. "I want to sign queer writers."

"Wow, yeah, that's awesome," Kim chirped. "We have stayed with the status quo for too long," she added seriously.

"I agree. Would you help me?"

"As if you need to ask," Kim smirked. "Actually, I have a couple of manuscripts waiting for your perusal. I know it's not right, but I put them to one side when they were sent in. I knew Marcus would dismiss them outright, and I knew you wouldn't be able to change his mind. I read a few and there are some outstanding books in the making."

"I'm just happy you had the foresight to keep hold of them. Let's go over them tomorrow afternoon. I've planned a meeting first thing with everyone, just to get a feel for it all."

"Brilliant, but I'm the one who plans the meetings, Anna, it's kind of my job," Kim chuckled. "I hope you're not trying to make me redundant?"

241

Anna rolled her eyes. "Kim, I couldn't function in my job or my life without you!"

Kim blushed at the compliment. "Well, good."

Anna held up her coffee cup. "Here's to our new adventures." They gently knocked cups.

* * *

Anna's first week had gone better than she could have ever hoped for. All the team seemed overjoyed that she was now in charge, they seemed to draw energy from it and they had been more motivated than Anna had seen them in a long time, especially after she announced that she was making it a mission of Tower Publishing to be at the forefront of queer publications. Anna hadn't realised that Marcus' refusal to sign writers he considered "risky" had severely impacted the team.

"It's not that we didn't love working for Marcus," Rachel said in the first meeting Anna had held, "It's just that we were passing on some wonderful manuscripts, we lost some excellent authors to competitors," she sighed.

It was true and a little unconventional that Marcus had insisted that he had the final say on any manuscripts. That was Anna's job and the job of her team. For whatever reason, though, Marcus wouldn't relinquish control. Acting that way had led Tower Publishing to become stuck. Why Marcus only accepted certain manuscripts, Anna could only guess.

Anna nodded along. She wanted her team to feel as if they could talk to her. It was the only way that Tower Publishing would progress and become more successful.

"Rachel is correct. I had a wonderful manuscript. It was practically ready to go, but it barely crossed my desk before it was rejected," Emanuel added.

"Okay, I hear you and I want you to know from the beginning that I trust all of your judgements. If you have something you think we should publish, but are unsure, bring it to my attention. We're a small company and we have to work together to make

242

it successful," Anna stated. Every person in the room seemed to sit a little straighter and their smiles grow a bit wider.

Anna had every reason to be on a high. She was over the moon that her employees were so responsive to her, and the bonus of her week was that Sam had sent her a message.

Kim had been right. Sam had waited a couple of days before making contact. Anna didn't realise how much she had been worrying about Sam disappearing until she got the notification on her phone. She'd let out the biggest breath when she'd seen it was from Sam. The message hadn't been long, but it was enough for now.

Another achievement in her week had been finally clearing all her belongings from her old place and moving them to her new apartment. Her nights had been spent unpacking and organising. She'd thrown away a lot of things that she'd kept over the years out of laziness rather than for any sentimental reason. They didn't bring her joy anymore, and she didn't want her new digs to feel cluttered with things from the past.

The transition hadn't been completely stress-free; James had turned up at the old apartment as she'd been removing the last of her boxes. Apparently, he still had a few belongings knocking around, which had surprised Anna. She thought he would have been long gone by the time she was ready to return to the apartment.

Their conversation had been awkward, to say the least. James had looked rough, unkempt even. His hair was longer, and he had a rough beard growing. He was the opposite of how Anna had seen him last.

"James, what are you doing here?" Anna couldn't hide her surprise at his appearance.

"Just collecting the last of my bits," he mumbled.

"Right, okay, well, I'll be done soon and then I can leave you to it."

James just nodded before packing some of his things into a box. Anna could see there was something wrong, but she wasn't

243

sure if it was her place to ask anymore. He just looked so dejected she couldn't help herself. "Is something wrong?"

"I miss you," he almost whispered.

The statement was so out of left field that Anna actually looked over her shoulder to see if he was talking to someone else. "Where's this coming from?" It was difficult to understand what the hell was going on. They had both walked away feeling better after the split.

"I just think we may have been a bit too quick to end things. We were okay together, comfortable. I think we should give it another go." The shock of what he was saying must have been clear on Anna's face, because he quickly spoke again. He was on a roll. "Just think about it, Anna, our life was good, we had some fun times. I can work on the more romantic side if that's what you need!"

"What I need is some clarification of where this is coming from, James. We both agreed many times over that splitting up was the best thing for both of us. Honestly, I thought you would be in England by now with your friend Amy. You were clearly attracted to her."

Anna saw tears pool in his eyes. That's when she understood. James was heartbroken, but not over her. It was over the woman in England. "You have been to England, haven't you?" James nodded sadly. "I take it that things didn't work out?"

James shrugged. "It is what it is. But maybe it's for the best. Maybe it meant I was supposed to be here, with you."

"No James, it means you're upset and you need to grieve the loss of your new relationship, not try to get back into one that was wrong from the beginning and before you try to talk me into anything you should know that... I'm gay."

James' eyes had snapped up to Anna's. "Gay?"

"Yes, gay. I've come out to my friends and family. I'm sorry if this upsets you, but you need to understand that we will never be a couple again. I would still like us to be friends in the future, if that's possible. I'll let you think about it, but now I need to get on. I *am* sorry James, I hope you can get yourself to a better place.

244

I'll see you around." Anna left the apartment and never looked back. She felt for James, but she wasn't about to get sucked into his drama. He had to sort his own life out.

So, with that minor exchange being the only downer of her week, Anna was overjoyed that her first week was drawing to a close on such a positive note. A timid knock on her office door drew Anna away from her computer. It was almost time for her to leave for the evening. She had a hot date with Kim and a bottle of wine.

Anna looked up to see Rachel waiting and looking a little nervous. "Everything okay, Rachel?"

"Oh yes, everything is great. I… I just have something that I think we should consider, but I can see you're busy, so I can speak to you on Monday."

"No need. I'd be happy to look." It wasn't a lie. Anna was thrilled that Rachel had brought her something new. "I told you to come to me if you had something, stop looking so worried," Anna chuckled and with that, Rachel visibly relaxed.

"I sent it to you. The author is Camille Richards. She writes lesbian romance. She sent me her first draft last week. I know her through a friend of a friend. She lives in Paris and England. Not sure of her situation completely. Anyway, the book is raw and beautiful. It really is something special."

"Well then, I'll read it this weekend and get back to you. How does that sound?"

"Wow, that's great, thanks Anna," Rachel beamed. "I'll see you Monday," she called as she left.

Anna couldn't contain her smile. She picked up her phone. There was only one person she wanted to talk to and share her week with. Sam.

* * *

The weekend had flown by in a blur. Anna had spent the entire time wrapped up in Camille Richards' manuscript. To say it had promise didn't do it justice. Camille had written a beautiful and

245

raw lesbian love story, not to mention the fact that she had written some of the steamiest sex scenes Anna had ever read. In fact, Anna had had to indulge in some self-service to relieve some of the excitement that Camille had stirred using her words.

Anna sat behind her desk, waiting for Rachel to arrive. Three cups of coffee later, she was almost shaking with excitement. She hadn't felt this good about her job, well, ever.

"Rachel!" Anna shrieked as soon as she saw her sit at her desk. "Can I grab you for a few minutes?"

Rachel dropped everything and rushed to Anna's office. She seemed just as excited as Anna. "Did you read it?" Rachel blurted, which made Anna chuckle. It was wonderful to see the energy radiating off of her. "Sorry Anna, I mean good morning," she grinned shyly.

"Morning, Rachel, and to answer your question, yes, I read it and your hunch was spot on. It is an excellent manuscript. I want you to set up a meeting with Ms Richards as soon as possible, please."

"Right away." Rachel rushed out of the office, already dialling on her mobile. Anna watched Rachel speak. She was becoming more and more animated as the conversation progressed. After a couple of minutes, she returned to Anna's desk with a triumphant smile stretched across her face. "Done. Camille will be with you this afternoon."

"Excellent, I will take the initial meeting and then fill you in once I know if we can proceed."

Rachel seemed more than happy with that idea. "Thank you, Anna. I'm so happy that you have taken over and I'm so grateful that you took the time to listen to my recommendation."

"No, thank you, Rachel. Keep them coming. I trust your instinct completely."

Anna's Monday was off to a flying start. The morning rushed by as Anna prepared for her afternoon meeting. She was a little nervous, which was ridiculous. She took these meetings all the time.

Anna was engrossed in paperwork when she was interrupted by Kim. "Ms Richards is here for you."

"Thank you, Kim. Send her in." Anna watched Camille as she approached the door. She was probably the same height as Anna. Her hair was almost white blonde and in a very cute pixie cut. She wore fitted jeans and a figure-hugging T-shirt. Anna noted how Camille fiddled with the strap of her messenger bag as she walked into the office; she was clearly just as nervous as Anna.

"Ms Richards, it's a pleasure to meet you. I'm Anna Holland."

Camille reached and shook her hand. She had a firm and steady grip. "Please call me Camille, and the pleasure is mine. I'm very grateful for your time."

Anna gestured for her to sit. Her brief bout of nerves was replaced with her usual confidence.

"Let's get straight to it, shall we? Rachel forwarded me your manuscript and, frankly, Camille. It's brilliant." Anna watched as Camille's face blushed. Had she never received a compliment about her work before, or was she just not good at receiving them at all?

"Thank you... that's very kind of you to say, Anna."

"I'm not being kind. I'm giving you my honest opinion. Have you sent it to any other publishing houses?"

Camille shifted in her seat. "No, I have only shown it to a couple of friends. Rachel didn't tell me until this morning that you had read it and were interested."

"Any reason you haven't sent it to anyone?" Anna couldn't for the life of her understand why Camille hadn't sent it to every publishing house from Paris to Edinburgh.

"I just never considered it going anywhere, if I'm being honest. I'm a little self-conscious about my work."

"Would you consider allowing us to publish it? We will show you the contract. You should have a lawyer look it over and then decide if you want to move forward."

"Wow, that's... well, wonderful. I would love to sign with you."

Anna matched the same radiant smile Camille wore. "That's fantastic news. I won't be personally handling you as a client. I think Rachel has earned that right. She will set up a meeting with you in the coming days to go over everything and explain what happens next. She will also be your first port of call if you have any worries or questions. How does that all sound?"

"Sounds great to me." Anna noticed a subtle change in her demeanour. Camille's nerves seemed to be replaced with something else. Anna couldn't put her finger on it. Camille cleared her throat, "So if you're not handling my book... does that mean I'm free to ask you out?"

Anna was *not* expecting that. She stared at Camille in utter shock. Had she missed something? Where was the timid woman that had walked into her office just a few minutes ago? Camille now looked like the most confident woman in the world. "Umm..." was the only sound Anna could make.

"Sorry, unless you're spoken for?"

"No, no, I'm single." A flash of guilt and pain coursed through Anna's chest as she thought of Sam. She had to wipe that out of her mind. Sam didn't factor into it anymore. Anna couldn't keep hurting herself repeatedly, hoping that Sam would magically appear and whisk her off her feet.

Sam was gone, and they were friends. Anna needed to move forward and maybe moving forward with Camille was the perfect solution. She was good-looking and even though Anna knew nothing about her personally, going on a date with her couldn't hurt. Right?

"I'd like to have a drink with you." Anna felt a little heat licking at her neck.

"Wow, I *am* having a good day," Camille grinned. "How about Friday evening?"

"Friday is good, shall we say eight? You choose the place and let me know. Here's my card." Anna produced her business card and handed it over.

"I'll be in touch." Camille stood and offered Anna another handshake. This time Camille held Anna's hand for a beat longer than normal.

After Camille left, Anna sank into her chair, a little confused how the meeting had turned from Tower Publishing signing a new author to Anna getting asked on a date. She could still feel the heat from Camille's hand on her palm. Heat pooled in her lower abdomen.

"How did it go?" Kim sat in the seat Camille had vacated a few minutes earlier.

"Really well. She wants to sign with us."

"That's great. We should celebrate this weekend," Kim chirped. "How about we head to a bar after work on Friday? We can kick the weekend off with a bang?"

Anna blushed. "I can't Friday. I have a date."

Kim sat up ramrod straight. "Date, since when?"

"Well, since about six minutes ago, Camille asked me out," Anna giggled nervously.

"Bloody hell, that's… that's good, right?" Kim was obviously trying to gauge how Anna was feeling about it being someone other than Sam.

"I think it will be good for me. I need to try, Kim." Anna was trying to convince herself more than anyone that it was the right thing to do.

"Hey you don't have to persuade me, sugar, you do what feels right for you. I know how you feel about the Sam situation, so you do whatever it is you need to do to move on. I can't wait to hear all the juicy details," she laughed.

Anna smiled, "Thanks, Kim." She hesitated. "Do you think I should tell Sam? She only left a week ago."

"You're trying to be friends, right? You *would* normally tell your friends about being asked out, so I would be honest with her. Look, it's one night out, you're not riding off into the sunset with Camille and in all honesty ,Anna, you and Sam decided a while ago that you wouldn't be more than friends. Sam left. You still have a life to live and if someone as cute as Camille wants to

249

woo you, then I don't see why you should feel anything but happy."

Anna nodded. She knew that what Kim said made sense, but she still had a knot in her stomach. It would *not* be that easy to get over someone like Sam, but damn it, she had to try.

"I'll give her a call this week," she sighed.

"You're not doing anything wrong, Anna."

"I know that in my head, but my heart is telling me something different."

Kim walked around the desk and wrapped Anna in a hug. "What's meant to be will be. I don't know what's in your future, love. Maybe you're supposed to be with Sam, but you can't wait around hoping for it. You have to keep going and see what happens. Have a drink with Camille and see how you feel after, no pressure."

Anna nodded. She had to see what her life looked like now without Sam.

Chapter Twenty-One

"There she is," Charlie practically screamed the first morning Sam was back at Bright Lights. "Fuck me. You're a sight for sore eyes." Sam laughed at her best friend. She really had missed Charlie. "Give me a hug, you gorgeous lez." Charlie didn't wait for a response; she flung herself at Sam and gave her a bone-crushing squeeze.

"Bloody hell, Char, let me breathe."

"Shut it, I need to love you," Charlie quipped. "Why didn't you let me know you got back on Saturday evening? I would have met you at the station."

Sam hadn't told anyone she had come back a day early. She didn't know herself until she had left Anna's apartment. The thought of being in such close proximity to Anna was too much. She'd had to get out of there as fast as she possibly could. She saw Helene briefly before leaving. It was only fair, and thankfully Helene had been more than understanding. They'd promised to call and message, which Sam had every intention of doing.

"I just didn't want to wait around, didn't see much point, and it allowed me a day of sleep yesterday before starting back up again," Sam lied.

"If you say so." Charlie clearly did not believe a word of Sam's bullshit. "Well, you're here now. You ready to get back on it?"

"Ready and raring, I just have to check-in with John." Sam dumped her stuff at her usual desk and headed to his office. Nothing seemed to have changed at all since Sam had left for Paris. Everything looked the same, felt the same. Actually, that was wrong; Sam definitely didn't feel the same.

"Knock knock." Verbalising her actions had obviously become a thing now. Queue an internal eye roll. John was expecting her, so she didn't feel bad about walking in and interrupting him.

"Sam, what an absolute pleasure to see you again," John beamed.

"Good to be home." Was it?

"Sit down. Coffee?"

"That sounds great, thanks."

John walked over to the coffee machine at the back of his office. Although "machine" was an understatement. The thing had to be industry grade, easily able to rival anything you would find at Starbucks or Costa. Sam wondered how much a thing like that must have cost. More than her monthly pay, she would bet.

"I know it looks ridiculous to have this monstrosity in an office, but the one thing I cannot forgo in life is a decent cup of coffee," he chuckled.

"After drinking French coffee, I completely understand the need to stay away from normal office sludge," she laughed.

John smiled as he made their drinks. After a few minutes of gargling and spluttering, the coffees were done and by god did they smell good. "I have to say, Sam, you seem completely different from the woman who left her all those weeks ago. You sound different, too."

252

"Honestly, I am. Paris… the project was just what I needed. I loved every second, so thank you, John, for having faith that I could pull it off." He would never understand just how grateful she was.

"You did more than pull it off, Sam. You really blew my expectations out of the water. I couldn't believe it when I saw your pieces. Rupert was overjoyed. He wants to schedule a call with you sometime over the next few weeks. Not sure when, he's busy taking over the world right now," John laughed.

"I look forward to talking to him. Now I'm back. What do you have for me?"

"Right, ready to get down to business. Excellent. Chat with Charlie, she has the details for all the upcoming projects. After Paris, you have earned the right to pick what you want."

What I want, isn't that a loaded question?

"That's great, thanks again, John." Sam chugged the rest of her coffee, she needed to get on with work, she couldn't let her mind slow down, that was dangerous, that led to thinking about the one person she couldn't think about.

* * *

"How'd it go?"

"Great, he's happy, so that's good."

"And you? You're happy to be home?" Concern clouded Charlie's eyes.

"Yeah, of course I am." Sam's reply wasn't very convincing, but Charlie knew Sam better than anyone, so she understood that whatever Sam was feeling, she wasn't ready to talk about it just yet.

"Cool, you wanna go for lunch and chat about your next project?"

"It's not even ten o'clock, Char, a tad early for lunch," Sam chuckled.

"Brunch then, c'mon, I can't be arsed to sit around the office all day. God, if I have to listen to Sally harp on about her chuffin'

253

cactus obsession for one more minute, I'm gonna snap, like legit snap."

Sam laughed out loud. She loved Charlie's dramatic nature. "Yeah, alright, let's go. We can head into town." They grabbed a cab into town and walked around, neither of them attempting to talk about work. They had too much to catch up on. Sam left out the parts about Anna. It was still too soon.

* * *

The rest of the week seemed to pass by quickly; Sam had spent some time going over some proposed projects, but there was nothing that really stood out. She'd had a taste of something wonderful in Paris and she wanted more. But as she perused through her options, she realised there was nothing on offer that even came close. A food shoot, a model shoot, nothing out of the ordinary at all. Was this what she was going to have to contend with from now on? She felt irritated at the thought, but what could she do about it?

Really, what can I do?

Sam was more and more in her own head. She couldn't get the idea out of her mind that she wanted to change things up, create something unique, something that she could be proud of, something that was hers and hers alone. The question was, how was she going to do it and could she do it at Bright Lights?

"You look serious," Sandy said as Sam sat staring into her morning coffee. She'd been back a week, and she wasn't settling in.

"Just got some stuff on my mind," she mumbled.

"Care to share, love?"

Sam let out a sigh. She needed to talk. Maybe getting her thoughts out of her head would help her decide what she wanted to do. "I just can't seem to settle back into work, Mum. It's not that I don't want to work, it's just that there isn't anything that inspires me. It's all the same shit, nothing new or original, nothing I want to put my name to."

254

"So make a change. You're not bound to the company forever, and honestly, Sammy, I thought you would have moved on long ago."

Sam looked at her mum with surprise. "Really? Why did you think that?"

"All you went on about at uni was being a freelance photographer. You said you could take on the odd job here and there whilst working on your own projects. Did I get that wrong?"

Had she said that? Sam sat and delved into her memories. She remembered saying something along those lines, but it flabbergasted her that her mum had taken her so seriously.

"I'm really surprised you remembered that, Mum."

"Why? You were so passionate when you said it. I was sure you would make it a reality and then... Well, you didn't."

Christ, her mum was right, well when wasn't she? Sam had planned to go freelance. She'd wanted the opportunity to work on her own projects, hopefully get her work into galleries.

Well, that hadn't happened, and she knew why. Jo, that's what happened. Sam rolled her eyes at herself. "Is there anything I didn't mess up when I met Jo?"

"Hey, enough of that, you're past it. Look at yourself. Look how much you've changed since being away. It's admirable and I'm so proud of you. Don't give that woman another second of your time or energy. If you want to do something different, love, do it!"

Maybe her mum was right. Sam had gained confidence in her work again. She knew she could create something wonderful if she had the chance, but could she risk her steady income? Could she leave a company she had been with for years without knowing for certain she could make it on her own?

As if Sandy could read her mind, she held Sam's hand. "Love, don't worry about money. I've got plenty, you can stay here or I can help you rent a place if needs be. Don't let fear stop you."

"I can't rely on you, Mum, it's not right. I'm an adult. I need to take care of myself."

"Normally I would agree, but this time you're wrong. It's not a case of you mooching off me, Sam, I wouldn't be giving you a handout. I would be investing in you because you have what it takes to succeed in anything you put your mind to. Think about it, seriously. If you're ready to step it up, I'm right behind you every step of the way and I know Charlie will be there with bells on, too."

Sandy gave Sam's hand one last squeeze before leaving her in the kitchen, still nursing her coffee cup. Now, however, she didn't feel dejected. She felt the stirring of something exciting. Could this be the opportunity to make her dreams come true?

* * *

Sam sat in the editing suite, skimming through her latest images. They weren't anything to write home about. Another model in another fashion shoot. *God, this has to change.*

It had been a few days since she had spoken to Anna. She was so pleased that Anna had understood her reason for leaving early. They were able to talk and message now like they had when they were living opposite each other — without the flirting, of course.

Sam rolled her neck from side to side, glancing at the time. Lunchtime in Paris. She could see Anna sitting in her favourite café sipping her coffee chatting with Kim. A smile crept on her face. God, she missed her. Without thinking too much about it, she pulled up Anna's number on WhatsApp and called.

"Well, if it isn't my favourite photographer," Anna chimed.

Sam's heart did a little skip. She couldn't help how her body reacted to Anna's voice. "Well, if it isn't my favourite publisher," Sam laughed.

"How are you? It's been a while? Are you settling in okay?"

That was the question, wasn't it? "Not really. I'm going out of my mind with the banality of the work. I think I want to do something different, but it could be risky."

"Tell me."

256

God, this woman was perfect. She always listened and took in everything that Sam was thinking and feeling, making her feel supported and heard. "In uni I wanted to do freelance work so I could have time to work on my own projects, you know, try to get my work into galleries. Obviously, I didn't do that and now I'm regretting it. Do you think I could try now? Do you think it's a good idea?"

Anna was silent; Sam knew she was mulling it over in her mind. "Forget about before. You aren't that person anymore. What do you want to do now?"

"I want to challenge myself, push myself creatively. Make something I can be proud of."

"Can you do that in your current position?"

"No, not without serious limits being put on me."

"Then there's your answer, Sam. If it's something you're passionate about, don't hold back out of fear."

"Mum pretty much said the same thing."

"She sounds like a clever woman."

Sam laughed, "Yeah, she is. You both are." Sam fell silent for a few moments. Her mind was made up. "Fuck it, I have to do it. I have to go for it."

"I'm happy for you. Let me know if I can do anything to help."

"You've helped more than you could ever realise, Anna."

Sam heard Anna sigh. It was a sigh she had heard time and time again after they'd resigned themselves to being friends instead of lovers. It was a sigh that signified Anna's disappointment and frustration at their situation.

Sam was painfully aware that Anna only agreed to stay friends, so she didn't lose their connection completely. Sam wondered if she was being unfair to Anna, keeping her close but not giving her what she really wanted, what they both really wanted.

"How's your week going?" Sam wanted to break the awkward tension that was hanging between them.

"Great actually, I signed my first queer author, well the account is Rachel's. She was the one that brought the manuscript to my attention. I met with the author on Monday afternoon. It went well, I mean really well." Anna was babbling. Sam knew she did that when she was nervous.

"Wow, congratulations. God, I'm so proud of you."

"Thanks." Silence. "She asked me out, the author. She asked me out on a date," Anna stuttered.

So this is what being stabbed in the chest feels like.

"Oh, right, wow." Sam's voice was shaky. "So when's the big night?"

"Friday, it's *just* drinks."

"That's so exciting for you. Let me know how it goes." Sam did her best to sound supportive, even though she felt her heart being crushed to a pulp.

"Umm, okay... I have to go, Kim is giving me side eye, I promised to take her to lunch and I think she's getting a little hangry," Anna chuckled although Sam knew it wasn't her genuine chuckle, it was forced.

"Yeah, of course, no worries. Message me when you can. It was great speaking to you, Anna."

"You too, Sam, bye."

Sam wanted to crawl under her table and take the foetal position. She had no right to feel anything but happy for Anna, no right at all. She'd been the one who had walked away. Of course, some gorgeous lesbian was going to come along and whisk Anna up. She was amazing and beautiful. Sam had no right, but it didn't stop her from feeling as if she had lost Anna all over again, though this time it felt more permanent. Sam had lost Anna to someone else.

Perhaps Anna had the right idea. Perhaps Sam needed to put herself out there, look for someone she could have a fling with, nothing serious, just someone to help her along.

Shit, that sounded shallow. Was that who she was now? A woman who could only think about getting into someone's knickers and then walking away?

Whatever, she had to do something. If she sat thinking about Anna and her upcoming date, she was going to go insane.

"Like I'm super happy we're going clubbing, Sam, er, just a little confused why, especially on a work night?"

"I fancied a night out, that's all," Sam lied. She hadn't told Charlie about Anna's date.

"Okay, fair enough. So, are we on the pull?"

"I'm not closed to the idea."

Charlie looked at Sam with a mix of concern and confusion, but she didn't question her motives — well, not to her face. "Alright, let's do this."

They opted to go to their favourite gay club. It was rundown and in desperate need of a good clean. The floors had been sticky for as long as Sam could remember. The bar area was crowded. The music pumped through the sound system at an obnoxious level, but it was just what Sam needed, something to drown out the noise of her own thoughts.

They threw back several shots in quick succession. The buzz of the atmosphere and the alcohol quickly seeped into every one of Sam's cells. They danced their hearts out and drank without care.

Sam watched Charlie chat up a woman who was dancing with her friends. Charlie had defiantly grown in confidence since their student days. She was smooth and charming, and she was clearly on to a winner with the pretty redhead.

Sam smiled at her friend, and then she smiled at the friend of the redhead. She was cute, with long brown hair, skinny jeans and a top that emphasised her boobs. *Fuck it!*

Sam danced her way over. The brunette was more than receptive. The dance quickly turned into grinding. Before she knew it, Sam had her hands all over the brunette's body. She felt nice, nothing compared to Anna's delicious curves. *Stop it.*

"I'm Lisa," the brunette shouted.

"Sam."

That's all the conversation they needed. Sam wasn't sure who made the first move, but in a flash, they were kissing furiously. Their mouths smashed together, their tongues fought, and their hands grabbed. Lisa took Sam's hand and tugged her towards the toilets, crashing through the door and into one of the stalls.

Sam had Lisa pinned up against the door, her hand cupping one of Lisa's breasts as the other snapped open her jeans. Sam thrust her hand into Lisa's knickers, not giving herself any time to think. She stroked up and down whilst Lisa bucked into her, moaning into her ear. It didn't take long until Lisa came, her body going slack in Sam's arms.

They breathed heavily, holding onto each other. Lisa unzipped Sam's trousers. She obviously wasn't done with their toilet encounter, but Sam was. She felt sick. She couldn't imagine anyone touching her the way Anna had. She didn't *want* anyone touching her that way, either.

Before she could do anything, tears sprang from her eyes. *What did I just do?* Lisa stopped and cupped Sam's face. "Hey what's wrong?"

"I... I can't. I'm sorry, we shouldn't have done that," Sam spluttered.

"Oh, shit, have you got a girlfriend?"

"No, no, nothing like that."

"So, what's the problem? You looked like you were enjoying it. I know I did," she smirked.

Sam couldn't speak. She wanted to run, hide away until the shame of what she had done ceased to exist. "I get it," Lisa said. "This was an attempt to get over someone, right?"

Sam looked into Lisa's eyes. "I'm sorry."

"Hey don't apologise to me. I've been there. But take it from me. You can't fuck yourself out of love." They stared at each other for a beat before Lisa shifted toward the cubicle door. "I'm gonna go. Will you be okay?"

"Yeah, fine, sorry again."

Lisa left the stall, closing the door behind her. Sam leaned against the wall, willing herself to leave, but all she could do was let her tears fall. Minutes passed, but Sam still couldn't move. The outside door opened. "Sam?" Charlie called.

"Yeah." Sam's voice broke as she spoke.

"Let me in."

Sam flipped the lock and opened the door. Charlie leant against the opposite side of the loo and waited. "Anna has a date tomorrow."

"So that's what inspired our night out."

Sam nodded. "I feel like an arsehole. I just screwed a random woman in a toilet of all places because I was so gutted that the woman I walked away from is going on a date. She's moving on."

"Well, since you brought it up, why did you walk away?"

"What do you mean, I live in a different fucking country?"

"And? You never heard of long distance?"

"That's bullshit and you know it. Long distance doesn't work."

"Whatever you have to tell yourself. There's more to it than that, though. Am I right?"

Sam shifted her weight from side to side. "I can't be in a relationship again, Char, not after last time. I'm only just getting myself into a good headspace. I can't afford to lose myself to someone again. I couldn't survive it."

Charlie pulled Sam into a hug, "Anna isn't Jo. Yes, you could get hurt, but that's how it is, mate. If you're not ready for a relationship, that's okay, but just make sure that you aren't denying yourself something that could make you happy out of fear. Not all relationships will end as it did with Jo."

Sam breathed in slowly, "Thanks, Char, I just need some time."

"That's fine. Take as much time as you need... but you can't expect Anna to hang around without the promise of you guys moving forward at some stage. It's not fair."

"I never asked her to wait around."

"Okay, but look how you've reacted to her going on a date. I think you have to decide if you can be friends. I mean really

261

think, Sam. You might not be together, but you could still hurt her. You're not great at hiding your emotions. It's only gonna take Anna to realise that you're jealous or unhappy when she meets someone, and then your 'friendship' will be ruined and you really will lose her from your life."

Sam didn't know what to say. She couldn't think clearly anymore. "Can we go?"

Charlie nodded. "Yeah, let's get out of here."

What a mess. How the hell had she ended up like this? How could she be so clear about what she wanted professionally but be so lost when it came to her personal life? The idea of committing herself to a risky future career-wise invoked joy and excitement, but the idea of risking her heart and letting herself be with someone completely terrified her.

How long could she keep doing this to herself and how in god's name was she going to sort it out? One thing was for sure: she would never again try to shag Anna out of her system.

Chapter Twenty-Two

Tap tap tap tap tap tap......... *tap tap tap tap tap tap tap.*

"Good lord, will you please stop tapping?" Kim shouted.

"Hmm?"

"The bloody tapping, Anna, you're driving me bonkers," Kim shot back. Anna looked at Kim and then at the metal straw she was holding. She'd been in a world of her own and hadn't realised she was banging the straw on the table. "We've been here for twenty minutes and so far we haven't had a single conversation. You keep drifting off and banging that bloody straw."

"Sorry, sorry. I'm freaking out."

"The date?"

Anna had been absent-minded every day since Camille had asked her out, even more so since she'd spoken to Sam. "I'm just nervous."

"Why though? I mean, it's not like this is your first ever date *or* your first date with a woman," Kim smiled. Her irritation at the straw banging had slipped away. "Is there more to it than that? Maybe something to do with a hot Englishwoman?"

"She wasn't happy. She didn't say anything, but I know her and I could hear it in her voice." Anna replayed the phone conversation with Sam in her head.

"Oh, doll," Kim sighed, "I hate seeing you like this. I wish I could make it all better for you, I really do."

"Me, too," Anna chuckled.

"Saying that, though, I still stick to what I have said a hundred times already. Sam left. You're still here and you need to live your life. Camille seems interesting. She's hot for one. Having a drink with her isn't going to hurt. If you aren't into her, then that's the end of it, but don't dismiss her without giving her a fair shot."

"I know." And in her head, she did know that what Kim said was right. She completely agreed with Kim's assessment of the situation, but she still couldn't get her heart to jump on the *moving on* bandwagon.

"Figured out what you're going to wear?" Anna groaned and let her head slump onto the table. "Stop, no need to get dramatic," Kim chimed.

Goddammit, why couldn't she just be happy? Happy that a gorgeous woman had asked her out. She wasn't being fair to Camille or herself. Tonight was something she should be looking forward to. She had the chance to meet and talk to someone new. A woman who was genuinely interested in getting to know Anna as a person. Maybe even wanting more than just a quick fling.

Enough was enough. Anna was going to put everything into this date and not think about anything else. Hopefully.

* * *

264

Anna listened to the music that she'd put on through her Bose speaker. It was filtering throughout the apartment. Her hips swayed to the rhythm. The random playlist offered her a mixed bag of songs to help her get ready for her date with Camille. Everything was going pretty well until she tried to decide what underwear to put on.

Time was ticking by, but Anna couldn't commit. Too sexy and she felt as if she was promising herself to Camille, even though Camille would have absolutely no idea what was beneath her clothes. But then again, too casual made her feel as if she wasn't giving the date a real chance.

Anna wasn't the type of person who had to have a set number of dates before taking things further. If she felt comfortable, she was open to exploring things sexually, no matter how many times she'd been out with the person.

Case in point, Sam, and that wonderful first date. A shiver ran down her naked body as she fingered the lingerie she had been wearing that night. *No, can't wear those.* Snapping herself out of her memories, she grabbed a matching set. Lace trim, but not too sexy. *Yes, they'll do.*

Camille had sent Anna the address to the bar they would meet at earlier in the day. It'd given Anna a chance to Google it and decide what clothes were fitting. Thankfully, Camille had chosen a laidback place Anna had been to several times. The atmosphere was light and often frequented by students. At least she could pop on some jeans and a T-shirt without feeling underdressed.

Anna gave herself a once-over in the mirror. Her black skinny jeans looked good and the red V-neck T-shirt gave a little peek of cleavage without being too obvious. She'd pulled her soft curls into a ponytail.

Her hair was longer than she'd ever had it before. She'd often shied away from having it long because of the time it took to keep it well groomed, but now with a bit of hair milk — which helped to tame the frizz — and a lot of conditioner, she was able to keep it looking sleek and soft with little effort.

Placing silver hoops in her ears and a couple of bangles on each wrist, finished off her look. Her makeup was flawless. The dark "smokey eye" look was a definite win. She looked good. *Yes, casual and a little sexy.*

The night air was warm, so a light jacket was all she needed. The bar was a ten-minute walk, which Anna appreciated. It gave her just enough time to walk off some of her nervous energy, but not enough that would allow herself to overthink and panic.

The bar came into view as she rounded the corner. All the tables on the pavement were full, but none of the patrons were Camille. Anna took one last deep breath before pushing through the door. Camille was propped at the end of the bar facing the door. Her face brightened as soon as Anna stepped in from outside.

"Hey," she called, waving. Anna made the quick trip over and gave her the obligatory two-cheek kiss.

"Good evening, you look lovely." Anna wasn't lying. Camille wore a long summer dress and tennis shoes. She'd only used a little makeup to highlight her sharp features, and it made an impact. There was no denying that Camille was a *very* good-looking woman.

"What can I get you?" Camille flagged the bartender.

"Rosé, please." Anna smiled, but her nerves were bubbling close to the edge.

Camille was obviously good at reading body language because she placed her hand gently on Anna's forearm. "Don't be nervous, let's just have a good time tonight and see what happens." Anna blushed at her obvious state of distress. *Good first impression, Anna.*

"Shall we go out to the terrace? It's not as crowded as in here and out front." Anna nodded and followed close behind until they reached a table set back from the main terrace. Vine leaves hung from beams that covered the entire outside area. It was beautiful.

"So, thanks for coming out with me," Camille said.

"Thank you for asking me," Anna chuckled.

266

"Can I ask why you're so nervous?"

Anna cleared her throat. "Honestly, you're only the second woman I have been out with. I came out a few weeks ago, so it's all still a little nerve-wracking."

"Wow, congratulations. How are you feeling about it all?"

"I feel great. I can't remember ever feeling so... me, I suppose."

"Oh, I completely understand. When I came out, it felt as if I had literally shaken loose all this weight I'd been carrying around with me."

Anna nodded emphatically. "Liberating, that's the word. I feel liberated."

"C'mon then, spill, tell me all about it... that's if you want to, no pressure."

Anna grinned. Camille made her feel comfortable, which was a major tick in the "Pros for dating Camille" column. She began her story only covering the Sam part of the tale lightly because, as happy as she was talking about her journey out of the closet, her and Sam's story wasn't for sharing.

"I'm so happy your friends and family were okay, I wasn't as lucky. My dad threw a fit and didn't speak to me for two years. Although it didn't really have anything to do with me liking women, but more the fact that I'd messed up his plans for me. He's a control freak, which is why I spend so much time in Paris.

"My parents divorced when I was sixteen. Mum is French, so as soon as they split, she came home. Thankfully, Dad is so wrapped up in himself he didn't bat an eye when I decided to live with Mum for the majority of the time."

"I'm really sorry to hear that, Camille. I can't imagine what it must have been like having to deal with that."

Camille shrugged. "No need to be sorry. Honestly, Dad is the worst; we always butted heads, so it didn't come as much of a surprise when he flipped his lid when I came out."

"What about your mum?"

"Different story entirely. She was thrilled, couldn't wait to set me up," Camille giggled.

267

"Just like mine then," Anna laughed. It was surprising how much they had in common. After just an hour of conversation, they covered all the usual topics such as books, music, art and family. It was nice to know that they had similar taste and interests.

They'd also had some playful banter and a little flirting. The only problem was that Anna kept comparing Camille to Sam. She compared their looks, their humour, how they drank, walked, talked, everything. Anna wanted to mentally slap herself.

"I just need to use the bathroom," Camille said as she popped out of her chair and headed inside. Anna's phone vibrated in her pocket, her heart skipped when she saw a message from Sam.

Sam: *Have a great night, enjoy yourself. Don't do anything I wouldn't do ;) Thinking of you xx*

Anna frowned. What the hell? She could've sworn that Sam had been upset when they'd spoken on the phone. Had Anna read the situation wrong? Did Sam really not care anymore?

Deciding that entering into a text chat with her, what? Ex? No they'd never put a label on it, past lover? Better description than ex, she supposed. Well, no matter what they were — past tense — it didn't seem like a good idea to start a text thread when she was in the middle of a date with another woman. She pushed the phone back into her pocket and tried her best to put all things Sam-related out of her mind.

"Fancy a walk?" Anna asked Camille as soon as she returned.

"Yes, that sounds great." Camille smiled at her enthusiastically.

"Great." Anna tried to match Camille's enthusiasm. It wasn't easy, not after Sam's message. The truth was that the text had severely pissed her off. The fact that Sam had sent a message in the middle of her date made Anna think she'd done it to screw up her night. She must have known what a message from her would do. Right?

268

Anna watched as Camille walked toward the bar to settle their bill. There was a decision to be made; Anna could continue to explore things with Camille and go home with her – which she was almost certain that Camille wanted, and maybe she did too – or she could say good night to her date and go home.

The problem was that she was still feeling some residual anger towards Sam and she was sure that if she went home, she would ruminate on Sam's message for the rest of the night. Hell, she was already ruminating, if she were being honest. Why did Sam want to ruin her date? She had to have known it would unbalance her.

"Ready to go?" Camille gently guided Anna away from their table and towards the door. Anna didn't reply, she only nodded as she walked. The air had turned chilly when they exited the bar. The long summer days were drawing in and Anna could feel autumn sweeping through the city. She took a big lung full of air. Decision time.

"So, tonight was nice." Not a lie. They really had spent a lovely evening together.

"Could I interest you in a drink at my place?" And there it was! The question Anna had been waiting for. She just didn't know how to answer it. Her brain was trying to untie all her feelings with little success. "Anna, I had a great night and I think you did, too. No pressure. Maybe I could just give you a kiss goodnight?"

Anna didn't move, she just looked into Camille's eyes. They were shining with want. Taking Anna's non-answer as a bad sign, Camille stepped back. The movement shook Anna out of her head and back to reality.

"Kiss me." There, decision made.

Camille leaned in and captured her lips. Anna closed her eyes, trying to be present in the moment, feel everything that was happening. The kiss was pleasant, soft and sensual, but it didn't make her heart skip as her many kisses with Sam had done.

Stop it. Sam's gone.

269

Anna placed her hands on Camille's hips and drew her closer. She was well and truly done thinking about Sam. Camille seemed more than pleased with Anna's response and deepened the kiss by brushing her tongue against Anna's lips. Anna opened her mouth and let Camille in.

For all she knew, the reason she was so hung up on Sam was because she was the first woman she'd dated and slept with. Maybe that's all it was, an infatuation, because Sam was her first. If Anna had a chance to move on, perhaps Camille could give her a hand, so to speak.

Anna pulled back slightly so she could look into Camille's eyes again. "Let's go back to your place." Camille grinned and turned to hail a taxi.

They rode in silence all the way to Camille's apartment, which turned out to be in one of the most expensive hotels in Paris. Anna looked out of the window before turning to Camille with a confused look on her face.

Camille smiled. "My family owns the hotel. Well, the brand, actually. I have the penthouse on the top floor."

"Wow, that's… well, that's a surprise. Why didn't you tell me earlier?" Anna was a little concerned that Camille had kept something so big from her.

"Honestly, I hate having to tell people. Too many unpleasant experiences with people who only want me for the family name and money that comes with it. Not that I'm implying you would be like that. In fact, I wouldn't have invited you here if that were the case. Sorry, I hope I haven't ruined our date."

"No, you haven't ruined anything. Let's go."

Camille was a kind and warm woman. The thought of someone trying to take advantage of her was unpleasant. Anna could fully understand why she'd kept that information to herself until she was sure she could trust Anna.

Anna didn't get to see much of the hotel. Camille was in too much of a hurry to get her upstairs. They moved through the lobby and past the bank of elevators. To the left of the lobby was a small corridor with a gold elevator at the end. Anna surmised it was a private lift for the penthouse.

The ride up to the top floor only took a few moments. When the doors slid open, one of the most beautiful sights of Paris Anna had ever seen unfolded before her.

Camille's penthouse boasted floor-to-ceiling windows that surrounded three-quarters of the building. Anna couldn't help but stare in wonder. She was still staring when she felt Camille wrap her arms around her waist, her mouth brushing against her neck. "You feel so good," Camille whispered in her ear.

Anna closed her eyes. The feeling of Camille wrapped around her was nice. She enjoyed feeling wanted. Camille continued to kiss her neck, whilst her hand wandered up from her torso. Camille gently caressed Anna's breast. Before Anna could register another thought, Camille slipped her hand under Anna's top, lifting it up and off her body. Anna's bra was quickly discarded next.

"Hmmm," Anna moaned slightly. Camille's hand felt good, especially when she felt her nipple being pinched.

"You like that?" Anna nodded, not wanting to break the moment. Camille used her other hand to unbutton Anna's trousers, slipping into Anna's underwear.

Anna gave a small moan. "Oh!" That felt good. Camille worked on her clit, slowly drawing circles. Anna closed her eyes and dropped her head back to Camille's shoulder. Her heart raced as she tried to let herself be taken. The rhythm was nice, but not enough. She just couldn't let herself go. Camille was doing everything right, but Anna couldn't open herself up. It didn't feel right.

Sam's face swam in front of her closed eyes. Anna hitched her breath. She could feel Sam's hands where Camille's were touching her. She could feel Sam's breath where Camille's breath danced on her skin. Anna snapped her eyes open and jerked away from Camille, who quickly withdrew her hands. "Are you okay?" she said with ragged breaths. "Did I hurt you?"

271

"No, god no, I'm sorry." Anna was breathing heavily, but it wasn't from excitement. It was from the shock of feeling Sam on her body when it was Camille that was touching her. "Oh god, Camille, I'm sorry, it's not you… really it's not." How the hell had the night gone so wrong?

Camille stood for a second, assessing Anna as she fumbled with her bra and T-shirt, trying to redress as quickly as possible. "Tell me what's happening." Anna looked at her, unsure if she could articulate what was going on in her head. "Please." Camille took a step towards her, her hand gently gripping Anna's. "God, you're shaking… Anna, did I go too far? Crap, did I pressure you into something you didn't want?"

"No, Camille, I promise that's not it at all. You did nothing I didn't want you to do, but it's complicated and I don't know what I'm doing," she sobbed.

Camille stepped into Anna's space and hugged her. "Talk to me, please."

Anna took a few seconds to steady herself. She owed Camille an explanation. "I told you briefly about Sam, my first." Camille nodded and waited for Anna to continue. "It was more than just a few dates. We got serious, but she had to leave and I don't think I'm really over it." Anna was still shaking.

"I see." Camille turned her head away from Anna.

"I thought I would move on once she'd left, but I'm really struggling. The way we met isn't your usual story. It was intense from the beginning," Anna blurted.

"Okay… tell me everything." Anna did as Camille asked. She explained her history with Sam. Camille didn't move the entire time Anna talked, she just listened silently.

Anna stared at Camille, waiting for her to say something. It had been a couple of minutes since Anna had finished talking. "Thank you for telling me, and thank you for stopping before we went any further this evening."

Anna sucked in a breath. She wasn't sure what she was expecting Camille to say, but that sure as hell wasn't it. "Um, okay," Anna mumbled. What more could she say?

272

"I like you, Anna, but I won't be your compromise. I deserve better than that."

"Of course you do, I'm so, so sorry, Camille."

"Don't apologise for being in love with someone else."

They stood for a second, looking at each other. "I really enjoyed your company tonight. I'd like to try for friendship if you think that's still possible?" Camille really was a great person. Anna would be lucky to have a friend like her.

"I'd like that, too. Maybe just give me a bit of time to get over tonight." Camille smiled, but it didn't reach her eyes.

"Of course." The night hadn't ended how Anna thought it would, but at least she hadn't completely buggered everything up.

On the way home, her anger resurfaced. *Fuck you, Sam. Fuck you for making me feel this way and fuck you for leaving.*

By the time Anna stepped through her apartment door, her hands were shaking with rage. She snatched her phone from her pocket and dialled Sam's number. It rang and rang until she reached her voice mail.

"You've ruined me, Samantha Chambers. Ruined me for anyone else. I hope you're fucking happy," she bellowed into the phone before cutting the call and throwing it across the living room.

"Fuck you, Sam," she shouted into the room before dropping to the floor in tears.

Chapter Twenty-Three

Sam couldn't ignore the incessant banging on her door any longer. She'd tried for the past ten minutes to block it out, but whoever was doing it was in no hurry to give up.

"For fuck's sake," she grumbled as she heaved herself out of bed. She stomped towards her bedroom door, only pausing for a second to unlock it before returning to her safe haven.

"What in Christ's name is going on?" Charlie shouted as she barrelled into the room. "You've been AWOL all weekend. I thought you were just working Friday when you stood me up, but then you go off the grid completely and now I find you hiding in your hovel. Jesus, Sam crack a window and then talk to me. Please."

Sam didn't move. Her bedcovers had kept her hidden for the past forty-eight hours and she wasn't ready to leave. Charlie had other ideas, though, because the quilt — or *cone of safety* as Sam thought of it — was abruptly ripped off of her and flung on the floor. Sam lay looking into the concerned eyes of her best friend.

"Well?" Charlie pushed. Sam couldn't take it. Her well-constructed walls took all of two seconds to crumble under Charlie's stare. Tears rolled down her face and her body shook.

"Bloody hell, Sam. What happened?" Charlie climbed onto the bed to comfort Sam.

"I fucked up, Char, I really fucked up," Sam sobbed.

"Okay, you're gonna have to narrow it down, mate. There are plenty of things you could fuck up, but surely it can't be that bad. You didn't kill anyone, right? It's okay. If you did, I'll help hide the body." She squeezed Sam as she spoke, offering comfort in her comedy.

Sam chuckled, but it came out as a weird hiccup. "I know you would," she sniffed, pretty sure she was getting tears and snot all over the place.

"What did you do that's so bad?" Charlie pressed.

"I fucked everything up with Anna," she cried. "I'm the world's biggest arsehole. I should have listened to you."

"Well, you should always listen to me, but remind me which piece of magnificent advice I gave you that you ignored."

"You told me I could still hurt her, and you were right. I did. I'm a selfish twat."

"Whoa, whoa, whoa, alright, enough of the self-hate. Fill me in on what happened."

Sam stilled her sobbing. "I sent her a message in the middle of her date. I told her to have a good time, and that I was thinking about her. I even threw in a 'don't do anything I wouldn't do' with a fucking wink face. I knew she would be out already, but I sent it anyway because I was stupid and jealous and I didn't want her to forget about me. I knew once I'd sent it, it was a dick move. I practically forced myself into her night and it got ruined and now she is so angry at me."

"Oh, mate," Charlie sighed.

"I know. I wasn't thinking clearly. I just couldn't stop the thought of her with another woman running through my mind."

"You chose to leave Sam; you can't stop her from seeing other women."

"I know," Sam screamed, pushing away from Charlie. "I know what I did. I know it was my choice to leave her."

"So make it right then."

"How? She left me a message on my phone. I saw her calling that night and I was a complete chickenshit. I let it go to voicemail. It took me two hours before I could listen to it." Sam cried again, her tears were falling rapidly. "She told me I had ruined her, ruined her for anyone else."

"Did you call her back?"

"I tried, but she doesn't want to know. She sent me a message telling me to leave her alone." Sam fell to her knees and sobbed.

"I think you have to leave her alone then, mate. It's clear that you can't be friends, there's too much emotion. You're just gonna hurt each other over and over." Charlie moved to Sam's side and stroked her back tenderly.

Sam nodded. Charlie was right. If she couldn't give Anna what she needed, she had no right to interfere any longer. The idea that they could be friends was laughable now. They'd shared too much. Their connection was too strong to just be friends.

Sam's heart ached. Why, oh why, couldn't she move past her issues? Anna was perfect. She understood Sam like nobody else except Charlie, maybe.

No matter what she did though, Sam just couldn't push past her fear and panic. She'd been hurt by Jo, but she knew that if she gave herself to Anna completely, she had the power to obliterate her heart if it went wrong. No, she wasn't prepared to risk it.

"I'll leave her alone," Sam whispered to herself more than Charlie. It was the right thing to do. Wasn't it?

* * *

"Mum... Mum... Mother!" Sam shouted as she flung herself down the stairs from her bedroom. It had taken her another twenty-four hours of feeling sorry for herself before she felt strong enough to leave her room. That had been two weeks ago and in that time, she'd heard nothing from Anna. Sam would stick to her word and leave her be. She wouldn't inflict any more pain.

"What's with the screaming? It's eight in the morning, Sam, Jesus," Andy groaned. Sam's bellowing could have woken the neighbours two streets down.

"Have you seen her?" Sam snapped.

"No, I was peacefully sleeping until you started screaming like a bloody banshee!" Sam ignored him and pushed past into the kitchen. Her mother was nowhere to be seen. *Studio.*

The morning was chilly, a slight frost had set on the ground, but Sam didn't care. She didn't even stop to put shoes on. The wet grass tickled her feet and soaked the bottom of her trousers as she marched towards her mum's art studio. None of that mattered though, she needed to speak to her mum pronto.

Sandy was in her studio, sitting in front of a blank canvas, when Sam stormed in. "What's this?" Sam demanded, pointing at her smartphone.

Sandy turned slowly. "It's your phone, love."

"Yes, I know that. What is *this*?" Sam thrust the phone toward her mother, pointing at the screen.

Sandy squinted and leaned towards the phone. "It's your banking app."

"Jesus fu... yes, it is, but what is *that*?" She demanded as she pointed at the enormous balance that was showing on her screen. She'd thought it was an obvious banking error at first, but then she saw who had made the transfer.

"That is your bank balance, love. Bloody hell, Sam, should I be worried that my daughter, who is in her thirties, doesn't know how to use her banking app?"

"Don't play dumb with me, Mum, why in god's name have you transferred that amount of money into my account?" Sam was losing patience, something that was already in short supply nowadays.

277

Sandy blew out a breath. "First, calm down, love. You're gonna give yourself an ulcer. Second, the money is yours. I've been saving for the last twenty-odd years, and now it's time for you to make use of it."

"No, you're going to need to do better than that, Mum. This amount of money doesn't just accumulate from you sticking a few quid away each month. This is more than I will probably ever make in my lifetime."

"Fine," Sandy said, rolling her eyes. "I made that tidy sum selling my paintings."

"Okaaaaay." Sam waited, hoping Sandy would elaborate a little more.

"You have your dad to thank, really." Hearing about her dad always brought a sense of deep loss to her, even though she had been too young to know him. "When I met your dad, I was a struggling artist, like most artists I suppose. We were so in love and he was so supportive of me. He worked like a dog, earning as much money as possible so I could paint without having to get a second job. He was a wonderful man," Sandy choked. Sam hadn't seen her mum upset about her dad in a long time, or maybe she was just a selfish shit and hadn't been paying attention. Too wrapped up inher own her own life.

Sam sat next to her mum and slung her arm around her shoulders. "Mum, you okay?"

"Yes, love, don't worry, it's just nice to talk about him. It reminds me of how wonderful he was. It makes it feel like he's still here." Sam nodded as she held her mum. "Anyway, once I had the time to commit to my art, things really took off. I sold several pieces. Your dad was over the moon. In fact, you were conceived after my fifth sale."

"Ew, Mum, gross," Sam shuddered, Sandy chuckled.

"The only part I didn't like was the publicity. It took me away from the simplicity of painting. I hated having to kiss the arses of gallery owners and stuck up art critics, so I began selling my work under a different name. I stopped doing public functions and large galleries. Your dad thought I was making a mistake.

278

He worried people would lose interest if they didn't see me or get to engage with me. He was wrong, bless his heart. For whatever reason, the mystery just poured fuel on the fire, and my sales exploded.

"I only need to sell one painting a year now and that's only for my pocket money, really. The house is paid for, and the rest has been put in savings for you. Your dad had done everything he could to support me, so after he died I knew in my bones he would have wanted you to have the same support, but he couldn't be here to do it, so I did it for him. That money, Sam, is for you to live your dream, just like I did. Take it and open your own business. Do what you dreamt of doing all those years ago."

Sam sat silently. She was in shock. Her mum had never, not once, divulged the fact she was loaded. "I don't know what to say," she stuttered.

"You don't need to say anything, my love. Just take it and make your dreams come true. Your dad would be so proud of you, button." Sandy turned and kissed Sam's head.

"Thanks, Mum, I... I can't thank you enough for everything. I don't mean the money, I mean everything. You're the best mum in the world, and I love you."

Sandy pulled Sam into a tight squeeze. "Love you too, darling. Now, are you ready to take the leap, take your future into your own hands?"

"Yeah, I'm ready." And she was. Her love life might be a complete shit show, but she knew her professional life was going to be just fine. She was a rock star behind a lens.

"I'm heading into the office. I think I need to have a chat with John."

Sandy nodded. "Go get 'em kid."

* * *

Sam walked into the office with a purpose. Her one goal for the day was to hand in her notice. "Cory, is John around?"

"You've got five minutes," she chirped as she typed manically on her computer, never once looking up. Well, that was easier than she thought it would be. Sam gave the door a confident knock.

"Yes," John shouted. Sam pushed through the door and approached John's desk. "Sam, how are you, everything alright?" He briefly looked up from the paperwork that was scattered across his desk.

"Absolutely fine, John. I wanted to tell you that I intend to hand in my notice by the end of the day."

She watched John's face drop, along with the paperwork he was holding. "Your notice? Why, what's happened?"

"Nothing's happened. The trip to Paris reminded me that all I ever wanted was to be independent. I've been in a rut for so long, John, but I finally feel like I can do it. I can go out on my own. I can't thank you enough for the kick up the arse you gave me. You'll never know how grateful I am. I'm sure it doesn't feel like that right now, with me buggering off and all, but I am... grateful, I mean. I need to do this, John, for me. I could and most likely will cock it all up, but I need to try."

John sat for a few moments processing what Sam had just said, she watched as he tilted his head from one side to the other, mulling over how he was going to respond. "Well, I can't say it's a total shock. After I saw your work from Paris, I knew you weren't going to be satisfied here for much longer. I thought we had a bit more time, but I understand. You're a gifted photographer, Sam. I have no doubt you are going to succeed."

Sam swallowed hard. "Wow, thanks, John."

"Don't thank me, just go out there and show everyone what you're capable of. That's all I want from you."

"You're like the coolest boss ever. Anyone ever tell you that?" she chuckled.

John laughed along with her and then sighed. "It puts me in a bit of a shitty position losing you and Charlie, though." Sam looked at him, not understanding his sentence at all. "She didn't tell you, huh?"

280

"Tell me what?"

"A few weeks ago, she popped in to tell me that when you came in here to hand in your notice, I was to accept hers as well. She said she had no idea when you would do it, but she was more than confident you would."

"Sorry, I'm a little confused. She told you I would hand in my notice a few weeks ago?"

"Yep, waltzed right in to let me know that when you go, she goes."

"Can you excuse me?" Sam was already walking towards the door. "I think I need to clarify what the hell she's playing at."

"Do that and then come back. Rupert wants to chat."

"Yeah, right, okay." Sam was only half listening. Her mind was firmly on her best friend. *What is Charlie thinking?*

Sam found Charlie lounging at her desk, her headphones blaring as she stared into space. "Oi." Sam jabbed Charlie in her shoulder.

"Hey, what was that for?" Charlie grumbled, yanking her earphones out.

"I could ask you the same question."

"What's got your knickers in a twist?" Charlie shot back, rubbing her shoulder.

"Oh, I don't know. Maybe finding out you told John you would be leaving."

"I only said that when you handed your notice in, I would, too."

"Why would you say that? You love it here. You've just been promoted, for Christ's sake."

"Yeah, I've loved it here, past tense. I'm ready for the next challenge as well, Sam. You're not the only one with bigger dreams. You're my best friend. I want to be with you for the next adventure. What's wrong with that?"

Sam couldn't find a single reason why Charlie shouldn't do exactly what she wanted. Who was she to dictate what her friend could do? "You really want to come with me?"

"Abso-fucking-lutely I do. I think we can do anything we want when we put our minds together, Sam, don't you?"

"Yes, I do!" Sam laughed. "Come here." She grabbed Charlie off her chair, yanking her up into a mammoth hug. "Are we really doing this, me and you, our own company?"

"Yeah, we are, but it's your company, Sam. I just want to be able to do my thing, no pressure, you cool with that?"

"I'm cool with that, Char."

"Glad we sorted that part out, then. We should probably make some time to sit down and come up with a proper business plan. I've got some savings I can put forward, but we might need to look at loans to really get us started."

"Yes, we need to chat, but no, we don't need to worry about money. I'll explain later. I have to go back to John's office. Rupert wants a chat. Pizza and beer tonight, okay?"

"Cool, check ya later, woman."

Sam rolled her eyes and left Charlie to lounge at her desk again. The morning was turning out to be better than she could've hoped for. At least one thing was going well.

* * *

The call connected after the second ring, Rupert's voice boomed out into John's office, "Samantha Chambers."

Sam hesitated a moment, unsure if Rupert had finished talking, "Hi, Rupert, good to finally put a voice to the money." *Shit, did I really just say that?*

Rupert's deep laugh echoed in the room. "You're a firecracker, but I wouldn't expect anything less. Your work blew my damn mind!"

Sam chuckled. It was difficult not to laugh listening to Rupert talk. He sounded like the poster boy of a Texan stereotype. He must be at home on his ranch right now in a Stetson and cowboy boots, chewing on a strand of hay or something.

"Thanks, I appreciate the compliment." She grinned at John, who wore a brilliant smile on his face, something akin to pride glinting in his eye.

"I want you to showcase the work before it's shipped over," he bellowed. The man didn't seem to have a volume setting that wasn't below shouting level.

"Showcase it?" Sam questioned, looking quizzically at John.

"John, you didn't tell her?" Rupert blustered.

"No, Rupert, thought it should come from you, my friend." John winked at Sam.

"Good shout! So, Sam, I want to throw a party, a party that shows off those remarkable prints and lets the world see what you're capable of. You worked hard and I want to show my appreciation. I want a real soiree, invites, champagne, tiny sandwiches that you English like, oh, and a gallery worthy of showing your work."

Sam was speechless. Her work had never been shown in a gallery. It was her dream, but she didn't think it would come true like this. "Are you serious?" she spluttered.

"As a damn heart attack. John set it up and put it on my account. You got it?"

"I got it Rupert." John laughed at Sam, who looked like a goldfish with her mouth gaped open.

"Next item of business. Sam, I've got another project for you. I'll need you to fly over here. I'm thinking next summer, you good with that?"

A sudden feeling of unease crept over her. She wouldn't be here next summer. She cleared her throat, ready to decline. She didn't think that many people said no to Rupert often. "I'm sorry, Rupert, I won't be here at the end of the year. I gave my notice today. I'm starting out on my own."

"Well, shit!" he exclaimed loudly, "Sorry John, you know I don't like to take my business away from you, man, but Sam's the photographer I need."

Sam snatched her gaze from the phone to John, searching his face for a reaction.

"That's okay, Rupert. I can still count on your commercial business, right?" He replied. Sam couldn't believe what was happening.

"John, you know my commercial business is always gonna be yours."

John nodded, seemingly satisfied with Rupert's answer. "Then I couldn't be happier that you will be Sam's first client. Congratulations to both of you." Sam felt the smile spread across her face. She had a goddamn client!

"Great, let me know about the party. I'll be there. Speak soon guys." And with that, Rupert hung up. Sam sat staring at the phone.

"You okay, Sam?" John chuckled.

"Yeah, yeah, I'm good. That was just a lot."

"Sometimes things happen for a reason, you know. Take the opportunities given and make the most of them."

"I'll try. Thanks, John, really, thanks so much for your support."

"Anytime, Sam, now bugger off back to work."

Sam left John's office, her mind buzzing. Today had been an almost perfect day.

Almost.

I miss you, Anna.

Chapter Twenty-Four

Anna ran her fingers over the gold-embossed writing for what seemed like the hundredth time. For a while now, she had kept herself in a routine. She would arrive early, grab a coffee, open her laptop and pray she could concentrate, which had been proving to be almost impossible since the disastrous date night with Camille.

Today hadn't started out any differently until she'd walked to her desk to set up her laptop. Her attention had been caught by a glossy black piece of card that lay on her desk. She was sure it hadn't been there the night before.

Curious, she'd abandoned her laptop to inspect the card. As she scanned the fine gold lettering, Anna's heart dropped to her stomach. The card was an invitation addressed to Tower Publishing. It was an invitation to celebrate Samantha Chambers and her project, simply named "Paris." There was going to be a formal soirée in London at one of the city's most prestigious galleries.

The invitation shouldn't have come as a shock. She'd been in talks with Rupert and John about the book and they'd wanted copies sent over for the party.

Anna hadn't spoken to Sam for almost a month now, not since she'd sent a message asking Sam to leave her alone. The text she'd received from Sam on her date with Camille had been the final straw. Anna knew now that she'd been kidding herself in believing they could remain friends. The way they'd left each other may have been amicable, but it had been far from resolved.

After a few bottles of wine with Kim the night after the date, Anna had worked through a few things. The most important being that she and Sam hadn't said goodbye to each other because they were incompatible or lacked feelings — in fact, that couldn't have been farther from the truth — they'd stopped their budding romance because Sam had needed to return to the UK and wasn't in the right headspace to make a relationship work.

So with that being the cause of their separation, how could they ever possibly be friends when they still had so much emotion and chemistry coursing between them? The short answer, they couldn't.

It was clear to Anna now that if they continued down this road, they would never be happy. Their unresolved emotions and feelings towards each other would be a constant source of jealousy. How could either of them watch the other start a relationship with someone else? It wasn't possible or healthy.

So here she was, sitting at her desk, running her hands back and forth over the invitation. It was a professional invite, that's all, but it didn't make Anna feel any better about accepting. Maybe she could get away with sending someone else in her place. That would be okay, right? No, of course it wouldn't, Anna knew before she'd even asked the question. She was the co-owner of Tower Publishing and she'd been the one to work alongside Sam on the book. It would be highly unprofessional to snub the party.

One thing was for sure though, Anna would need reinforcements — also known as Kim. If she was going to get through the party in one piece, she needed her support. She looked at the date. Still two weeks away, leaving her plenty of time to prepare herself, both mentally and emotionally.

"Kim," Anna shouted as soon as she saw her walk in the door, "Can I borrow you for a sec?"

Kim dropped her bag and skipped into Anna's office. "Alright, doll, you have a good evening?"

"TV and wine. That counts as a good evening, right?" Another depressing routine she'd formed: arriving home from the office late, showering, dressing in her baggiest and comfiest clothes before sitting in front of her TV with a bottle of wine and takeout.

"Nothing wrong with a bit of self-indulgence, if that's all it is." Kim raised her eyebrow, her tone laced with concern. Anna didn't answer. She slid the invitation across the desk to Kim and waited. Kim scanned the card, letting out a little sigh before looking at her friend. "You okay?"

"Fine, I'm fine. Can you put the date in the diary, arrange the transport and hotel for us both? I'd like you to come along if that's okay with you." It was taking all of her resolve not to let her voice crack, revealing the fact that she was far from fine.

"Of course, I'll do it this morning." Kim paused. Anna could see that Kim wanted to say something else, but was conflicted about whether to say it.

"Just say it." Anna sighed.

Kim nodded resolutely. "Fine, I'll say it, but I'm not sure you're going to like it." She took a quick breath before continuing. "You're not okay, Anna, you haven't been for a long time, not since Sam left. I can't speak on Sam's behalf. She had her reasons for leaving, but I can speak on behalf of what I've observed with you.

"You've had a tremendous year so far, so much has changed for you and you have done yourself proud with how you've handled it. Coming out must have been so daunting — hanging your life just as scary. But Anna, you did it. I have watched you embrace everything except for this thing with Sam."

287

Anna was shocked. What did she mean she hadn't embraced her relationship/fling or whatever the hell it had been with Sam? "How can you say that? You've seen what a mess I am."

"Yes, I've watched you cry and mope, but what I haven't seen is you fighting, fighting for her, for your relationship."

"There's nothing to fight for! Sam made it painfully clear when she left."

"Oh, bollocks did she! If Sam or you didn't want this, you would have said goodbye and left it at that, but no, the both of you have been hanging on to something pretending it's friendship. As I said, I don't know Sam well enough to understand why she ran away when clearly she wants nothing more than to be with you.

"Everyone who saw the two of you could see that you were both in lo... both wanted to be together. You wouldn't have been so conflicted about Camille, and Sam wouldn't have been jealous enough to interrupt your date if there was nothing serious between you." Kim took a breath. Anna was not feeling very friendly towards her best friend right now, but she said nothing. She waited to see what else Kim had to say, no matter how wrong she was.

"Stop kidding yourself that this was just Sam's decision. You didn't fight her on it, you let her leave without being honest about how strongly you felt. Feel. Why are you so scared to go after what you want? You've done it in every other aspect of your life, Anna, why not with Sam?" Anna was speechless. "Truth time," Kim added.

"Truth...you want the truth! I don't know what the truth is," Anna shouted, her emotions no longer bubbling at the surface. They had burst free and were on the warpath. "What do you want me to say? We had a wonderful time together. I've never felt a connection like that with anyone. She swept me off my feet and took my breath away and then she left, ran away without looking back."

"She looked back every time she contacted you, but why did you let her go if you feel like this? Why didn't you fight for her?"

"Because what if all I'm feeling is infatuation? What if I only feel like this because she was my first?…"

"I call bollocks again, Anna… your connection with Sam came well before you fell into bed. You connected with her on a level I can't even understand. You dreamt about her before you met in person, for heaven's sake."

"That's all well and good, but it makes no difference how I feel if she doesn't want the same thing."

"Well, did you ever ask her why she didn't want to commit? Or did you let her give you a half-arsed excuse and let it go?" Anna felt her face turn red. She knew she hadn't pushed the reason Sam couldn't be with her. She hadn't questioned her reasoning at all, she'd just accepted it. "I'm guessing by that look on your face that I hit the nail on the head."

"Yes, you're right, I didn't push, but so what? Even if I knew the reason it wouldn't mean anything, I can't force her to be with me. I deserve better than that, Kim."

"Of course you do, but you're assuming she doesn't want to be with you because she doesn't feel as strongly as you do for her. Her reason could be something that you guys could work through together."

Anna puffed out a breath. She was done with this conversation. "Have I got anything going on that can't be rescheduled until Monday?"

Kim was taken aback by the abrupt change of subject. "Er… no, I can rearrange your schedule."

Anna couldn't look Kim in the eye any longer. Her friend had thrown her into a tailspin and she needed to get away. "Do it. I'm leaving for the weekend. I need some space." She gave a curt nod, signalling her friend's dismissal.

Kim nodded and left the office. It was the first time they had come close to an argument, and it felt awful.

Anna would deal with that later. Right now, she needed to get out of Paris, out of her head, and she knew exactly where to go. For the first time in years, Anna couldn't wait to go home to her parents.

289

* * *

Anna called her mum when she was already halfway into her journey. To say her mum sounded surprised at her impromptu visit would be an understatement. She wasn't looking forward to explaining her reason for visiting. She wasn't sure she had the energy to go through it all again.

Thankfully, her mum had left her to her own thoughts as they travelled to the house from the station. They'd shared a quick hug, and Anna noted the worry on her mum's face when they greeted each other.

Her emotions stirred as they drove up to the house. She wasn't sure why the sight of her childhood home made her feel like crying.

"So?" her mum said as they sat on the terrace looking out onto the farmers' fields that surrounded them. Anna sat silently, unsure where to even begin. She felt her mum's hand gently squeeze her knee. "You don't seem like yourself, love."

"I don't feel like myself." It was true. She hadn't felt like herself for a while now, even if she'd tried to convince herself otherwise. "I met someone, but it didn't work out how I thought it would. Now I'm confused and hurt."

"Tell me all about it, darling, let your old mum help." Anna gave a little chuckle. Maybe if she'd let her mum help her in the past, she wouldn't be struggling now.

The situation felt like déjà vu, having to recount everything that happened with Sam, just like she'd had to do with Camille on that disastrous date night.

Steeling herself, she forced her way through another explanation of her and Sam's time together. Once she'd finished, she glanced towards her mum, waiting for her to comment. She

290

didn't know what to expect. This was the first time in her adult life she'd confided in her mum and asked for advice.

"First, darling, I'm sorry you have been going through this, but I'm so happy you told me. I know it's difficult for you to share with me." God, did Anna feel like an asshole of a daughter!

"Second, I have to say I'm over the moon that you're going through this, too."

Anna whipped her head round to stare at her mum. "What do you mean?"

Her mum laughed, "Oh, love, don't you see? You're finally feeling what it is to be head over heels in love with someone and sometimes, honey, love hurts." Anna shook her head wordlessly. What on earth was her mother talking about? She felt her hands being clamped between those of her mothers. "My sweet girl, I'm going to tell you something and believe it or not, it's really very simple. You're struggling because you're scared. Falling in love for the first time is terrifying, you have no control and for you, Anna, that's the scariest thing of all."

"I don't think it's that easy, Mum," Anna mumbled.

"Yes, it is. You shared something real with Sam and that scared the living daylights out of you. Loving Sam and having her love you back is everything you want, but you've self-sabotaged. You let it slip away because the thought of having everything means that you have to think about the possibility of losing it, too. I would put money on it being a similar reason for Sam running away, just like you're doing."

"But I already lost it, so that makes little sense."

"No, you didn't *lose* it, you let it go. You let her go on *your* terms before you got any deeper. The pair of you buggered it up for no other reason than fear. Can I also mention that you didn't dispute the fact that you love her?" Yes, she'd tripped Anna up on that one.

Sidestepping the comment, Anna straightened her shoulders. "What do I do?"

"You decide whether you are brave enough to put yourself out there. Talk to Sam, honestly, without holding back. I'm not saying it's going to magically fix everything. You could end up hurt, but to be fair, love, that's already happened. My advice, honey, go to London, first to celebrate Sam's achievement because aside from all this, she still deserves that from you. Second, talk to her and see where that goes. Just communicate, flower."

Was it really that easy?

Her mum was right about one thing. Anna hated feeling out of control. That's why she'd stayed with James for so long. There were no surprises, no actual risk of her heart being hurt permanently with him. Was her mum right about being in love? Anna had thought so, but then, after Sam left, she'd convinced herself it was just infatuation.

Mon Dieu, yes, I love her, of course I do. I knew from the moment I saw her.

Now, it all came down to whether or not Anna was willing to put it all on the line? Could she risk her heart for everything she ever wanted?

* * *

What felt like the biggest decision of her life still rattled around Anna's head almost two weeks later, and she was still no closer to knowing if she could do what her heart wanted her to do.

Things with Kim had been awkward. They hadn't spoken about their last conversation since Anna returned from her weekend away at her parents' house. They'd just carried on as if nothing had happened. "Kim," Anna shouted.

"Yes," Kim replied politely. God, this was awful.

"Close the door, please, and take a seat." Kim did as she was asked, sitting with her pen and paper ready to do whatever it was Anna wanted her to do. Anna knew Kim would always be professional in the office, no matter how pissed she was. She loved that about her. "I'm sorry." Kim waited for her to continue. "You were right."

"Right about what?"

"About all of it."

"Hmmm."

"What does 'Hmmm' mean?"

"Want to tell me where you ran off to after you left?"

"I went to my parents. I spoke to my mum about it all."

"Good. Did she get through to you?"

Anna nodded, "I really am sorry, Kim. You're my best friend and you've only ever been supportive and I didn't handle the conversation well, I shouldn't have left and I shouldn't have waited this long to talk to you, please forgive me."

"Of course I forgive you."

Anna smiled from ear to ear. "Really?"

"Yes. Listen, I know I could have been a little more sensitive when we spoke–"

"No," Anna interrupted, "You were right. I needed to hear it, just like I needed to hear it from my mum. This thing with Sam scares me. It scares me because of how much I feel about her. I've never felt like that, never felt so out of control and surprised by my own emotions. I feel like my heart doesn't belong to me. It's as if she took it with her when she left. I *am* in love with her and the thought of her not returning that love is overwhelming."

"Oh, Anna, come here." Anna rounded her desk and fell into Kim's embrace. "So, what's your plan of action?"

Anna thought for a second. There was only one plan of action. Talk to Sam. "I'll find some time after the party to talk to her and see how she feels. It's going to be difficult after I told her to leave me alone."

"Difficult but not impossible."

Anna tightened the embrace before releasing. Having Kim back in her corner certainly gave her the boost of confidence she so badly needed if she was going to face her fear and fight for Sam.

293

* * *

Anna sat stock-still in one of the cushioned chairs that lined the hall of the Eurostar waiting area. With her eyes closed, she took in a breath to the count of five and slowly let it out to the count of eight.

Forcing herself to concentrate on her breathing; she listened to her heartbeat slowly mellow. She was so different to the woman that had roamed these halls months ago after breaking up with James. Everything had changed. She had changed.

The next twenty-four hours were going to either make or break her. That's the only way she could describe it. In twenty-four hours, she would see Sam again after weeks apart. She would breathe the same air as the woman she had fallen so hopelessly in love with. She could only hope and dream that Sam would reciprocate her feelings, even if they weren't as strong as hers.

If Sam didn't feel the same way, Ann would be heartbroken. Never in all thirty-three years had she connected with someone like she had with Sam. It was far more than a sexual connection. It felt almost spiritual. She only hoped that turning up and declaring her love would not turn out to be the biggest mistake of her life.

The truth was, she was miserable without Sam. She'd let her go without putting up any fight because she knew that settling for something easy was her go-to method of coping, her way of safeguarding her heart. If she stayed in control, she was okay. But now, as she thought of her future, she couldn't bear to picture it without Sam by her side. She'd been a coward, letting their relationship break so easily.

She opened her eyes, blinking rapidly as she adjusted to the neon lights hanging above her. The area wasn't very busy. Their departure time was set for the middle of the afternoon. Most passengers had taken early trains by the looks of it. Kim sat next to her reading. Anna was appreciative that Kim had given her some space, knowing she needed a bit of quiet to sort herself out.

Kim's phone buzzed a few minutes later. She saw out of the corner of her eye that Kim's reaction to whatever she had just read had surprised her. She was about to ask if everything was okay when Kim shot to her feet; her phone clutched to her chest. "Toilet." That's all she said before rushing off toward the restrooms. *Odd.*

Dismissing Kim's strange behaviour, Anna gathered her things and headed to WHSmith's. She needed a book, something to take her out of her own head for a few hours. She browsed and selected a couple that piqued her interest.

The voice over the speaker interrupted her browsing. Boarding had begun. Anna quickly paid for her books and headed toward the toilets. Kim still hadn't returned. Just as she was about to turn the corner to the ladies' room, Kim appeared, looking flustered.

"You okay?" Anna was starting to get a little worried.

"Absolutely fine. Did I hear we can board the train?"

"Yes, I was just coming to get you. Let's go."

Okay, Kim was definitely acting strange, but if she didn't want to talk about it, Anna wasn't going to push.

They boarded the train and slipped into their seats, happy they'd reserved a table so they could spread out. The train pulled away from the station. There was no turning back now.

One way or the other, in a few short hours, she would have her answer.

Chapter Twenty-Five

The countdown to the biggest night of Sam's life was on. T-minus twenty-four hours. So much had happened in the last two weeks that Sam was happy to have a morning to herself.

Although, in reality, that meant she was not by herself at all. No, she had Charlie and her mum hounding her every five minutes with questions relating to her new business, S.C. Photography. Not a very creative name, but she liked it. Seeing her initials printed on business cards gave Sam a warm feeling.

In twenty-four hours, most of the people she'd ever worked with would gather in one of the most prestigious galleries in London to celebrate her work. The invitations had gone out a couple of weeks ago and Sam had been surprised to see that so many of the guests had R.S.V.P'd so quickly.

Amongst the names listed were some photographers that Sam had been following since university. It felt a little unreal to know these people. These distinguished artists and photographers were going to be commending Sam on her own work.

The evening *would* be the biggest of Sam's life, but not because of the aforementioned artists that would attend, but because Sam had seen that Tower Publishing had confirmed their attendance and that meant she would finally see Anna after weeks of silence.

Sam's mind had been a hive of confusion and excitement since she'd seen the acceptance list for the party. She knew she'd fucked up royally. She'd thrown her friendship away with Anna over jealousy, a feeling she wasn't all too familiar with. Sam had never been the type of person to let the green-eyed monster overtake her, but she had no control when it came to Anna.

Charlie and Sandy had done everything they could to help her over the last couple of weeks, but she was pretty sure — no, she was one hundred percent certain — they were tiring of her moping. She wished they could understand the battle that was raging in her mind.

Her heart was telling her to jump in feet first, beg Anna for another chance, not at friendship but an actual relationship. It had felt like they were in one when they were together in Paris, no matter how much Sam told herself they'd kept it casual.

Her brain, on the other hand, was screaming at her to let it all go, to stay away from the danger of losing herself to another woman, inevitably getting her heart crushed when Anna let her down. The battles were unrelenting.

Sam had thrown herself into her work. She'd finished her last day at Bright Lights Photography two days ago. It had been an overwhelming feeling leaving the office she'd known for so long. Charlie had managed it a lot better than she had. As soon as 5 p.m had rolled around, Charlie had thrown her bag over her shoulder and declared herself a free woman, shouting "Later, bitches" as she left laughing. Thankfully, the office found her funny and not insulting.

After arriving home from her last day at the office, she found her mum waiting in the kitchen with a magnum of Champagne. Andy stood beside her in a party hat that read "Happy 60th." Jeez, she felt so honoured that he'd put in so much effort. She'd given him the biggest eye roll she could muster before she'd laughed and thrown her arms around him for a hug.

Charlie joined them and they'd spent the night drinking and laughing about all the different things they'd been through since they'd left uni. Chatting about all the things they wanted to do in the future.

Regrettably, they'd gotten carried away with their celebrations and had overindulged. A full magnum of Champagne and a bottle of rum left them worse for wear. The next day had been super unproductive. No shock there, really. Sam certainly wasn't able to bounce back after a night on the piss anymore, so she'd stayed in bed the entire day until she'd felt a little more human. That had occurred around ten o'clock in the evening when she'd been able to take a shower and eat some dry toast.

This morning, though, was the proper start of it all. Her first day as a self-employed woman. "Sammy baby, I've got some fantastic news," Charlie shouted from the front door. She never knocked. The house was much a home to her as it was to Sam.

"Lay it on me."

"Well, my useless fuckwit parents have actually done me a solid," she chirped.

Sam was used to hearing Charlie speak about her parents in a less than generous way. They'd practically left Charlie to raise herself, too busy with their own lives to bother about their daughter. The only thing they ever contributed was money. They had the idea that throwing wads of cash at Charlie could make up for the fact they'd been really shitty parents.

"Okay, sounds interesting."

"They've agreed to rent us Bowman Manor."

Sam just stared. Bowman Manor was a house — no, more like a mansion — that had been in Charlie's family for generations. It had sat empty for years after Charlie's parents had moved away in search of warmer weather.

Sam had visited it once before. It wasn't a very homely place. Sam struggled to see Charlie living there happily. The place was

298

so vast. She thought it must have been a very lonely place for a child.

"How the hell did that happen?"

"Well, I just asked, to be honest. I remembered you telling me how good it would be for offices. Plus, they've missed every birthday and Christmas since I was twelve, which I reminded them on the phone and wotcha know, they were happy to lease it to us at a stupid rate," She laughed, her face lighting up like a Christmas tree.

"Char, that's perfect!"

"Right!" Sam pulled her in for a hug and a few sloppy kisses on her face. "Get. Off. Me!" Charlie yelled, laughing. "We just need to go over and start shifting some old crap down to the cellar. Wanna go now?"

"Does a bear shit in the woods?"

"I'll take that as a yes then," Charlie grinned. "Get your coat."

The house was only a five-minute walk away, which was ideal. The behemoth building was hidden from the street behind massive conifers. The driveway was long and winding. It led to a set of grand oak doors. There were more windows than Sam could count. She didn't want to think about the amount of money it took to keep it clean, let alone the repairs. Thank god they were only renting.

They let themselves in and stood in the lobby. Charlie looked as if she was filtering some good and probably painful memories. Sam knew this hadn't been a happy home for her best friend. "You alright?"

Charlie nodded, silently walking to the first room on their right. "Thought we could start in here. This would be the best room for our office." Her voice was quiet and timid.

"Yeah, I was thinking the same." She walked over and squeezed Charlie's shoulder before ducking into the room. It looked as if the space had previously functioned as an office, looking at the furniture that was left behind. Boxes were piled in every corner.

"Any idea what all this is?"

299

"Crap, from my old room. They wanted a second gym so obviously my childhood bedroom had to go," Charlie mumbled, her face creased with sadness from decades of feeling unwanted.

"C'mon, let's get started." She hated that she couldn't do anything to take away Charlie's pain.

They spent a good two hours lugging boxes down to the cellar. Sam was more than happy she'd resumed her daily workouts, especially when she saw how red and sweaty Charlie was.

They only had a couple left, but the boxes were heavy and in awful shape. Sam just reached the door to the cellar when she heard the box rip, the entire contents falling to her feet. "Bollocks," she shouted.

Throwing the broken box to one side, she bent down to retrieve the items. Pausing when she saw they were photo albums. Picking one up, she flipped through the pages. She cracked the biggest smile when she saw the pictures were of her and Charlie at university.

"Charlie, come and look at these," she shouted down the stairs. She heard Charlie panting as she walked/hobbled up the stairs.

"Oh my god, are those what I think they are?" She laughed.

"Too right, our golden days lady." Every picture was of Sam and Charlie, either drunk or well on their way.

"I don't know how we actually graduated. We were hammered ninety percent of the time," Charlie mused.

They continued flipping the pages, laughing now and then. Just as Sam went to turn to the last page, Charlie slammed her hand on the album. "Holy fucking shit," Charlie gasped.

Sam looked from Charlie to the page. She saw the two of them with their hands on each other's shoulders smiling at the camera; Charlie was a few drinks in by the looks of it. Sam knew instantly which part they'd been at. She would never forget it. *The dance.*

Sam scrunched her eyebrows, bringing the picture closer to her face. It wasn't the image of Sam and Charlie that had caught her interest. It was the young woman at the back of the crowd

300

that she couldn't take her eyes off. "It's not possible," she whispered. Her head whipped up to look at Charlie, who looked equally stunned. Sam gently withdrew the photo from its protective sleeve, running her finger over the image in utter shock. "It's her," she stuttered, "My god, it's her."

Charlie relieved Sam of the album, putting it back on the pile that had fallen to the floor. "Think we should have a drink, mate." Charlie led Sam back to the office and plonked her down into the closest chair. Sam sat, stunned. She couldn't take her eyes off of the picture.

A short while later, Charlie emerged with two glasses of rum. "Drink up," she said, shooting her own glass, coughing a little as the rum hit the back of her throat. Sam tore her eyes away from the picture. She looked into Charlie's eyes before gulping down her own drink.

"I need some air." The room felt like it was drawing in on her.

Stumbling out of the manor, Sam numbly began to walk. A few minutes in and she realised she'd automatically walked home with no recollection of the journey.

Once home, Sam locked herself in her room. The outside world would have to wait. She had far too much to process. That image changed everything. It put all of Sam's fears into perspective. She finally had the answers she'd been searching for.

Sam knew what she had to do. She just needed to find a way to do it. Time for reinforcements. After sending the message, Sam sat and waited. She could only hope that she would get a reply quickly. The sound of her ringtone jolted her into action. "Kim, thank god, look I need your help."

* * *

Anna's knee was bouncing at an incredibly fast rate. In less than ten minutes, she would arrive at the party. She'd taken nearly four hours to dress herself in preparation, and now, as she sat in the back of the taxi, she was second guessing how she looked.

301

"Doll, will you relax! You look gorgeous. I mean really stunning." Kim squeezed her knee, halting its movement.

Anna took a few big breaths in, trying to contain her nerves from spilling out. "You really think so?"

Anna had brought three different outfits with her; she'd tried them all on several times but finally settled on a midnight blue floor-length strapless dress. She'd complemented the outfit with a simple white gold teardrop necklace and matching earrings. "I promise, you're a knockout," Kim reassured her. Anna unconsciously fiddled with the hair that she'd left down, straightened hanging over her left shoulder.

She gave Kim a nod. "Thanks, Kim, you look wonderful too."

Kim sported one of her pin-up style dresses. It was black with white trim, the neckline dipped to show off her ample cleavage. She was also in the biggest heels Anna had ever seen. It was a wonder she could walk, but honestly, Kim made it look so easy. You would think she was strutting around in trainers.

"Thanks, doll," Kim winked. Anna chuckled, trust Kim to help dispel some of the tension that was radiating off her in waves.

The black cab finally pulled up outside the gallery. Kim grabbed Anna's hand as they stepped out of the taxi and onto the red carpet. They didn't make an immediate move to enter. Kim was allowing Anna to collect herself first. Anna adored this woman.

After a few moments, Anna signalled to Kim that she was ready — well, ready as she would ever be. The gallery was in a large industrial-looking building. There were metal rails along the foyer ceiling, the walls were bare brick and the floor a smooth concrete. It was modern and beautifully maintained.

Posters of the soirée had been mounted at the front of the gallery entrance. Anna could see through the door that the room was lit by a blanket of LED lights, making it feel as if they were walking under the stars.

"Ready?" Kim held her hand.

"Yes." It was now or never.

They stepped through into the gallery. Anna almost stumbled. Her chest swelled with pride as she took in the scene in front of her. Sam's photographs were mounted on the walls and on metal partitions that were expertly placed throughout the room. Dozens of people dressed in gowns and black ties milled about, taking in Sam's breathtaking work. A few had already picked up a copy of the book.

Waiters and waitresses picked their way skilfully through the crowd, offering wine and champagne. Liquid courage, just what the doctor ordered. Anna grabbed a couple of glasses, swallowing the first one in two gulps. She brought the second up to her lips, only then noticing Kim's grin. "Thanks for the drink, doll," Kim said sarcastically.

"Sorry," Anna mumbled, her lips still on the glass. Kim rolled her eyes and chuckled. After a quick sweep of the room, Anna was sure that Sam wasn't there. *It's her party. Where could she be?*

"Let's have a mooch around." Kim threaded her arm through Anna's. They followed the general direction of people walking around the gallery. They stopped at every piece, marvelling at Sam's talent for capturing Paris in a way they'd never seen before.

They'd just completed a full lap of the work when the sound of a knife clinking on a champagne glass caught their attention. A tall man in a brown suit, cowboy hat, and boots stood on a little platform. This had to be Rupert Downes, billionaire and man responsible for commissioning Sam.

"Howdy," he bellowed. Anna almost winced at the volume of his voice. "Y'all won't have a clue who I am and that's fine because tonight I'm not very important. Tonight we're here to celebrate a wonderful and talented young photographer who I commissioned for this project." There was a smattering of applause before he continued to shout/talk.

"I gave Sam the enormous task of capturing one of my favourite cities and, as you can see by the quality of her work, she blew the project out the water," he laughed. The crowd was enjoying Rupert's energy and positivity. He had them all captivated. "I'm not gonna jabber on all night. I just want y'all to welcome to the stage the woman of the hour... Ms Samantha Chambers."

Anna felt her breath catch in her throat as she watched Sam weave through the crowd to join Rupert on the stage. *My god, she's beautiful.*

"Now I promised Sam she wouldn't have to make a speech, so let's just raise our glasses and toast." Rupert raised his glass towards Sam, who bowed her head graciously. Ann couldn't take her eyes off Sam, who had yet to see her. She knew it was now or never. Pushing herself towards the stage, her heart thudded wildly. She hoped she could get to Sam before she lost her nerve.

The crowd had swallowed Sam up by the time Anna had fought her way through. Sam was gone. *Did she see me and leave?* The possibility of that sat on Anna's chest like a lead weight. Fighting back tears, Anna retreated to the side of the room. She needed a minute to compose herself. She was still at an important function and she was still representing her company.

Kim made her way over. "Let's take a walk." Placing her hand on the small of Anna's back, she guided her to a door at the back of the room. They stepped through into a smaller gallery area. This room had been lit by candles of all shapes and sizes, hundreds of them.

Anna came to a stop in the centre of the room, her eyes drawn to the photographs displayed on the walls, black and white portraits of her. They were the photos that Sam had taken. Pictures of their adventures in Paris. Anna brought her hand up to her mouth. She was speechless. Movement from the door caught her eye. She turned slowly round. Sam stood leaning up against the doorframe. "What's going on?" Anna whispered.

"You look beautiful, Anna," Sam breathed. Anna couldn't move, couldn't form words. Sam walked slowly, stopping a couple of metres away. "Can I talk, and will you listen until I'm finished? No interrupting." Her eyes revealed a mix of emotions that Anna couldn't decipher.

304

"Okay." What else could she say? Anna watched Sam shuffle from one foot to the other, squaring her shoulders, readying herself for whatever she was going to say.

"Leaving Paris, leaving you was the single hardest thing I have ever done," she began. Anna raised her eyebrows at her opening statement. She didn't feel that Sam had found it *that* hard to leave. "You probably don't believe me, considering I snuck out of your bed and vanished without saying goodbye, plus all the times I told you I couldn't be in a relationship. It was all bollocks, Anna. I lied to myself just as much as I did to you." Sam cleared her throat. Anna wanted to go to her, to reassure her, but she needed to hear the rest of what Sam had to say.

"We briefly brushed over my ex, Jo. I didn't want to taint our time together with all the baggage from my past, but now I think I should've spoken more openly about it." Sam paused, taking in a deep breath. "Jo didn't just cheat on me. She spent years gradually tearing me down, stripping me of my confidence and self-belief.

"So much so that when I found her cheating, I spent so long blaming myself, thinking it was something that I had done which drove her into the arms of someone else. It took me so long to believe that I was worthy of something more, that I deserved to have happiness. I only started thinking that way when I arrived in Paris, when I met you." Sam inhaled sharply.

"I started to get myself together again. Charlie and my mum certainly helped, but it was you that made me realise that I could have a future again. When we met, the feelings between us became strong so fast, it scared me to death." Anna took a small step towards Sam. God, she wanted to touch her, make her feel safe.

"I could handle the changes to my career and I felt good about all the positive things that were happening to me. I loved feeling my confidence return, but with you... Christ, Anna, I was terrified. It felt like Jo had permanently scarred me, broken something inside me that allowed me to give myself to someone again." Sam took another sharp breath, "But I was so wrong,

305

Anna, and the worst part is that it took me so long to realise that after all these years, I'd already given myself to you completely."

Anna felt her brow frown. What did Sam mean after all these years? "I don't understand."

"I need you to trust me for a few minutes. Can you do that?" Anna trusted Sam. She might have been upset with her, but she'd always trusted her. She gave a little nod and watched as Sam turned her head to signal someone in the corner of the room. Anna looked over. Kim was walking towards them, holding two satin ties. What the hell was going on?

Kim quietly manoeuvred herself behind Anna. "Trust her," she whispered, before wrapping the blindfold snugly around Anna's eyes. Everything was dark. A little sliver of panic crept its way up Anna's neck.

Before it could take root, Anna heard the soft melody and opening line to a song she would never forget. "If I should stay... I would only be in your way." She felt a body push gently into hers. The memories of that night, that dance, came flooding back.

It wasn't possible, but Anna knew the truth. She felt Sam's breath next to her ear as the song continued. She felt her own arms take hold of Sam's waist, slowly drifting up and around Sam's back as they swayed so seamlessly with each other. Anna gasped. "Mon Dieu."

"You said that the last time we danced, too," Sam whispered.

Anna stilled. She had to see Sam's face. She felt Sam take a small step back, giving her the opportunity to take her blindfold off. She opened her eyes and basked in the beauty that was Sam standing before her.

Sam stood with her hands clasped in front of her. She looked radiant in wide-leg pinstriped trousers. Tucked into them was a simple bright white tank. Her golden-red hair was scooped up into a messy bun with a few strands left to frame her face; it seemed to shimmer in the candlelight. Anna had to look up to see Sam's eyes. She was an inch taller than Anna, the pair of black high heels accounted for her added height. She took Anna's breath away.

"How is this possible?"

"I've asked that question a million times since I found out that it was you that stole my heart at that party all those years ago," Sam stated simply.

"When did you find out?" She needed to understand.

"Yesterday. Look." Sam handed Anna a photograph she took from her back pocket. The photo was of a younger Sam and Charlie in a one arm hug. People crowded around at a party. Anna looked from the picture to Sam, confused. Sam stepped forward and pointed to a young woman in the background. Anna's eyes opened wide. Good god, it was her.

"I came here to fight for you," Anna whispered as she caressed the picture in her hand. She felt Sam move quickly into her space.

"You should never have had to fight for me. I'm so sorry, Anna, I'm so sorry for letting you think you were the only one who felt so strongly. I'm sorry for not being brave enough. I want to be though. You've been with me every day, in my thoughts, in my heart. Seeing this picture and seeing you in it finally made everything fall into place.

"I realised that Jo could never break my heart, not really because you've been carrying it with you for over a decade, keeping it safe for when I found you again. I fell in love with you that night. I just didn't know it was you, but now, after everything, it makes perfect sense," she chuckled.

"I was angry at you. You left me." Anna noted Sam drop her head to her chest. "But it wasn't entirely your fault. I let you go without telling you how I felt. I didn't fight for you because I was scared, too."

"We're a right pair," Sam smiled.

Anna beamed back at her. "I'm in love with you, Sam. I don't care how hard it is. I want to be by your side."

Sam slipped her arms around Anna's waist and pulled her in. The moment their lips met, Anna felt at home. There was nothing in this world to fear when she had Sam next to her.

"You know, Dolly is right," Sam grinned against her lips.

Anna cocked her eyebrow, Sam brushed her lips over Anna's again, "I will always love you, Anna. I have no doubt in my mind."

Well, who in their right mind could argue with Dolly Parton?

Epilogue

1 Year Later

It wasn't the sound of rain hammering on Sam's bedroom window that made her stir from her deep dreamless sleep; it was the warm sensation of lips kissing her leg. She kept her eyes closed, enjoying the delicious caress of Anna's mouth, soft yet strong. Her body betrayed her as her hips automatically rolled when Anna placed an open-mouth kiss on her inner thigh. "Morning," she rasped as Anna travelled higher.

"Shh, I'm not done waking you up," Anna replied, her voice muffled under the duvet.

"But I'm awake," Sam giggled.

"Mmm, no, I don't think you're fully awake yet. Hang on." Sam gasped as Anna spread her legs apart, sinking her mouth into Sam's need.

"Oh, fuck."

"Mmm, now I think we're getting somewhere," Anna mumbled. She wrapped her forearms around Sam's hips, anchoring her to the bed.

"Oh god, Anna," Sam panted. There was nothing in the world as exquisite as Anna's mouth.

"Come for me mon amour."

"Oh… oh, yes… yeeesss!" Sam screamed. Anna held her close until her body stopped shaking and her breath steadied.

Anna crawled up Sam's body and popped her head out from under the cover. "Mmm, I think that's my favourite way to wake you up," she sighed dreamily.

"I wholeheartedly agree," Sam laughed. "I think you still look a little sleepy, though."

"You know, come to think of it, I am a little sleepy. What could we do to remedy that, do you think?"

"I've got an idea," Sam chuckled before swiftly manoeuvring Anna so she was flat on her back, her legs instinctively wrapping themselves around Sam's hips. They kissed each other deeply, their breaths becoming ragged. Sam pulled herself away to look down at Anna. Their eyes held equal amounts of lust and love.

"I bought us a little present." Sam had bought them a strap-on. They'd talked about buying one for a few months without following through. Sam had seen this one and couldn't help herself. Anna was a rocket in the bedroom and always up for trying new things, which made Sam insanely happy.

"Is it a strap-on by any chance?" Anna smiled, her cheeks flushed from their heavy kissing.

"How'd you know?"

"Darling, you left the packaging in the bin," she chuckled. Sam felt her face burn. So much for the surprise.

"Are you okay with it?"

"Absolutely," Anna blurted.

Sam smiled. God, she loved this woman. "Don't laugh when I put it on!" She slipped out of bed and began digging through her suitcase.

310

"Out of the two of us, Sam, it's not me who will laugh, is it?" Sam grinned. She definitely was the one who would laugh out of nerves. She couldn't help it. It was how she coped with awkward or embarrassing situations.

Anna watched as Sam slipped on the harness and turned around. "Oh, wow," she gasped. Sam stood in the Superhero pose, deliciously naked, with a rainbow dildo hanging between her legs. "Get over here," Anna ordered. Sam raced back to the bed, ripping back the covers. She slid on top and with no time to waste, they began kissing, their hands roaming, searching for each other's pleasure points. "I'm so wet," Anna gasped.

"You ready?" Sam watched Anna, her eyes searching.

"Yes."

Sam reached between them and rubbed the dildo through Anna's folds, coating it in her essence. After several moans of pleasure from Anna, Sam guided the tip to Anna's entrance, slowly pushing herself forward.

"Are you okay?" Anna nodded furiously. Sam needed no more confirmation than that. She slid herself in and out, picking up a steady rhythm. Anna's hips worked alongside hers. The base of the dildo was doing magical things to Sam's throbbing clit.

"I'm close," Anna panted.

"Touch yourself," Sam ordered. The sight of Anna adding to her own pleasure was almost enough to make Sam come. She had to fight to keep control of herself. Anna's fingers sped up. Sam matched her speed, thrusting faster. She could feel Anna shake. Her head snapped back before her whole body shook. Her orgasm ripped through them both. Sam allowed herself to tip over the edge. They cried out in unison.

"Oh," Anna stuttered between gasps of air. "That was amazing."

"Yeah, it was," Sam giggled.

"Although..."

"Although?" Sam repeated, her eyes darting to Anna's. "Did I hurt you?"

"No, not at all, mon amour, it's just that as good as it was, nothing beats your hands and tongue." Anna wiggled her eyebrows.

Sam chuckled. "Don't worry, honey, there is no toy on this planet that will ever replace my hands and mouth. I love touching you too much."

"Excellent, maybe you could remind me how good it feels, then?"

Two hours and two showers later, they finally emerged from Sam's old bedroom. Andy had gone to stay with his family for a few days, so it was just Sam, Anna, and Sandy. Sam was grateful that Andy had given them some time alone. Sam hadn't realized how much she would miss her mum and their time together when she moved to Paris six months ago

They slowly descended the stairs, stealing kisses and touches as they went. Sam could hear her mum in the kitchen. It sounded as if she was having a fight with the pans — and losing.

"Morning, Mum." Sam kissed her on the cheek with Anna following suit. Sam couldn't have been happier with the way Anna and her mum interacted. Sandy had embraced Anna instantly, welcoming her into their little family.

"Morning, my loves, have a seat. I made breakfast," Sandy chirped.

"You made breakfast, really?" Sam could count on one hand the amount of times Sandy had cooked a breakfast for her.

"Don't sound so surprised. I love cooking. It's not my fault you only ever wanted to eat toast in the mornings, growing up."

"Fair point," Sam chuckled. They sat at the breakfast bar, nursing their coffee. They all turned to the door as they heard Charlie enter through the back.

"Morning, beautiful people," Charlie exclaimed loudly. They returned the greeting in unison.

"So, last day, huh?" Charlie directed her comment at Sam.

"Yeah, last day. I'm excited but sad at the same time."

"It's going to be fantastic," Sandy said as she pushed a plate of pancakes into the middle of the worktop.

"I know," Sam sighed. She really was happy to be leaving for the US. Rupert had followed through on his offer to employ Sam's services again. It was a wonderful opportunity allowing Sam to have free rein in Texas for three months. The obvious downside was leaving Anna again.

They'd spent less than a few hours apart for six months straight. Sam's stomach dropped at the thought of not seeing her, not touching her for twelve weeks. Anna had constantly reassured her it was too big of an experience to pass up.

"Hey, stop that." Anna lifted Sam's chin, so she had to turn her head to face Anna. "It's going to be amazing. I'm not going anywhere." She placed a soft kiss on Sam's lips.

"Samantha," her mum barked, jolting Sam's attention away from Anna's loving eyes.

"Why are you shouting?"

"I've said your name three times."

"Oh, sorry." It wasn't the first time she'd lost herself in Anna's kiss and it wouldn't be the last.

"It's fine, love. You have done so well for yourself this last year. I'm very proud of you."

"Thanks, Mum."

"Anyway, you've got to be off your rocker if you think Anna's going anywhere. From the sounds you've been extracting from her this past week, I doubt you ever have to worry about her straying too far."

Sam looked at her mum, confused. Anna had gone bright red, and Charlie was trying desperately to suppress her laughter. It finally dawned on Sam what sounds her mum was referring to. "Mother, for Christ's sake," she yelled.

"I don't know why you get to do the shouting, It's me that hasn't had a good night's sleep for a week, I mean really, Samantha, you're going to wear the poor girl out," Sandy retorted with a wicked grin.

"Oh, right, I'm the insatiable one."

"Hey!" Anna shot.

"Sorry," she grumbled.

313

"Well, either way, the trip to the US will at least give you both time to rest your vaginas. I imagine they need a bit of rest and relaxation after the way you've been at it."

"Oh, my god!" Sam shouted.

Charlie couldn't hold her laughter in any longer. She doubled over with tears in her eyes. "That's fucking fantastic," she cried, thrusting her hand to get a high-five from Sandy, who was now laughing as equally hard.

"Calm down, I'm only teasing," Sandy wheezed through her laughter. "You're just too easy to wind up, love."

Sam instinctively looked at Anna, who was hiding her face behind her coffee cup, laughing.

"You're the worst." Sam fanned her face, hoping it would go back to a colour lighter than beetroot.

"You packed?" Charlie asked once she'd composed herself.

"All done. Just need to close the case; you still okay to take me to the station?"

"Yeah, no worries, mate. What you lovebirds got planned for your last night?"

"I think we're all fully aware of what they have planned, Charlie," Sandy piped up.

"Yes, you're right, Mother, that's exactly what we have planned." God, she wished she didn't let her mum's teasing get under her skin so much.

"Excellent, but before you retire for long hours of debauchery, do you think you could take an hour to have dinner with your old mum?"

"Of course, Sandy, I'm sure I can tear myself away from Sam for a little while," Anna grinned wolfishly. It still took Anna a bit of time to feel comfortable with Sam and her mother's back-and-forth teasing. She was getting better at joining in, though. It helped that Sandy and Charlie welcomed her into the fold like she'd known them forever.

"Wonderful, Paddy's at seven then."

"Paddy's? That's where you want to spend an evening with your only daughter before she goes travelling to the other side of the world for months, Paddy's shitty pub?"

"Yes, Paddy's, that's where I took you for your first pint. The night before you left for uni, I thought it would be appropriate." Oh god, Sam could really be an insensitive tosser sometimes.

"Oh balls, sorry, Mum, of course, Paddy's would be great," Sam looked frantically from her mum to Anna. Upsetting her mum was the last thing she ever wanted to do.

"Oh, for god's sake, Sam, you really are too gullible. As if I'd take you to that shithole again. The last time you went there, you got the shits from their dodgy burgers." Sandy laughed. "I thought a pizza and a beer would be better. Nice night in with my girls."

Sam let out a long breath, "That wasn't teasing, Mum, I thought I'd really upset you."

"A night in sounds lovely." Anna squeezed Sam's knee.

"What time do we need to ship out for you, Anna?" Charlie was taking her role as the designated driver seriously.

"I'm on the last train tomorrow evening, so we have a few hours between dropping Sam off and taking me."

"Okay, great, I'll check the traffic tomorrow."

"Come on, girls, let's get on with the day," Sandy clapped, ushering them all to move.

* * *

Sam's last night with her family had been better than expected. They'd shared two large pizzas and watched a couple of trashy films. Sam was over the moon when Andy stopped in to wish her well on her travels. He ended up staying for the night along with Charlie.

But that was then. Now as she loaded her suitcase into the back of Charlie's car, the only thing rattling around in Sam's

315

mind was the fact she was willingly leaving her girlfriend, the woman she loved.

The past year couldn't have gone any better for Sam and Charlie. S. C. Photography had taken off quickly, and Sam had gained a lot of recognition from her "Paris" project. Both Sam and Charlie were so much happier in their professional lives, and even though Charlie had originally said that she only wanted to be an employee of Sam's, it hadn't taken her long to come round to the idea of becoming a full partner. Sam was delighted. She trusted Charlie with her life and she knew the business was in safe hands whilst she was away.

The trip to the US was going to be the first project since Paris that Sam could really sink her teeth into. To get S. C. Photography off the ground, she'd had to take on whatever work she could, which had paid off in the end because now she could step back and focus on personal projects that challenged her creativity.

The "Texas" project was perfect. She'd enjoyed working for Rupert, and thankfully he trusted her to work her magic behind the lens, which meant she would have complete freedom again. She should be on cloud nine, but she wasn't. So what was the problem? The problem was leaving Anna. It just didn't sit right in her stomach.

Anna had had just as much of a busy year as Sam. She'd made some major changes at Tower Publishing that had allowed them to branch out. Sam couldn't have been prouder. Anna was born to run that business.

That had been the deciding factor when it came to their living arrangements. For six months they'd gone back and forth visiting each other as much as possible, which had been great in the beginning, but the distance soon took its toll.

Sam had decided to relocate to Paris. The offices in England were in safe hands, and Sam was excited to branch out. Sam didn't need a second office in Paris because she could easily work from home. She moved in with Anna and it had been a perfect six months.

Sandy had visited on several occasions. They'd even taken her to meet Anna's parents and brother, which had been an interesting experience. Sam was pretty sure Anna's parents hadn't known what hit them when storm Sandy blew through.

Thankfully, by the end of the stay, they'd all got on so well that now Sandy regularly Skyped with Anna's mum, negating Sam and Anna from the equation, which thrilled them both. Everything in their lives was settled, their businesses, their parents and friends.

"Ready?" Charlie called from the driver's seat of her VW bug. She'd already settled herself in the car, allowing Sam and Anna time to say goodbye.

"Yeah, let's go before I change my mind." Sam kissed Anna before turning away. God, this felt awful. "I love you," she called over her shoulder.

"I love you, too." Anna smiled and waved. Sam was a little taken aback; Anna didn't seem anywhere near as disturbed as Sam did about her leaving. Maybe she was just being super sensitive?

The car journey took forever. Sam was thankful they'd left a large amount of time to get to St Pancras because it seemed that Charlie had lost the ability to find the accelerator. "Bloody hell, Char, I could walk faster than this," she grumbled.

"Hey, I'm not getting a ticket just because you're impatient," she snapped. Charlie seemed on edge.

"Alright, keep your knickers on." God knows what was wrong with her. Maybe she was just upset Sam was leaving. She certainly seemed more nervous than Anna had been. "You know, you could have taken me to the airport instead of making me drag my ass there by train." She hadn't understood why Charlie was adamant she couldn't take her to Heathrow directly.

"I told you I haven't got time, and your mum is busy with some art thing. Jeez, Sam, when did you get so precious? We're not here to cart your arse around, you know," Charlie grinned.

Sam mumbled something under her breath. It was going to be a royal pain in the arse, dragging her luggage and equipment

317

through St Pancras and then the airport. Fuck, it was going to be a long day.

"We're here," Charlie announced. Sam was too lost in her souring mood to realise that they had finally arrived. Charlie jumped out of the car and unloaded her bags. "Giz a smooch then." Charlie dragged Sam into a hug, kissing her face until Sam squirmed to be released.

"Get off me, you tool," Sam laughed. "I'm gonna miss you, mate."

"Me too, but you're gonna rock this. Enjoy it okay, embrace it all." With that, Charlie stepped back. "Go, you don't want to miss your train." Sam inhaled deeply. She was really doing this.

The double doors to the station swished open. It took her several minutes to locate the board that told her where she needed to be. Shit. She was going to be late if she didn't get a move on. Well, okay not super late. She still had thirty-five minutes, but Sam's nerves were getting frayed and the thought of missing her train was overwhelming.

She grabbed her suitcase, adjusted the equipment that rested on her shoulder, and began the trek to her platform. She was completely lost in thought as she rushed past throngs of people until something stopped her in her tracks. Almonds and cherries. She'd know that smell anywhere.

Stopping dead in the middle of St Pancras, Sam slowly turned around. Standing there leaning against a pillar was Anna, with a smile that could have lit up the entire station. Sam froze. She wasn't sure she could trust what she was seeing. "Anna?"

She watched her girlfriend stroll over, her suitcase trailing behind. "Hey, baby."

"What's happening? Your train isn't until this evening. What are you doing here?"

"I'm not going back to Paris, Sam. I'm coming with you."

Sam felt her knees go weak. "You are?" This was too good to be true.

"Sam, your adventures are my adventures. I couldn't be away from you even if I tried. I could have told you, but I thought it would be a pleasant surprise and fitting to meet you here. After all, it was the first time I glimpsed you for the first time, well, the first time after a decade," she chuckled. "Do you mind?"

"Do I mind? Are you joking? This is the best thing ever and you're right, meeting you here is perfect. Jesus, if I'd have known then that the beautiful woman I saw briefly after her douchebag boyfriend smashed into me was the love of my life, I would have chased after you that very day and done what I'm about to do."

Anna smiled, but a crease formed on her forehead. "What do you mean? What are you about to do?"

Sam reached into her jacket pocket—something she'd been doing a lot recently, ever since she'd bought the ring, in fact. She'd kept it on her at all times, terrified she would lose it. She'd planned to wait until she returned from the US, but this was the perfect time. She felt it in every fibre of her being. Sam dropped to one knee, not caring one bit about the people who were having to divert themselves around the pair as they held up the flow of foot traffic.

"Mon Dieu," Anna whispered.

"Anna, you're my person. I knew from the second my body felt yours as we danced. I knew it the moment I heard your voice. It took me too long to find you again, but I know I'm meant to be yours now and forever. Please do me the biggest honour and be my wife." Sam held her breath as she waited for Anna's answer. She saw the tears pool in her lover's eyes, pure emotion washing down her face.

"Yes… yes… yes, of course, yes," Anna cried. Sam jumped up and embraced Anna, lifting her off the ground. She hadn't noticed the cheering that surrounded them as they hugged and kissed. It seemed they'd attracted quite the audience.

Sam kissed Anna with everything she had. Without a doubt, Sam had given herself to Anna wholeheartedly. There was nothing holding her back; the fear of losing herself had vanished. She wanted Anna to have all of her. She knew Anna would hold her heart forever, keeping it safe along with her own.

"I love you," Sam gasped in between kisses.

319

"Mon amour, I love you, too. I'll always love you."

They were home, safe in each other's arms, even in the middle of a crowded train station. The sound of music drifted over from the piano that stood in the middle of the hall. Sam kissed Anna softly. "Dance with me?"

"Always."

The dance was a promise between them both, a promise of forever.

Acknowledgement

I never thought I would have the confidence to write a book. It was a life goal that I never thought would be made into a reality. I have to give all my love and thanks to my wife for helping me make this book happen. From the moment I mentioned the idea of writing it, she supported me without question. Throughout the entire process, she has been there, reading my first, second and third draft. Offering her thoughts and opinion on the story, helping me to flesh out the characters and muddle through writer's block. Even after her long days in the office, she was always happy to help.

Thank you, my love. For everything.

About Author

Alyson was born and raised in the heart of England. She moved to Paris in 2015 when she met her wife. Together they moved to the west of France where they now live with their two dogs and pet bird. Alyson spends her time running a small campsite and holiday home. During her off time, she loves to read lesbian romance books, write and Scuba Dive.